RE-ENTER THE SAS

RE-ENTER
THE SAS

THE SPECIAL AIR SERVICE
AND THE MALAYAN EMERGENCY

by

ALAN HOE and ERIC MORRIS

LEO COOPER

LONDON

First published in Great Britain in 1994 by
LEO COOPER
190 Shaftesbury Avenue, London WC2H 8JL
an imprint of
Pen & Sword Books Ltd
47 Church Street, Barnsley South Yorkshire S70 2AS

ISBN 0 85052 383 4

A CIP record for this book is available
from the British Library

Typeset by CentraCet Limited, Cambridge
Printed by Redwood Books
Trowbridge, Wilts.

CONTENTS

ACKNOWLEDGEMENTS

The authors wish to acknowledge the many people who have given freely of their time, dredged their memories, entrusted them with precious photographs and otherwise so willingly assisted in putting this book together.

In particular they would wish to thank: Brig. 'Mad' Mike Calvert, DSO; Lt. Col. John Woodhouse, MBE, MC; Bob Bennett, BEM, MM; the late Harry 'Bosun' Sandilands, MM; Col. Ian 'Biffo' Cartwright, CBE; the late Maj. Dare Newell, OBE., and his wife Hazel; Col. Patrick Winter, OBE; Maj. Alistair McGregor, DSO, MC., and his wife Magda; the late 'Paddy' Winters; Maj. Mike Jones; Edward 'Tosh' Bates; John Davis; Donald Palmer, MBE; John Leary; Bill Harvey; Huw Griffiths and Brian Lloyd both of the 'Helicopter Operations (Malayan Emergency) Association'; the Imperial War Museum; the Public Records Office (Kew); Little, Brown & Company (UK) Ltd., (publishers of 'David Stirling: The Authorised Biography' by Alan Hoe) and the many veteran soldiers who were involved but would prefer not to be named. In addition we have a debt of gratitude to Pamela Morris for her painstaking work on the word processor and Leah James for her research assistance.

Tom Hartman read the manuscript. His recommendations in both substance and syntax has improved the work out of all recognition. Last but by no means least we thank Leo Cooper for his infinite patience and tact.

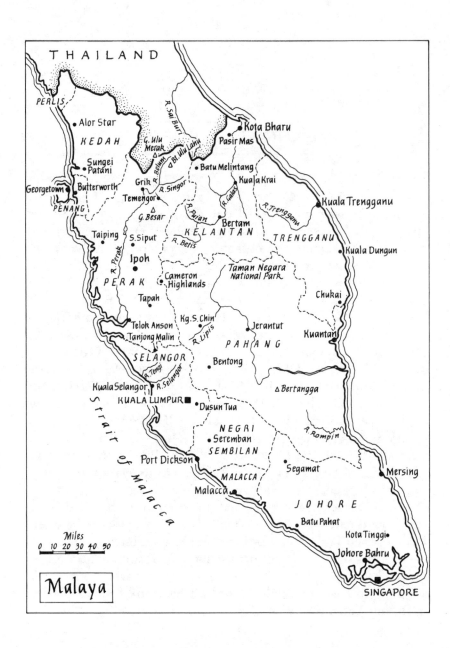

THAILAND

PERLIS

• Alor Star

KEDAH

G. Ulu
Merak

R. Sai Buri

• Kota Bharu
Pasir Mas •

• Sungei
Patani

• Batu Melintang

Bt. Ulu Lahu

Georgetown

Butterworth

Grik

R. Belum

R. Singor

• Kuala Krai

PENANG

Temengor

R. Purian

R. Galas

Kuala Trengganu

R. Trengganu

Taiping

G. Besar

Bertam

• S.Siput

KELANTAN

TRENGGANU

R. Beris

Ipoh

Kuala Dungun

PERAK

R. Perak

• Cameron
Highlands

Taman Negara
National Park

Chukai

Tapah

Kg. S. Chin

Telok Anson

Tanjong Malin

R. Lipis

• Jerantut

Kuantan

SELANGOR

PAHANG

R. Tengi

• Bentong

Kuala Selangor

R. Selangor

△ Bertangga

KUALA LUMPUR ■

• Dusun Tua

NEGRI

• Seremban

Strait

R. Rompin

SEMBILAN

of

Port Dickson

Malacca

MALACCA

• Segamat

Mersing

Malacca •

JOHORE

Batu Pahat

Kota Tinggi •

Miles
0 10 20 30 40 50

Johore Bahru

Malaya

SINGAPORE

INTRODUCTION

The SAS is very familiar to the public today as the modern version of David Stirling's wartime concept. Utilising the same tenets of personal determination, self-discipline and diligence to guide the selection process, it has become the best known Special Force in the world. A unit which is the model to virtually all other countries, it stands on the pinnacle of excellence. In the post-war years the regiment has come into the public eye as the result of nine active service campaigns and many high interest incidents such as the Iranian Embassy siege in London; it has gained a prominence which it does not welcome. The SAS became redundant at the end of World War II and was disbanded on the cessation of hostilities – yet six years later it reappeared.

This book is not a campaign history. This is the story of the 'missing years'; the story of a set of political and military circumstances which came about during a twelve-year guerrilla war in the Malayan Peninsula. Neither is the book a history of the Malayan Emergency. There is sufficient detail for those who may be unfamiliar with the campaign to provide a backdrop to the rebirth of 22 SAS which had many parallels with the original formation of 'L' Detachment, 1st Special Air Service Brigade. It was the faith and dedication of a few outstanding officers and men which prevailed against heavy military bureaucratic odds to ensure the retention of the SAS in the British Army Order of Battle and thus into the modern history books.

GLOSSARY

Malay

Basha	Improvised shelter
Belukar	Thick growth of secondary jungle
Bukit	Hill
Gunong	Mountain
Hantu	Ghost or spirit
Jahat	Bad or evil
Kuala	River or stream junction
Kris	Traditional Malayan sword
Ladang	Cultivated area
Lalang	Long grass (can be in excess of 6 feet)
Orang	Man or people
Orang Asli	Aboriginal people
Parang	Jungle machete
Sungei	River
Ulu	Headwaters (familiarly used by SAS to mean deep jungle)

Thai

Sai	River

1

THE ORIGINS OF THE SAS

During the spring of 1941 two Celts of quite different backgrounds and temperaments were discussing the conduct of operations in North Africa. One of the officers, Captain 'Jock' Lewes, was a Welshman; a dark-haired, stocky individual, he was a serious, taciturn man to whom inactivity was anathema. Superbly fit, the ex-Oxford rowing blue was just itching to get on with the war. His companion, six feet five inches tall, was a much more fun-loving character. Lieutenant David Stirling came from an ancient and aristocratic Scottish family and had a penchant for the nightlife of Cairo which had not escaped the attention of his superiors (neither had his habit of appearing late for duty in the mornings). A Cambridge man, Stirling had not enjoyed either the academic or sporting successes of his brother officer. They were both members of 8 Commando and had seen action together. The common bond between them that Spring in Africa was boredom.

Lewes told Stirling that he had discovered a quantity of parachutes which had been destined for India and unloaded by mistake in Cairo. There was no parachuting role in North Africa and it had not been difficult for him to persuade his commander to let him conduct some experiments. To Lewes it was merely a way of making life a little more interesting during the interminable resting up phase before the next major offensive. It took Stirling, caught up by his companion's enthusiasm, only a little time to persuade Lewes to take him along. This simple agreement between friends was to have far-reaching effects.

The first jump, from a Valentia aircraft, took place on 15 June, 1941. For Stirling it was a disaster. His canopy snagged on the tail of the aircraft and, spilling air through the ripped silk, he came down fast and hard onto the rocky ground. The resultant shock to his spine was sufficient to paralyse both his legs. Confined to a hospital bed Stirling put his mind to work. He had been on a number of operations with 8 Commando as part of Layforce and they had all taken the form of raids on German positions along the coast of Cyrenaica. Such raids were, in Stirling's opinion, quite fruitless. Launched from gunboats or destroyers it was normal for about one third of the force to be committed to establishing and then defending a beachhead. Even if surprise had been achieved by the 'thundering herd' there would inevitably be a fighting withdrawal for the assault force back through the beachhead resulting in heavy casualties. Time on target was very short during these expensive ventures which placed such heavy demands on manpower and resources. At best they delivered only pin-pricks to the enemy and, in Stirling's opinion, actually bolstered German morale as they were usually the 'victors'. These operations had, however, become the norm and were anticipated by the Germans who constructed very strong defences facing the sea and the open flanks to each side.

Hospitalized and poring over maps of the North African coast, Stirling was struck by a phrase, 'The Great Sand Sea', covering the vast desert areas to the south. Surely this was one flank that the enemy would not be watching, one sea on which his sentries did not have their binoculars trained because of the enormous difficulties presented by the inhospitable terrain. But, were the difficulties really so great? This was just another sea – an unob-served sea at that. The more Stirling considered the prospect the more excited he got. The key elements to success in mounting operations from the south would be surprise, mobility and the ability to inflict maximum damage to the enemy. The approach right up to the target (and off it again) had to be secure. This meant that the soldiers had to get in and out without being noticed and therefore explosives with delay fuses had to be the main armament – this fulfilled the surprise factor and the maximum damage factor. What about mobility? The parachutes of course – he had just been unlucky. The matter of extraction was pushed aside for the time being. His first problem would be in refining the strategic possibilities and persuading someone in the Middle East Headquarters (MEHQ) that he had a viable concept.

He gave little thought at the time to recruits. Although he was not enamoured of the Commando tactics, he had a very high regard for the quality of their fighting men. They were fit and they were loyal and were already volunteers for hazardous operations. There would be a requirement for special training for he envisaged working in small numbers in a manner which would be at first alien to the Commandos, used as they were to operating at troop strength. These were all minor problems to be faced later.

Stirling had realized that a unit such as he proposed would have to come under command of the highest authority if it was to be used correctly in a strategic role and not get lost in the tactical battle by being used by a local commander as a conventional force. This dictated that he would have to present his case to the Deputy Chief of General Staff (DCGS) who at that time was General Neil Ritchie. For a mere Lieutenant to gain access to the DCGS would not be easy and if he was successful he would have to present his case quickly and cogently. In anticipation he drafted a paper which he entitled, '**A Special Service Unit**', covering all his thoughts on the vulnerability of the enemy airfields, transport and fuel parks to attack from the undefended desert front. He pointed out the great advantage to be gained from the use of a special unit based on the principle of the fullest exploitation of surprise and making the minimum demands on manpower and equipment. One of these special sub-units of 12 men could cover a target previously requiring the deployment of 5 troops of a Commando (200 men).

Using such a force should mean that up to 50 aircraft could be destroyed by any sub-unit. It therefore followed that a properly trained and equipped special unit of 200 men could attack up to 10 different targets at the same time on the same night compared to only one objective using current Commando techniques. This mean that only 25% success with the special unit would be equivalent to many times the maximum result of a Commando raid. The effect on German morale would be very significant.

The corollary was that such a unit must be trained to arrive at the scene of operation by every practicable means, by land, sea and air, and using only those means which were immediately available and not valuable in tactical scale operations. As an example he stated that if a unit was to be parachuted then it would use conveniently available aircraft and not demand those which were specifically modified for the role. (In their jump from the Valentia he and Lewes had simply tied their static lines to the aircraft seats!) The unit would be trained to use folboats or caiques in order to infiltrate from submarines or destroyers. By land, he argued, the unit could be dropped off as close as possible to their targets by experienced troops with whom they could meet up again after the attack. It followed that the unit had to be responsible for its own training and operational planning and therefore the commander of the unit must operate directly under the order of the Commander-in-Chief. Stirling ended his dissertation with the comment that it was well-known that an offensive was being planned for November, 1941, and, in anticipation of agreement, he appended his plan for the use of the unit in that manoeuvre.

PLAN FOR THE NOVEMBER OFFENSIVE

1. Target: Enemy fighter and bomber landing grounds at TMIMI and GAZALA

2. Method: In the night of D minus 2, 5 sections to be parachuted onto drop zones some 12 miles south of the objectives; this will preserve surprise. Each section is of 12 men (i.e., 3 subsections of 4). As cover a heavy air raid is required on TMIMI and GAZALA using as many flares as possible to aid navigation to the drop zones.

3. After re-assembly on the drop zone each section will spend the balance of night D minus 2 in getting to prearranged lying-up points from which they will observe the targets the next day. The following night (D minus 1) each party will carry out its raid so as to arrive on the targets at the same time.

4. Each party will carry a total of about 60 incendiary cum

explosive bombs equipped with 2 hour, ½ hour and 10 minute time pencils in addition to a 12 second fuse. The time pencils will be used on a time de-escalating basis to ensure almost simultaneous detonation.

5. After the raid each party will retire independently into the desert to a pre-arranged meeting place south of the TRIG EL ABD to rendezvous with a patrol of the Long Range Desert Group (LRDG).

The rendezvous was some 50 miles south of the targets in almost featureless desert but there was a small hill on which the LRDG were to be asked to leave a red hurricane lamp at night and keep a watch by day for returning patrols. Stirling later admitted that the figure of 50 miles 'seemed a sensible distance'. He had paid no real attention to the reality of having to cover such a distance in one night. The suggestion of using the LRDG was an inspired guess. Stirling had heard of this deep penetration unit consisting of brave, highly skilled men operating in an intelligence capacity. It was to be the beginning of an extremely happy and effective alliance between the two units.

Stirling approached the problem of getting an audience with Ritchie in typical fashion. He knew that if he put his paper forward in the proper military fashion it would never reach the DCGS – he had to present it in person. He was now able to walk short distances with difficulty and in great pain and so he decided on subterfuge. On crutches he managed to bluff his way into MEHQ and arrived at Ritchie's office unannounced and seconds ahead of the guards who were chasing him. In obvious pain he burst into the office and handed over his documents. Ritchie read them without asking a single question on the contents. He admitted that the proposal had much merit as a way of tying up German manpower and that he would discuss it with the Commander-in-Chief (General Auchinleck). He dismissed the young officer with the promise that he would hear from him soon.

Auchinleck, having only recently taken over from Wavell, was under pressure from Winston Churchill to strike out at Rommel's forces. Stirling's idea was attractive in that it was undemanding in terms of resources and thus of little risk to material aspects of his command. If it did work it would be a great morale booster at the same time as being of positive assistance. Three days later Stirling was summoned to a meeting with both Auchinleck and Ritchie and questioned in detail about his concept. At the end of the meeting he was promoted to Captain and given authority to recruit 6 officers and 60 other ranks with a high proportion of senior NCOs. His recruiting pool was to be the remnants of Layforce. The name was to be selected from the files of Brigadier Dudley Clarke who was responsible for deception operations throughout the Middle East. He had created a non-existent unit called the First Special Air Service Brigade. In support of the myth, dummy parachutists were dropped close to prisoner of war compounds and mock gliders parked in the desert, which all gave credence to the existence of the unit when reported to enemy intelligence. Clarke was keen for Stirling to use the name and, because his initial unit was to be small it became 'L' Detachment, SAS Brigade. Stirling was under way.

As a base the detachment was obliged to use Kabrit. This Canal Zone village lay roughly 100 miles to the east of Cairo and about the same distance south of Port Said; on the edge of the Great Bitter Lake, flat and fly-ridden, it was totally exposed to the full power of the desert sun. It was not an attractive camp. 'Jock' Lewes was one of the first volunteers, along with a hard core from Layforce, many of whom had served alongside both Stirling and Lewes in earlier Commando operations. Lewes took on the onus of setting training schedules, whilst Stirling carried on recruiting his officers. One of his early acquisitions was the great Blair 'Paddy' Mayne. In order to construct a habitable camp the early volunteers were obliged to raid a neighbouring New Zealand compound and steal the essentials.

Training programmes were dominated by navigation, survival, fitness and weapon training lessons. Tactics were devised on the spot as exercises began to become more realistic and many men failed to meet the exacting standards of Lewes. The physical aspects of the selection process were a series of lengthy desert marches by day and night carrying heavy loads and using the minimum amounts of water. Each patrol was to have a man trained in first aid, a driver/mechanic, a navigator and an explosives expert. A deeper philosophy behind the four-man patrol and separate skills was that the system created a dependency which helped to prevent the emergence of a leader and the possible acrimony which could result. Parachute training was run on a self-help basis and was very hit and miss with all training aids being constructed from within the detachment's meagre resources. There was no assistance from the Parachute Training School at Ringway and consequently there was at least one parachuting fatality which could have been avoided.

It was Lewes himself who overcame the knotty problem of producing a home-made explosive charge which would rupture fuel drums and then have a positive incendiary effect. He used the simple expedient of mixing fuel oil with the plastic explosive; there was a small but acceptable demerit in using this technique in that if the gun cotton primers were inserted too early they could absorb some of the liquid and become ineffective. Stirling had a major battle on his hands in trying to get supplies and equipment from a MEHQ which was jealously husbanding all resources and where the middle level staff officer viewed the young Scot as something of a 'Johnny-come-lately' who was bound to fail. Despite all the difficulties the calibre of the officers and men was such that by the end of October, 1941, 'L' Detachment, SAS Brigade was ready for action.

Auchinleck planned to start his major offensive on 18 November, 1941, with the aim of relieving Tobruk. 'L' Detachment's role in the operation was to be exactly as Stirling had planned it in his original memorandum to Ritchie. Five Bristol Bombay aircraft of 216 Squadron were to parachute the 62-man force into areas close to the airfields of Tmimi and Gazala on the night of 16 November. At this point Mother Nature took a hand in the matter. Stirling was advised that the weather conditions over the drop zones were going to be hazardous in the extreme. He took a deliberate decision to ignore the weather and parachute anyway. His men were raring to go and once the offensive started in earnest it would be difficult to distract either Auchinleck or Ritchie from the duties of command in order to get them to agree to an alternative target. The likelihood was that 'L' Detachment would have been sent to reinforce a tactical fighting unit and the concept would be lost forever. Stirling pulled no punches with his men and he told them exactly what the weather forecast held. Nobody questioned the decision to go ahead.

The venture was indeed disastrous. The weather was everything they had been warned about and the pilots quickly lost their bearing in the foul, stormy night. Lieutenant Bonnington's aircraft had to make a forced crash landing on the coast close to an enemy stronghold and although he managed to take off again he was soon down once more and all survivors were taken prisoner. Lieutenant McGonigal's plane was never heard of again and from the three remaining aircraft only 22 men made it back to the rendezvous with the LRDG, having been unable to attack their targets due to depleted numbers and the loss of most of their equipment.

Shocked though he was by the losses, Stirling refused to accept failure. He decided not to return to Cairo but to use the remnants of his force to prove that the German airfields were vulnerable. By striking a deal with the very willing LRDG, Stirling's small force was lifted back to Jalo Oasis which had just been captured by Brigadier Denys Reid's 'Flying Squadron'. Reid was able to offer food, weapons and explosives aplenty. He also told Stirling that he had been ordered to take his Squadron and deploy in the Agedabia area and he knew that he was going to be very vulnerable to attack by the enemy aircraft at Agedabia, Sirte and Agheila. This was a challenge to Stirling. His men would attack those airfields, lift some of the pressure from Reid's men and firmly establish their credentials.

The detachment split into small groups and, with the LRDG lending a hand to ferry them, over the next few days they achieved resounding success by destroying no less than 90 enemy aircraft, setting fire to massive fuel dumps and blowing up a large quantity of trucks. They were all to comment later how easy it had been in those early days. All German defences were indeed facing the ocean and coastal flanks. The attention of the sentries was also in those directions and the infiltrators quietly walked onto the airfields and set about placing their explosives before regrouping and marching out to their rendezvous to enjoy the sounds of the success from a safe distance. It was a confident Stirling who made his way back to Cairo to demand more men for 'L' Detachment.

From that point on the unit went from strength to strength, despite the tragic loss of 'Jock' Lewes and many others. Operations became more difficult as the Germans improved their defences and reactions, but somehow the patrols of 1st SAS, as it had become, stayed one jump ahead. They constantly switched tactics. For a period they would attack only during good moon conditions and then they would change to attacking only on the darkest of nights. They began to use the armed jeeps which Stirling had 'requisitioned' to carry out fast-moving raids to great effect. A legend grew up around them and Stirling became the 'Phantom Major' with a heavy price on his head.

He was still engaged in major battles with the MEHQ hierarchy, where he and his men were viewed as being somewhat piratical figures, despite their huge successes. Stirling was getting little time off between operations but he always seemed to get what he wanted even though it was at the cost of his own health. He was getting more and more tired, but he ignored the need for medical treatment for worsening desert sores and recurrent debilitating migraines.

Short of men, he managed to get permission to recruit Captain Georges Bergé and his band of Free French parachutists. 2nd SAS was forming up in the UK under the command of David's brother Bill Stirling, but meantime in North Africa operations carried on at an intensive pace. On the journey northwards through the Gabes Gap to link up with the 1st Army in February, 1943, Stirling's luck finally ran out and he was captured. At the age of 27 years he was a Lieutenant-Colonel, DSO, with command of a regiment that he had raised, trained and personally led. There is little doubt that at the time of his capture Stirling was in a state of near exhaustion due to his unceasing efforts on operations and in the rear echelons. His force had been responsible for the destruction of some 400 enemy aircraft, along with countless quantities of trucks, spares and fuel dumps.

Despite six escape attempts, Stirling was to remain (latterly in Colditz Castle) a prisoner until the end of hostilities in Europe. The SAS (now four regiments – one French and one Belgian) continued on in their now established tradition of daring and excellence through Sicily, Italy, France, Germany and Norway, causing damage out of all proportion to their modest size. At the end of the war they had every reason to expect that they would retain their identity. Indeed when Stirling was released when the

Germans surrendered in Europe he fully expected to be taking the SAS Brigade to China to attack the Japanese lines of supply, but that was not to be – the dropping of the atom bombs saw to that. On 8 October, 1945, HQ SAS, 1st and 2nd SAS Regiments were paraded for the last time and disbanded whilst under command of Brigadier Mike Calvert, DSO. Stirling, not waiting for personal demobilization, moved out to Rhodesia.

The War Office in its infinite wisdom had decided that any future conflict would be on a much lesser scale and controlled directly by those forces which possessed the atom bomb. Smaller limited-intensity conflicts would not require the use of forces such as the SAS. In the light of what Stirling had proved it seems a strange decision to disband such an effective organization in an army which was shortly to look long and hard at the cost-effectiveness of all its units.

The SAS had shown conclusively that it was possible to select and train men to work in very small numbers for long periods in the most inhospitable conditions. As a strategic tool they should be invaluable in any conflict, whether they be set to intelligence gathering or sabotage. Time, circumstances and the dedication of a few ex-SAS officers and men was to show that there would always be a place for special forces within the orbat of any professional army.

2

THE COMMUNIST REVOLT
IN MALAYA

The time and the circumstance first came together in the summer of 1948 when the British colony of Malaya was torn apart by a communist uprising. Communism in the colony can be traced back to 1930 when the Malayan Communist Party was formed. An important meeting was held that year in Singapore. Ho Chi Minh was there; he had come with a small delegation from Hong Kong where he lived in exile as the leader of the Vietnamese Communist Party. He also represented Russia's Far Eastern Bureau in Shanghai, from where Moscow controlled the Communist parties in Asia. The British Special Branch were also in attendance; their agents monitored every move that the communists made.

One of their agents-in-place was Lai Tek, a young Vietnamese protégé of Ho Chi Minh. Lai Tek came to Singapore, rose rapidly through the Communist Party hierarchy and became Secretary General in 1939, a few months before the outbreak of the Second World War. Throughout this time he kept his handlers in the Special Branch well informed and later, when the Japanese invaded, probably signed up with the Kempetai as well.

The outbreak of the war in Europe had little impact on the communist underground in Malaya, though they probably took heart from the early defeat of the Colonial powers of Holland and France, and rejoiced at Britain's military humiliations. The situation changed in 1941, however, when Germany invaded the Soviet Union. The Soviet Union and the British Empire were now allies and Moscow ordered the MCP to cooperate with the colonial administration. There was an uneasy truce but no cooperation, and the fault lay very much with the Malayan Civil Service who were dismissive of support from the communists and convinced of British superiority should the Japanese be so foolhardy as to attack. In circumstances such as these it was difficult for them to see what the communists had to offer.

Such arrogance spread to the military establishment and half-hearted talks were held between the General Staff and representatives of the Chinese community on the ways and means in which the latter might contribute. Little progress was made as the war clouds gathered in the Far East and the British raj looked to the conventional defences of their Empire.

The military establishment blocked other initiatives. By the summer of 1941 special forces had become the in-thing in so far as Winston Churchill was concerned. But the reluctance of the military establishment was still evident despite the success of organizations like the LRDG in the North African Campaign and the Commando raids against Occupied Europe. Elsewhere in the Middle East the commandos of Layforce, as we have seen, languished for want of proper employment.

In the Far East it was a similar tale. In Malaya No 101 Training School had been established to undertake all the training, civilian and military, of Europeans and Asians, in irregular warfare and clandestine intelligence gathering. Spencer Chapman* was commando trained in Britain and posted to the school along with a number of others as an instructor. There he languished. Officialdom and the military establishment treated talk about guerrilla warfare with disdain if only because the premise for their deployment in the field was the failure of conventional force of arms.

In December, 1941, the Japanese crippled the American Pacific Fleet at Pearl Harbor and turned their full force and fury on the Philippines, Hong Kong and Malaya.

Malaya was primarily a military defeat. The beaches at Kota Bharu, close to the Kra Isthmus and the northern border of Malaya with Siam, had long since been identified as a possible invasion point and were defended by battalions of the 8th Indian

* Later to write about his experiences in Malaya in his masterly book *The Jungle is Neutral* (Chatto and Windus)

Brigade. What caught the defenders by surprise was the speed and ferocity of the assault by an enemy willing to accept higher casualties than they, and the surrender of their air cover to an enemy flying more and better machines than the Royal Air Force could muster. The loss of the *Prince of Wales* and the *Repulse* on Wednesday 10 December was a terrible shock which, when combined with enemy success on land, caused morale to plummet among the fighting troops and the High Command to surrender the initiative on the battlefield.

Most of the British, Imperial and Commonwealth forces were only partially trained and poorly led. In too many instances they fell back in disarray as an orderly retreat took on the dimensions of a shameful rout. Singapore town was full of Australian deserters. In the face of military calamity, General Percival, the Commander-in-Chief, summoned his special forces to unleash guerrilla warfare upon the enemy.

The problems were immense. While one element of 101 Special Training School assumed responsibility for the Chinese, Spencer Chapman concentrated on creating guerrilla groups to be run by the British. The Chinese operation had to be a separate affair because there were few Chinese-speaking British officers; such was the colonial conceit that it was inconceivable the Chinese could be entrusted to run their own show.

Before that Sunday in mid-February, 1941, when 80,000 troops in Singapore surrendered in the worst defeat in British military history, some 200 stay-behind teams had been hurriedly deployed. Most infiltrated into the jungle, armed and supplied, but none was adequately trained in the techniques of guerrilla warfare.

Very few of the British teams survived beyond a few months, often simply because there was nowhere for a European to run. Many British and Australian soldiers also evaded the Japanese and took to the jungle, determined to fight it out. Very few lasted more than a year, often simply because of attitude. Some saw the jungle as a primitive paradise. They quickly succumbed to one or other of the many hidden dangers which entrapped the unwary – disease, poisonous fruits or reptiles.

Inadvertently Spencer Chapman was forced to stay behind. He survived because he appreciated that:

The truth is, the jungle is neutral. It provides any amount of fresh water and unlimited cover for friend or foe: an armed neutrality, but neutrality nevertheless.*

The British Government created Force 136, an SOE-type organization which eventually was to number forty officers and some 250 NCOs/Radio Operators. Force 136, with its headquarters in Ceylon, was tasked to coordinate local resistance in the enemy-occupied countries. In Malaya many of the people, brutalized and persecuted by the Japanese, joined the resistance groups in the jungle. By the end of the war the Malayan Peoples Anti-Japanese Army numbered about 7,000 fighters in regiments and there was that shadowy array of supporters and logisticians, the Min Yuen.

A rising star in those bleak days was Chin Peng. In 1944, when he was appointed a liaison officer to Force 136, he was just 22 years of age. Chin Peng was totally committed to the Communist cause, but in his naivety apparently believed that a People's Republic in Malaya could be achieved by cooperation with and the eventual support of the British authorities.

The end of the war caught the MPAJA by surprise. Although they had an abundance of arms, the leadership needed no convincing that they were not in any condition to make a play for power, even though there was an interregnum before the British put in an appearance. There was barely time to conceal the bulk of their weapons in caches and ensure that the infrastructure was in place through a 'front organization,' called the 'Old Comrades Association,' before it was time to march out of the jungle and back into civilian life. The situation that prevailed in the immediate aftermath of the Japanese surrender is vividly recalled by John Allen Harvey who was a First Assistant Secretary in the Colonial Secretariat in Kuala Lumpur in 1942.

In 1945 Allen returned to Malaya at the head of the first detachment of Colonial Administration Officers. Subsequently he was Senior Civil Affairs officer in Pahang. His account, which is part of a long letter written to his wife is as follows:

* ibid

As the Japs had left Ipoh 36 hours before our advance troops arrived, every house had been looted except a few. I was here, in the stronghold of Chinese communism, and they soon made themselves felt. Early talks with Miss Eng Min Chin, the Chairman of the Party, made it clear that we were in for feigned cooperation but, in reality, underground opposition. The Malayan Communist Party (MCP) set out to stir up all the trouble it could for the British Military Authority. Looting, intimidation, and all the tricks of the Chinese secret societies were used. I realised that a showdown must come and on October 22 (Sunday) we had it. The MCP had told Chinese coolies that if they demonstrated they would receive from the government $30 a head and 5 gangtangs of rice (which we had not got to give) and wages of $5 a day.

There were demonstrations all over Perak and in some cases we had to open fire. They continued for several days. I was personally involved in the one at Sungei Siput. Here Force 136 paratroops, who had been dropped into Malaya at various times during the Japanese occupation, had their HQ. They had acted as liaison troops with the Chinese guerrillas and had procured for them arms, ammunition and equipment.

The Chinese guerrilla forces were known as the MPAJA (Malayan People's Anti-Japanese Army) or 3 star from their uniform. There was also a small force of 1 star who were not communists but the MT (Chaing Kai Shek's party). The 3 star were largely communist and controlled by them. Well, to proceed – the Chinese coolies, some 2500 in number, lured by the false promises referred to above, surrounded Force 136 HQ and would not go away. I went out with my successor, Colonel de Crespigny. We arrived at about 9.30pm and had no difficulty in getting through the crowd to the house. We asked what the demands were and received the usual answer. We told them bluntly that these could not be accepted. We then tried to leave, but the crowd resisted and would not let us out. Finally we gave them a half-hour warning to disperse or we would fire; another warning at 27 minutes that fire would open in 3 minutes and this was greeted with a shout of defiance. We opened fire at the half-hour and the crowd went like a whirlwind. Two were killed and two injured. Colonel de Crespigny and I returned to Ipoh.

A week or so previously I had been warned that I was wanted as Senior Civil Affairs Officer in Pahang. The incumbent could not speak Malayan and it was desired to have someone at the head of the state administration who could. On 26 October, I arrived in Kuala Lipis to take over. Two days before my arrival they had had an incident in Lipis at the Secretariat very much on the same lines as at Sungai Siput. One Chinese was killed. This was later referred to by the MCP as the *Lipis Massacre*. The shootings which took place were effective and dampened the ardour of the trouble makers, especially as we flatly refused their demands for compensation to the deceased's relatives and the injured.★

The communist tactics were to leave the British with all the headaches in sorting out the country after the Japanese deprivations and trying to return it to some condition of normality. In the meantime the communists sought to infiltrate and subvert the trade union movement and other bodies such as the Teachers' Association etc. In what is usually referred to as *salami tactics*, the intention is to chip away at the fabric of society until the party was in a commanding position, namely to have the power to orchestrate an escalating campaign of protests, strikes, civil disobedience and sabotage aimed at provoking the authorities into an over-reaction. The terrorist in these circumstances sees himself as a catalyst, goading the security forces into over-reaction by inflicting a collective misery on the population, which would then convert more to the cause, and so wear down government resistance until eventually it lost the heart and the will to resist. This is borne out by John Harvey's comments:

> The MCP is working underground and the latest efforts are in the forms of strikes. Innumerable unlicensed associations and unions have sprung up – all more or less under the influence of the MCP.

★ The authors are most grateful to Harvey's son Bill who kindly gave us his father's papers and permission to quote them in our account.

It is often a moot point in the study of war as to whether one side proved overwhelmingly superior or whether the opponent contributed to its own defeat. In the issue of the Malayan Emergency the verdict is less than ambiguous. It is quite clearly the case that the communist forces lost the campaign rather than the Government forces who won.

The communists – CTs – lost the struggle because they were isolated and alone. They received no material aid or assistance from either the Soviet Union or the newly-founded Marxist regime of Mao Tse Tung in Peking. But even these were not the critical factors. The communists lost because they failed to win the support of the one and a half million Chinese urban population who lived in Malaya. If a majority of that population had sympathized with their cause, no military tactics, elite special forces or clever devices in counter-insurgency could have saved the country.

The Chinese were, after all, aliens in a foreign country; their homeland was China even though very few had been there. The Chinese gave little thought and no sympathy to a free Malaya. This feeling of cultural alienation was reinforced by the fact that the bulk of the Chinese population lived in 'Chinatowns'; these distinct, ghetto-type communities, quite isolated from mainstream Malayan life, were to be found in almost every town in the Malayan peninsula.

There were just two sections of the population who were to prove vulnerable to CT recruiting. The first were the aborigine tribes. They numbered, at the most, 100,000 people, animists who lived in long houses deep in the jungle and hunted with the blow pipe. The aborigines are not a homogenous people and fall into three broad categories – the Negritos, the Senoi and the Aboriginal Malays.

Their existence, so remote from government, made them easy prey when they encountered the CTs as the latter were, in turn, forced by military pressure to retreat and establish bases deep in the jungle. Aboriginal recruits performed indifferently in the cause of the CTs, but it was a different story when they came under the protection of the Special Forces who won their 'hearts and minds'.

The second group posed a more serious threat. There were

perhaps 500,000★ Chinese who 'squatted' on abandoned land along the edge of the jungle. Many were refugees from the rundown rubber and tin industries in the years of the depression and subsequent Japanese occupation. Many had lived that way, in surly resignation at their appalling conditions, for a generation or more. In 1948 the squatters represented about 1 in 10 of the population. Accessible and resentful, these people proved to be both a more fruitful reservoir of recruits and at least easier to intimidate into obedience until the government saw fit to acknowledge their plight and address their grievances.

From the outset the CTs were organized into two distinct arms, very much as they were during the days of resistance to the Japanese occupation. The fighting arm comprised what eventually and belatedly became known as the Malayan Races Liberation Army. There were about 4,000 guerrillas who eventually took to the jungle in 1948.† They were organized in exactly the same way as they had been against the Japanese and indeed were, for the most part, veterans of that campaign. Although guerrillas, they were organized on conventional military lines. There were eight regiments posted in strategic parts of the country. We still have no precise knowledge of the size of these regiments. Some were large, perhaps a thousand men, others numbered less than 300 in their ranks. Accounts are confusing, but it would seem that not all the CTs lived in the jungle. About 3,000 lived in the jungle on a permanent basis and were attached to the regiments. There were perhaps as many as 7,000 who were 'part time', living in towns or kampongs and occasionally being called upon to commit acts of terrorism.

In the early years those CTs who were guerrillas mostly lived in large camps, normally of company strength (i.e. in excess of one hundred men and women) with sub-units of platoons and sections. Many of the camps were elaborate affairs complete with drill squares, barrack blocks and classrooms; these had been placed on a care and maintenance basis after the ceasefire.

The second arm was called the Min Yuen. They were respon-

★ There is no accurate figure; some government sources quote 423,000 but some contemporary sources list the number as high as 600,000.
† The call to mobilize came in March, 1948, but of the 10,000 ex-MPAJA members registered, only 3,000 answered the call by the Emergency in June.

sible for intelligence gathering and supplying food to the fighting arm. The term is a shortened version of 'Min Chong Yuen Tong' which means 'The People's Movement'. All activities by the Masses and the Masses' leaders in aid of the Party were covered and so it followed that a Min Yuen worker could be a Party sympathizer living in the jungle but engaged in controlling the Min Yuen Organization. The term 'Min Yuen' is adjectival and is not a noun. In essence the group acted in support at all levels to the MRLA which was the 'fighting' arm.

Chin Peng described the Min Yuen as the 'eyes, ears, hands and feet of the Army.' Theirs was a crucial role. Besides providing vital intelligence on potential targets and the strength and activities of security forces, they fed the guerrillas. The fighting men could grow some food in the jungle, but this was a time-consuming occupation and, in any case, once the security forces had got their act together and introduced an effective and comprehensive air reconnaissance, cultivated plots in the jungle were an obvious give-away. Thereafter the CTs were even more dependent upon the Min Yuen.

Some government reports at the time speak of half a million members of the Min Yuen, but this is only a guess, and not even very educated. The Min Yuen wore no uniforms, and neither did they draw pay. Some were more part-time than others. They were organized on a traditional cell basis, so only a small number, the leaders, had physical contact with the guerrillas. These were called the Masses Executive, trusted ones who were often related to the CTs in the field. The Chinese tradition of closeknit families was an additional asset when it came to security. Indeed the Chinese were the majority and largely drawn from the ranks of the squatter communities. In their small holdings along the jungle fringe they were highly accessible and therefore vulnerable to CT attention. But even in the towns, where the Chinese might keep themselves to themselves and live in ghettos, in business and work they permeated colonial Malaya. Thus Min Yuen members were to be found serving the drinks in the anteroom of an officers' mess; they were doctors, journalists, school teachers, clerks and taxi drivers, shopkeepers and street traders.

The Min Yuen reached into the top echelons of colonial society. In 1952, following the assassination of the High Commissioner,

Sir Henry Gurney, there was a concerted effort to root out the subversives. In the course of investigations the butler at King's House, the official residence of the High Commissioner in Kuala Lumpur, was discovered to be a member of the Min Yuen.

The Min Yuen were organized and structured through a parallel civilian chain of command with committees at state, regional, district, town and village levels. The Min Yuen were vital to success. Operationally, members spied on the British, provided recruits, screened the terrorists, acted as an early warning system, carried passengers and fed the fighters. The guerrillas also needed people to whom they could boast of their prowess and their exploits; they needed an audience of admirers because they wanted recognition as heroes in their own lifetime.

The Min Yuen were also Chin Peng's barometer; by their numbers and enthusiasm the Politburo could assess the success of the campaign. If their numbers swelled, then the CTs could be on target to achieve a mass popular uprising which would sweep aside the colonial trappings of British rule.

The critical role that the Min Yuen played as a lifeline to the CTs was recognized very early on in the campaign, and the organization was quickly singled out as a target for penetration by the fledgling Special Branch.

Controlling and coordinating the activities of the CTs and Min Yuen, albeit imperfectly through means of hand-written messages and couriers, was the over-elaborate structure of the Communist Party and its hierarchy.

Supreme power resided in the Central Executive Committee of the Malayan Communist Party which comprised about a dozen members who were scattered nation-wide and therefore could meet only on occasion and then with great difficulty. Effective operational authority was delegated to a three-man Politburo of Chin Peng, Yeung Kwo, who was Deputy Secretary of the MCP and Chairman of the Selangor Committee, and the outstanding Lau Lee, Head of the Propaganda Bureau.

Lai Tek had departed the scene. In March, 1947, he failed to answer a summons to attend a special Politburo Committee which had been established to investigate his behaviour. He disappeared and was never seen again.

Conspiracy theories abound but he was most probably executed by his own people and Chin Peng was appointed General Secretary in his place. At the age of 28 years this was a quite remarkable achievement.

Chin Peng headed an organization which was cumbersome, top-heavy and overly bureaucratic. The problem was further exacerbated because of primitive communication between the various hierarchies. Messages had to be sent by couriers, who, at best, could make use of public transport, and important committee members who also belonged to the fighting units; they spent a lot of down time travelling between committee meetings and their units.

As with the Chinese and Soviets before them, the key elements were the political commissars. They too had their own rank structure and were to be found at every level in the political and military hierarchy. The commissars ran courses on ideology, maintained discipline and had the authority to override military orders.

Even though Chin Peng received nothing from the Russians or the Chinese, his strategy for operations was based almost entirely on that developed by Mao Tse Tung in China. Conquest in Malaya was envisaged in three phases, of which only the first was ever fully defined.

Phase One of the campaign was devoted to economic warfare. The aim was to cripple the economy by attacks on the rubber estates and the tin mines.

It was intended in Phase Two, the timing of which had yet to be determined, that in true Maoist fashion the countryside would surround the towns. The government forces would find the countryside so hostile that they would be loath to leave the towns and maybe the coastal strip. In the countryside, in the meantime, liberated areas would be established under communist rule.

In Phase Three the British would be presented with an impossible situation. Confronted by a mass uprising orchestrated through the Min Yuen in the towns and with the CTs controlling the countryside, their position would become increasingly untenable. The High Commissioner would be forced to sue for peace. The British would leave Malaya and the Communists would establish a multi-ethnic Soviet state.

The strategy worked in China, it worked in Indo-China and Vietnam and it failed in Malaya.

For the CTs, success depended upon either the British managers, especially those in the more isolated areas, abandoning their posts or the labourers in the tin mines and the rubber plantations staying away from work.

With the white management killed, the local population would be open to CT influence and control, as well as a source of new recruits.

Chin Peng had underestimated white resolve and the stoic loyalty and endurance of their workers who were not about to surrender their livelihood. Planters and managers stayed put, barricaded their houses and, in some instances, armed their workers. Between them they bought time for the security forces to respond; their collective contribution was critical.

The planters were also able to acquire weapons. The secretary of their association was a recently retired brigadier from Headquarters Far East Land Forces (FARELF) with all the right connections. In contrast, the miners fared badly until the American-owned Pacific Tin Corporation flew in two Dakotas loaded with Thompsons, carbines and other small arms for the exclusive use of their managers.

The theories of Mao Tse Tung are fine on paper, but in practice other factors tend to take control. In Malaya the cosmopolitan nature of the population probably worked against the almost exclusively Chinese communists. The Malays, who made up practically half of the five million population,* were farmers and fishermen deeply immersed in their history and culture with loyalties for the most part centred on their Sultans, their hereditary rulers.

The Chinese were cantankerous, independent in thought and bloody-minded. The bulk of the Chinese population spent much of the Emergency sitting on the proverbial fence, defying the efforts of both sides to make a commitment. The communists could, on occasion, secure some measure of temporary compliance because their powers of coercion were less restrained.

The Indians, half a million in number and mostly Tamils from

* Excluding Singapore.

Madras, had no long-term commitment to the country either, but returned home once they had earned sufficient money to buy a plot of land. In the rigidly stratified society imposed by the British raj, the Indian community was at the bottom of the social scale and, in those days, of little consequence. The British, of which there were about 12,000, were no longer held in awe; the Japanese had destroyed the myth of Western invulnerability. This was manifest in many forms at the local level in terms of attitudes and the lack of respect shown to the whites.

Thus there were considerable difficulties in civil administration and trying to return Malaya to some normality. None of this was helped, of course, in the immediate post-war years by a disturbing increase in the tempo of industrial sabotage and political violence in line with the communist master plan. Innumerable unlicensed associations and trade unions had sprung up, all more or less under the influence of the communists. John Harvey wanted a firm hand; he wrote:

'I have tried to get the British Military Administration to insist on registration of the unions and the associations and to reintroduce banishment, but to no avail. If this had been done I could guarantee stable administration.'

But it is also the case that Britain's colonial policy contributed to the breakdown in law and order and the belated declaration of a State of Emergency in June, 1948.

The Crown had no intention of remaining in Malaya, and that is about all that can be said in its favour. The postwar Labour Government gave no great priority to the Colonial Office and was, in any case, grappling with the near-insuperable problems encountered in the partition of India and the withdrawal from Palestine.

In Malaya the plan was to create a single multiracial parliamentary democracy called the Malaya Union. As an interim measure the Sultans in their nine states ruled with British advisors; the exceptions were the three settlements of Singapore, Malacca and the island of Penang. The Chinese and Indians had no say in political affairs.

The Malayan Union was a disaster. In 1947 the Government

was forced into ignominious retreat and fell back on the constitutional device of a Federal Legislative Council, an advisory body appointed by the High Commissioner. This was intended as an interim measure while the Colonial Office in London groped about for an alternative path to self-government.

It is hardly surprising that in its confusion and disarray, the Administration failed to anticipate the communist uprising. There were those who were informed of the coming uprising and there was a general awareness of impending trouble. But in the event, the intensity and extent of the onslaught caught the administration by surprise. Much of this was probably exacerbated by bureaucratic confusion and poor crisis management, of bumbling between the disparate arms of the colonial administration, the police and the military.

Intelligence is a case in point. Earlier, in 1946, a new intelligence service was created in Malaya. The Malayan Security Service (MSS) was established by the Administraton with responsibility for intelligence gathering. The MSS was entirely separate from either the police or the military, was piteously under-funded and thereby understaffed. There was a Director and a headquarters in Singapore, and a Deputy with a small outstation in Kuala Lumpur.

In June, 1947, the Director ordered his deputy in Kuala Lumpur to penetrate the Malayan Communist Party. At this stage the MSS knew nothing about the MCP; such information was the preserve of the Police CID and they were not about to share the knowledge with anyone, least of all a rival.

Despite these constraints, the MSS was able to predict the militancy and intentions of the MCP, but their advice was spurned. The High Commissioner, Sir Edward Gent, also chose to ignore the advice and warning of impending trouble that was being fed in quite independently from the British plantation and mine managers.

In some mitigation to Gent's obstinacy, he was not well served by his police chief. Commissioner of Police H. B. Langworthy commanded a divided and bitter force. Those who had stayed at their posts in 1942 until the bitter end and then endured the hell of prison camp could not forgive those who had escaped the Japanese onslaught.

Military Intelligence also warned Gent, but to no avail. Against a background of rising violence Colonel John Dalley, a senior officer with vast experience in Intelligence, reported that the communists were training up their cadres in jungle camps and would shortly launch 'the armed struggle'. He even predicted with remarkable accuracy a guerrilla strength of 5,000 fighters and a quarter of a million people in the Min Yuen. Major General Boucher, GOC Malaya, was a Gurkha officer of great experience but an arrogant soldier of limited vision. He disagreed with Dalley's assessment and, in his submission to the High Commissioner, dismissed the CTs as of little consequence, a minor problem compared to the Greek communists whom he had recently fought.

Sir Edward Gent had a boss. Malcolm MacDonald was Commissioner General for South East Asia. The Labour Government did not trust the Colonial Office and so this political appointment – he was the son of a famous father, the first Labour Prime Minister, Ramsay MacDonald – was tasked to oversee the region.

Colonel John Dalley brought matters to a head. There had already been a number of killings and the British planters and miners were clamouring for arms, all of which had been brusquely dismissed by Gent. Dalley's career was about over, retirement beckoned, but he cared passionately about the country. So he went over the heads of his military superior and saw MacDonald directly. The latter read the intelligence assessment and believed what he read. But MacDonald played it by the book. He showed the Dalley Memorandum to Gent and told him that it would be forwarded to London with a recommendation that the High Commissioner should be recalled.

The reasons which prompted Chin Peng to launch the armed struggle at this time, to switch from the city to the countryside, has never been adequately explained. Some analysts have pointed to the influence of returning MCP delegates who, in February of that year, had attended a Communist Youth Conference in Calcutta. Other observers have claimed that he had a number of advisors sent to him by Mao Tse Tung, but there is no evidence to substantiate this claim. The most likely reason is that Chin Peng had become frustrated by the failure of the MCP to provoke the urban revolution. Perhaps the call to the jungle was also a cleansing, a purging move, away from the temptations of high living in the case of the Politburo.

The immediate result was that guerrilla raids became more effective and the casualty toll increased. Even so, most of the casualties were Malayan or Indian and no interest was elicited by the Colonial Administration. Then, on 16 June, 1948, the MCP signalled the start of the armed insurrection by killing three British, two miners and a planter.

Matters came to a head on 17 June when a delegation which had carefully rehearsed its case gave a very clear picture of the internal security situation in Malaya. As a result Gent agreed to introduce a limited State of Emergency in troubled areas such as Perak and Johore. But by this stage the public and the press had lost patience and respect for his administration.

The English language *Straits Times* carried banner headlines; 'Govern or Get Out.'

The public outcry in support of sterner measures was overwhelming. A few days later, on 23 June, 1948, Gent was forced to declare a State of Emergency throughout Malaya. It was not until 23 July that the Malayan Communist Party was declared an illegal organization.

Within days the Federation was transformed. Police on traffic duty carried side arms, planters walked the streets with Lee Enfields and American carbines slung on their shoulders. In the Long Bar at Raffles and the Cricket Club in Kuala Lumpur there was talk only of war.

Poor Gent was not alone in his complacency; there were other, very senior people who were caught by surprise over events in Malaya. General Sir Neil Ritchie, the man who had given Stirling his blessing in 1941, was by now Commander-in-Chief Far East Land Forces, with his headquarters in Singapore.

In a report, the Handover Notes, to his successor General Harding, Ritchie, in a masterpiece of understatement, wrote:

It was not until the evening of 22 June, 1948, that I was appraised by the civil authorities of the conditions of unrest existing in Malaya. An undercurrent of serious internal trouble already existed and in fact it is true to say that the communist-inspired Cold War in the country was by that time under way.

That this state of affairs came as a great surprise to the Services is possibly best illustrated by recalling that I had just returned from a brief visit to the United Kingdom where I had told the Chief of the Imperial General Staff (CIGS) that in my view Malaya could be regarded as one of the relatively stable areas in an otherwise disturbed South East Asia. I understand from the C in C Far East Air Force (FEAF) that he had expressed much the same view to the Chief of Air Staff (CAS). The GOC Malaya District was equally in the dark regarding the internal situation and had, in fact, at that time (early June 1948) a small body of troops acting in aid of the Civil Power in Perak operating against an unruly element of the KMT (Chinese Nationalist sympathizers) there; a body which is violently opposed to Communism.

It is unnecessary to stress what a disadvantage it is to be caught off-balance in such a way.*

The High Commissioner was made to pay for the failure to prevent civil insurrection. Gent was sacked and on 29 June left for London. Before his departure, however, he had a meeting with Colonial Dalley and apologised; he accepted unreservedly all the points in the Dalley Memorandum.

Four days later Gent's official aircraft, an Avro York of RAF Transport Command, crashed while on its final approach to London's Northolt Airport. In poor visibility the York was in a mid-air collision with a Skymaster of Scandinavian Air Lines. All thirty-nine people on board the two aircraft were killed.

* Ref WO 106/5884 para 8

3

THE COUNTRY, THE CHALLENGE
AND THE MEN

'If only we can double the ratio of kills per contact, we
will soon put an end to the shooting in Malaya.'

General Templer
High Commissioner and Director
Operations, Federation of Malaya.
1952

The Malay Peninsula, which can also be called the Kra
Peninsula, is a 700-mile-long, narrow appendage to mainland
South-East Asia. It stretches from a point parallel to Bangkok,
south through the Isthmus of Kra bordered by the Andaman Sea
(to the west) and the Gulf of Thailand (to the east) on through the
Straits of Malacca and the South China Sea to the Singapore
Straits which separate it from the island of Singapore. At its
northern origins the peninsula contains terrorities belonging to
Thailand and Burma but it is the 400-mile stretch south from the
Thai border – Peninsular Malaya – which is of interest to us for
this was the scene of the Malayan Emergency. The peninsula is
divided by a slightly offset mountain spine which rises to 7175
feet (Gunong Tahan) at its highest point; consequently more than
one half of the total area of Malaya (approximately 53,500 square
miles) is over 500 feet above sea level.

The western coast is exposed to the south-west monsoon
during the period June to October and the eastern coast suffers
from the north-west monsoon which occurs during the months
of November to March. The monsoons deliver a mean annual
rainfall of 100 inches. The effect of the offset mountain spine is

that the western rivers have comparatively short courses with navigation being limited by widespread silting along the coast which results in some districts in vast expanses of swamp. On the eastern side the rivers are longer with less precipitous gradients in the upper reaches.

Typical annual temperatures range between 77° to 86°F on the mountains. Vegetation is typical of such a hot humid climate with over three-quarters of the country (at the time of the Emergency) being covered by forest. Tree types are many and varied and include teak, bamboo, camphor, sandalwood and many more. Between them they can result in a canopy of interwoven vines and top growth as high as 200 feet above the height of the soldier on terra firma. The vegetation in Malaya is principally governed by two factors; altitude and history. The higher and drier the ground the more open is the bush at ground level. This 'virgin', or primary jungle, is usually quite easy to move through and the canopy of the trees tends to be lower than in the valleys. Along the rivers can be found the huge clumps of bamboo which can cover a number of acres – these present map reading problems as circumnavigation is often the only way to deal with them. Within areas of virgin jungle it is not uncommon to come across abandoned cultivated areas and these are a mess of low tangled growth as the plant life fights for its share of the sunlight. Such areas are uncomfortable, hot and difficult to move through where visibility is down to a few feet. Towards the foothills and the coasts, as the land flattens out, will be found the guardsmen-like ranks of the huge rubber plantations providing good visibility and allowing fast movement. Along the coast there are areas of waist-deep, stinking swamp where again visibility is poor and progress difficult.

Movement by the natural inhabitants of the jungle, be they animal or human, is usually along main river lines or the spurs and ridges of the mountain range. Once off these 'highways' the soldier will encounter a number of problems. The minor rivers, although principal aids to navigation, can be steep-sided, rocky and treacherous as can the minor spurs which drop steeply into them. The tree tops house what is one of the world's most varied collections of bird life. At lower levels there is an equally prolific collection of wild life, much of which is rarely seen by the soldier.

There are elephants, wild pigs, wild oxen and tiger, to say nothing of panthers, snakes and a huge conglomeration of gibbons, orangutans, monkeys and even rhinoceros.

The challenge to British soldiers operating in the jungle was in essence both physical and psychological. Soldiers were able to acclimatize to the heat and humidity once they were physically fit but the military equipment in use in the early fifties was not suited for jungle operations in company strength when soldiers were not always travelling along tracks or through open spaces. The 1944 pattern webbing was restrictive, uncomfortable and cumbersome given the slightest obstruction from vines, creepers and low brush. The early machetes are well described in military parlance – 'treebeaters'. Long, heavy and seemingly incapable of holding an edge for more than a few slashes, they were virtually useless for track-cutting purposes. Magazine pouches which sat nicely in front of the soldiers' lower chest were cleverly designed to hit the diaphragm with a resounding blow which winded the soldier who fell flat to take up a firing position; at the same time he was assaulted from behind his head by the back pack which, with a mind of its own, flew upward and forward. It was virtually impossible to take a quiet drink from the aluminium water bottle due to the squeaking of the lid (of the same material) as it was removed.

The issue jungle boots of poor quality canvas welded to a rubber sole were designed by a thoughtful boffin to release water as the boots filled during river crossings and the like, but their average life was about six days! If the hapless soldier was forced to march any distance at all on a road or hard track when he quickly found that the boots which let out the water so easily let in the sand just as rapidly and blisters soon resulted in an environment where infection sets in fast. Socks shrank and issue aertex-type underpants had an uncomfortable habit of inexorably creeping up between the buttocks to spread the sort of itching rash which the soldier had probably not experienced since his days in nappies.

The rations were wholesome enough but all packed in tin cans which, if not carefully stowed in the packs, soon created their own pressure points on shoulders and spines. On top of this they were heavy out of all proportion to their calorific value and there was no disguising the smell of British rations being cooked. The debris from a day's worth of rations was quite remarkable and if not buried deeply it soon displayed to every jungle traveller the fact that the British 'Tom' had been this way.

Given the inadequacy of his equipment it is remarkable that the resilience of the soldier allowed him to move over the distances he was called upon to cover when the effects of the ground and climate were added to this factor. In the main the infantryman tended to use the compass bearing as his prime means of navigating and this could mean miles of 'yo-yoing' as he went up and down the innumerable ridges and spurs only to find that he had travelled but a few miles on the plane surface of the map. It was likely that only one person had a map and compass and so those behind the leaders saw only the back of the man in front as he slipped and skidded along.

Psychologically the soldier was fighting two enemies; the environment and the Chinese Communist. The jungle, to the westerner, has always presented a picture of horrors – a strange and evil dampness within which lurked indescribable beasts and insects; a permanent malodorous, impenetrable wall of clinging, barbed vines and the webs of malevolent spiders; a land of blood-sucking leeches which infiltrated themselves into a man's most private parts leaving infection in their wake; snakes like the banded krait and the bamboo 'bootlace' which were rumoured to leave a man in agonizing death throes. Such stories and fears came from a multitude of sources: the post-war tales of Burma; the new genre of horror films and, not in the least, from the old sweats in the regiments.

And what of the CT? A hard, elusive enemy who had lived in the jungles for so long that he was part animal himself; the yellow-skinned zealot who killed from ambush or by booby trap and who had subverted the primitive tribesman to his will so that not one of them was to be trusted. Numbered in many thousands they moved out of the deep jungle, struck and were back in their wild habitat before the British soldier had time to gather his wits. More than this they were all around. Even when the soldier was in barracks he did not know who he could trust; was the 'char-wallah' part of the Min Yuen? Were the tailor who made the cheap shirts and the attractive bar girl part of the organization reporting every detail of the soldier's off-duty habits? How had the supreme commander described the CT? General Templer in the first edition of his pamphlet, *The Conduct of Anti-Terrorist Operations in Malaya*, defined the CT as:

Those who in any way actively further the subversive communist campaign for the purpose of overthrowing the Government of the Federation by resorting to or instigating violence and who:

(a) By the use of any firearm, explosive or ammunition act in a manner prejudicial to the public safety or to the maintenance of public order.

(b) Incite to violence or counsel disobedience to the law or to any lawful order by the use of any firearm, explosive or ammunition.

(c) Carry or have in their possession or under their control any firearm without lawful authority therefor.

(d) Carry or have in their possession or under their control any ammunition or explosive without authority therefor.

(e) Adhere to the CT gangs as couriers or camp followers.

A pretty all-encompassing description.

This then was the challenge which faced the generally honourable and basically clean British soldier as he stepped from the troopship on to the humid soil of Malaya. A dirty war in a filthy environment against an unscrupulous enemy surrounded by friends.

If there was challenge to the individual soldier then there was also a challenge to his supporting arms. Mapping was still crude in the early 1950s. It was not at all unusual, particularly when operating in deeper jungle, to find huge patches of the map totally blank with just the cryptic words 'Cloud Cover' written before them. Eventually these gaps were filled in as better air photographs were taken, analysed and transcribed to the charts, but initially it made things quite difficult. Even in comparatively well-mapped areas it took time for the soldier to adjust to the niceties of jungle navigation. Distances were confusing as obstacles were circumnavigated or patches of very slow going were encountered. Although the main rivers and the few roads were accurately recorded the same could not be said for the minor rivers and streams. The impossibility of seeing more than a few yards at the best made position fixing very unreliable in some areas; if a supply drop zone was found and the position not given accurately there could be long delays while the crew of an aircraft searched for it; a clearing which seemed quite large on the ground could be just a glimmer to the aircraft navigator.

Although as a rule the clouds which shroud the hillsides and the mists which cover the valleys and ravines disappear by mid-morning, this is not an absolute prediction. The weather is fickle and in any event there may only be a window of a few hours before clouds and mists descend again. The broken nature of the country produces phenomenal turbulence upsetting the balance and direction of light aircraft. In short, resupply was yet another uncertainty thrown into the equation by Mother Nature. The officer calling for artillery or mortar support would have anxious moments until the first shot fell. Small wonder that the soldier thought the odds were unfairly balanced against him.

From 1948 to early 1952 the operations of the security forces changed little. The role was in many areas reactive, with troops being despatched to specific areas as a result of a CT action. Their role was likely to be a hastily mounted 'Search and Destroy' mission into an area which may well have never hosted an actual CT, such was the paucity of the information. British and Gurkha troops became rapidly disenchanted with these long, sweaty, fruitless 'bashes' into the jungle. It is a strange anomaly but both opponents in the battle at that time actually credited the other with being the likely victors. On the one side the CTs saw better armed, numerically superior, trained soldiers with good air and artillery support and reasonable communications and on the security forces side they saw an intangible enemy who rarely closed for action; thus each saw the other's capabilities in a highly exaggerated form. In terms of men on the ground the security forces held a comfortable 2:1 majority over the CTs, but the actual bayonet figures of the force was probably in the region of 4500. A large percentage of these were relatively untrained, certainly in jungle warfare, and a great number were national servicemen with a suspect morale. The infantry battalions bore the brunt of the operations and leadership at all levels was of a fluctuating standard in those early days. Yet when the formation of a special force began there was no initial shortage of recruits even from the ranks of the conscripts as we shall see. What was in their minds as they volunteered? A little can be gleaned from the memories of two young officers who were to opt for 'special service':

We landed in Singapore and were unceremoniously put on the overnight train to Kuala Lampur. I can remember listening all night for the first shots fired from a terrorist ambush position. The trip, however, was uneventful. Arriving in Kuala Lumpur we were soon breakfasting at Wardieburn Camp. But, before we could consider settling down we were taken to the operations room and given a general briefing and then a specific operational brief for 'D' Squadron. We were to join them in the Ipoh area the next morning.

We spent the remainder of that day being kitted out. Our feet didn't touch the ground. We were allowed to choose what weapon we wanted. I selected a US M1 carbine – it looked the smallest, lightest one available, and I had seen John Wayne use one to great effect on the cinema screen. After an overnight stop at Brigade Headquarters we were flown in by helicopter to the 'D' Squadron Headquarters at the 'Dorset LZ' in primary jungle east of Sungei Siput. We were welcomed by John Woodhouse the squadron commander, to be told that he had no room for us until the next day. We would have to look after ourselves that night and find a basha site nearby. He gave us an escort to help us settle in. Peter de la Billière (who had arrived a few days earlier) was already with 'D' Squadron. He, too, was expelled from the main base to join us!

That first night in the jungle was terrifying. I didn't know what to expect. The night noises were very loud. I later learned to wake up when it went quiet at night. And I had never built a basha before. Somehow we survived and the next day returned to the 'Dorset Base'. It was a well-built jungle camp with good bashas and log sangars. We were taken there for a few days receiving excellent practical tuition from John Woodhouse.

Just after dark one evening a single shot rang out, amazingly loud amongst all the other jungle noises; we dived for our stand-to positions and stared into the darkness. We then heard John Woodhouse speaking to the dog handler. A second shot rang out. We were then told that we could stand down. What had happened was that Trooper McComb had been cleaning his handgun and let off an accidental discharge. When he was showing John Woodhouse what had happened he let off the second round. Apparently Woodhouse then snatched the gun from McComb, took out a 36 grenade, removed the pin and thrust it into McComb's hand saying: 'Now let's see you let that off accidentally.'

McComb worked for quite a few days thereafter armed only with his grenade minus its safety pin!

After about a week at 'Dorset', we were sent off on an individual navigation exercise. We had to rendezvous with the Training Troop at Long Jim's ladang. It was a two-day march and we were given an escort of two troopers who were forbidden to help us in any way.

On the first day I was travelling as number two in the patrol when the leading scout stopped, put up his hand to his ear to indicate that we should all listen. He pointed and then gave a thumbs down sign signifying enemy presence. I suddenly heard a noise as if the whole Chinese army was charging us. Bravely I stood my ground and released the safety catch on my carbine. The magazine dropped from the weapon – I'd pressed the magazine release lever instead. At that instant I realised it was only a troop of monkeys in the tree tops (a fact that the lead scout had known only too well). My escorts laughed their heads off and I learned that never again would I select a weapon with which I was not familiar.'

There were early experiences of another sort.

I came awake suddenly and rolled off my hammock, grabbed my rifle and crawled across to my stand-to position. It was still dark and I was conscious of the other members of the patrol to the left and right of me, blurred in the gloom and perfectly still. I heard the one on my right mutter softly, 'Wait for it. Wait for the crack.' What bloody crack? I thought. What have I missed? What were they expecting? I tried to make the guy conscious of my question by raising my eyebrows towards him. He merely looked back at me and muttered again, 'Wait for it. Wait for the crack'.

I really didn't know what was going on; what to expect. Was there a group of CTs even now crawling forward into attack position. Would the crack be the detonator of the first grenade some Chinese bandit would throw to open the attack? I tensed and eased my rifle into a more comfortable position. My movement drew the low, hissed comment, 'Wait for the bloody crack.' Dawn came quickly and as the light amplified I could see nothing untoward and I then became aware of the other chaps easing their muscles and beginning to relax. I turned to my right and questioned,

'What was the flap? What were we waiting for? What bloody crack?'

'The crack of dawn, of course. What did you think?'

Of course everyone creased up and I learned a bit more about the humour of the SAS.

Such are the recollections of two young officers on their initiation into 22 Special Air Service Regiment; both clearly show some trepidation but also an eagerness to get into the action. What was the attraction of this new unit involved in a war which virtually carried on from the cessation of hostilities of World War II, was to involve over 60,000 troops and last for fourteen years? What conditions were to materialize that would persuade the British Army to reverse the decision to disband the SAS and how did that regiment evolve under conditions so totally different from those of its initial conception in the North Africa of the early forties? What forces and which people were to shape its future?

4

CALVERT'S BUILDING SITE

'In the beginning it was like a building site . . . and he [Calvert] knew that building sites are muddy, rough places.'

Anon.

When Gent declared a State of Emergency in Malaya the British Army was largely shorn of its splendid array of special forces, many of whom had made such an important contribution to victory in the Second World War.

The dropping of the atomic bombs on Hiroshima and Nagasaki in August, 1945, sparked a chain of events which, insofar as the SAS Regiment was concerned, spelled disaster. David Stirling's concept had resulted in a rare situation in that the regiment he had formed had been accepted directly into the Order of Battle (orbat) of the British Army. On his release from Colditz in April, 1945, Stirling had fully expected to lead an SAS Brigade into action harassing the Japanese Army along the great Manchurian railway and also cutting off the lines of supply further to the south through which the enemy in Malaya was being fed and supported. The rapid collapse of Japanese resistance due to the devastation caused by the atom bombs brought all such plans to an end. On 21 September of that year the Belgian SAS Regiment was formally handed over to that country's national command; a short time later (1 October) the same thing happened to the French SAS; both regiments retained their formation and identity within the peacetime defence orbats of their respective countries. On 8 October, 1945, HQ SAS, 1st and 2nd SAS Regiments were

paraded for the last time. The officer in command of the disbandment parade was Brigadier 'Mad Mike' Calvert, DSO.

Calvert had formally taken over the SAS Brigade from Brigadier 'Roddy' McLeod in late 1944 and had remained in energetic
command until that final parade. He was bitterly opposed to
disbandment but it was inevitable and no doubt his reflections at
the time were that, sadly, he would see no more of the SAS. A
man of great military foresight (along with Colonel Sir David
Stirling and General Sir John Watts) he was, though, on this
occasion, quite wrong.

The legendary British officers of World War II do not make a
long list – for that is the matter-of-fact nature of the Briton, but
one only has to meet Mike Calvert, even after all the intervening
years, to get an inkling as to what placed him on that short list.
He is not a tall man but in later life his barrel chest is still
impressive and his arms, shoulders and powerful handshake
indicate the phenomenal strength of his earlier years. The flattened
nose, direct stare and pugnacious set of his jaw tell the story of a
thousand rounds inside and outside the boxing ring. He looks
tough and is tough, but the blind man, hearing only the soft,
quiet voice expressing his views on the welfare of his fellow man
could be forgiven for thinking he was talking to a philosopher or
priest rather than a hugely competent fighting man. The stories
of 'Mad' Mike's exploits as a Chindit Brigade Commander are
legion but usually they are heard from third parties, rarely from
the man himself.

At the end of the war the British Army underwent a massive
reduction in its establishment and Calvert, like very many others,
reverted to his substantive rank of Major. By this time he was
already something of a legend. In the early stages of the war he
had resigned his commission to fight as a volunteer in Finland
with the 'Snowballers'; as a private he became one of the founding
members of the Commando. A tough fighter and hard drinker,
Calvert was above all an idealist and a thoroughly determined
man and he was quickly commissioned once more. His experience
during the war is perhaps best known for his three years' fighting
the Japanese in Burma, much of this period was spent behind
enemy lines.

An indication of Calvert's unorthodoxy can be gleaned from

his post-war actions as CRE, 1st Indian Armoured Brigade. In his words, 'At that time it was a muddle of the Bombay, Bengal and Madras Sappers.'

Calvert felt he had to draw the unit together and give it a sense of identity. It was decided that the brigade would move from its base in Bangalore to Hyderabad, a distance of some 2–300 miles. Calvert marched his command to its new location but not by road; he chose instead a cross-country route which took his men over rivers, mountains and ravines. He personally led this mammoth march and arrived 'with a much healthier command'.

After Staff College, which he was unable to take seriously, Calvert moved to Trieste to take up a staff appointment as Head of Boundaries Commission for Jugoslavia and Italy and received congratulations from United Nations for his perspicacity in the settling of many border arguments and debates. From there he was sent to Hong Kong as G1 (Air).

On the way he was to make many new friends and reinforce a number of wartime acquaintances which were to have some effect on his future moves. An amusing story hints at the mutual regard between himself and General Sir Bernard Montgomery (at the time Chief of the Imperial General Staff [CIGS]): at a high table dinner, Montgomery is said to have remarked, 'Now, Major Calvert, why is it that here I have all my Generals; here's a General; there's a Quartermaster General; here's an Adjutant General and over there, a Military Secretary. I ask them questions and what do they say? They say, "Well, I'll have to look into that. I'll have a meeting about this or I'll give you my views in a fortnight's time," or something like that. But you, Major Calvert, when I ask you something, you say, "It should be done like this or like that." Now, why is it that you have these views and my Generals don't?'

Calvert's succinct reply was, 'Sir, I'm the only one, I think, who's in his substantive rank. You can't reduce me without a Court Martial.'

At a later stage Calvert was made to stand up in front of all the staff oficers and relate the story which was then finished off by Montgomery saying simply, 'I want more of you officers to be like Major Calvert.'

It will be seen that Calvert impressed his superiors just as much as he impresed the troops he led. We shall return to him.

Meantime, back in Malaya, General Sir Neil Ritchie who handed over to Lt-General Sir John Harding as High Commissioner and Director of Operations for the Federation, had completed his *Report of Operations in Malaya* for the CIGS. It is interesting to note some passages from this:

QUALITY OF BANDITS IN MALAYA

- They are terrorists and thugs and show no more courage than any others of that ilk.
- While cunning in their planning, they have on the whole proved indifferent in the execution of military plans.
- They are not well led on the lower levels, nor are they well equipped. For this reason they seldom stand and fight. Indeed one can scarcely expect them to do so, for their position is hopeless when facing regular troops or police when well trained and led.
- On the other hand their propaganda is good and their strength lies in the fact that they can so easily disperse and disappear amongst the squatter population.
- Despite being the aftermath of the MPAJA and having been trained to some extent by us in the FORCE 136 days, they appear to be generally unenterprising in their tactics. For instance, they have so far failed to make any really all out effort against communications, which are particularly vulnerable in Malaya.
- In fighting quality they are not in the same class as the Pathan of the North East Frontier of India. I would class them as of about the same calibre as the Palestinian Arabs who opposed our rule in Palestine in the rebellion of 1938/39.

PRIVATE ARMIES

- There has been some desire here on the part of certain civil authorities to form specialised ad hoc units of the commando type for operations in Malaya.

– As an instance the 'FERRET FORCE' was thought to be the very sort of unit needed here. The fact that the more senior officers were all civilians, who held local commissions and were paid for by the Federal Government was the thin end of the wedge for certain civil officials to feel that it was within their province to direct its operations. Its disbandment put an end to this, but nevertheless military commanders must be on their guard against this happening. The object of 'FERRET FORCE' was to raise the general standard of 'jungle warfare' of the troops. In consequence it contained the pick of the personnel in units and naturally produced high standards and results.

– The civilian cannot appreciate the strain that the provision of picked personnel for special units of this nature imposes on battalions. Moreover, once the regular units in Malaya had themselves become 'jungle-worthy', the young and well trained soldier showed himself to be at least as good and often superior to the 'FERRETS'. Once this stage had been reached the usefulness of the scratch 'FERRET FORCE' was over. Such units if needed at all, should be avoided as a permanent or semi–permanent commitment.

Ferret Force was in fact raised as a result of Ritchie's realization at an early stage that there was a definite requirement for highly trained teams to operate deep in the jungle for protracted periods. The main constituents of the Force were ex-Force 136 and volunteers from some of the regular battalions; the Force 136 operators in particular had an intimate knowledge of the country and the enemy and all had spent long periods within the jungle environment. There were 6 Ferret groups formed up in July, 1948, and they were highly successful in a number of areas, though this was not necessarily fully acknowledged by the military at the time.

Without a doubt they brought in a lot of intelligence on the CT organizations and tactics; they discovered significant caches of ammunition and food (some of these hidden before the end of the war as a result of Chin Peng's foresight); they located major training sites and 'transit' camps and they provided an enormous amount of 'going' information as well as providing many regular soldiers with a first class indoctrination into the ways of jungle warfare.

No such informal force could last long. The civilians who were leading it had other equally important functions to fulfil, as had the regular officers and SNCOs. Ferret Force was disbanded in December, 1948, but its activities had brought to the attention of a few senior military commanders the fact that there was a role for a deep penetration force. Not all such commanders, however, were to agree that the role was worthwhile.

By the end of the first quarter of 1950 it is fair to say that at least in terms of statistics, the Communists were 'ahead on points'. In the UK General Sir William Slim was now CIGS, a man very aware of Mike Calvert's background and capabilities from his Burma days. He made the suggestion to Harding that perhaps there was a study role in Malaya for Calvert who was 'mouldering' in a staff job in Hong Kong. The suggestion was accepted with reservations by Harding but with alacrity by Calvert.

On his way to Malaya, Calvert considered the position of the British Army in the post war years:

In 1947 the United States had called back all of their troops from all over the world; reduced them to ten percent of war strength. Britain alone was carrying out the defences of the world. About 1,000,000 troops of the Army, Navy and Air Force were looking after North Africa, Abyssinia, Eritrea, etc. There were missions in Australia, Germany, Indonesia, Indo-China and we had not then handed back Madagascar, India, Iran, Iraq or Syria. But – there was simply no money; we were utterly dependant on US lend-lease which stopped abruptly.

It appeared to me that the British Army had gone back to a stultified set-up in Singapore and to a certain extent in Malaya also. Many of the force were ex-POWs who had been promoted whilst being prisoners of war and come back into the army as senior staff officers. Many had little idea of all the advances made between 1939 and 1945. All they knew was to bring things back within the scope of peacetime regulations.

As far as I remember when I went to see Harding, his briefing was along the following lines:

'Things aren't going nearly as well as we had hoped. General Slim says that you know all about guerrilla warfare – I give you *carte blanche* – go where you like – see who you like and discover what is wrong. The police aren't working well with the army; the civil government isn't doing this and that; there's the problem of the Sultans; the Chinese versus the Malays; the mercantile interests of the rubber plantations, the tin mines and the like. We've tried to form a Ferret Force run by Robert Thompson and two or three ex-Force 136 officers who stayed in Malaya. They haven't got on well with the army at all. Look at all this and report back directly to me.'

The governorship of Malaya and Singapore was in the hands of Malcolm Macdonald who was the Prime Minister's representative and as such reporting back directly to a Labour government who were at variance with Harding's reports. I wondered whose side who was on!

As I saw it, it is the job of the guerrilla to attack the economy of a nation and to wear it down and go on attacking it until that nation's government concedes to some of the guerilla's demands as it realizes the true financial drain – perhaps it will give way to all of the demands. So the guerrilla should be attacking enemy roads, communications and factories etc., with a psychological warfare effort to support all of this. In our case the guerrillas seemed to number between five and seven thousand with recruiting areas deep in the ulu where they also had their training areas and headquarters.

I made a simile to the situation: 'A malarial germ is inserted into the bloodstream. It circulates in the blood weakening the body. If we put in an antibody like quinine it also circulates in the bloodstream in the same way as the malarial germ. If it works the antibody can destroy the enemy if it is strong enough.' I then took full advantage of my freedom to travel anywhere and speak to whoever I wished.

Calvert drove himself hard; far too hard in the manner of Stirling and Lewes before him in North Africa, and, like them, he makes light of this. He was singular in his task and analysis, and illnesses which were to make him less effective at a later stage were mostly incubated during his reconnaissance operation. His 'study period' took just under seven months to accomplish during which he physically covered well nigh 30,000 miles (including a trip to Rhodesia). He tacked himself onto patrols and companies of regular troops conducting conventional operations and travelled the many miles between such groups unescorted as like as not. He was ambushed twice during this period and one such occasion he recalls with a wry smile:

> We were subjected to a hail of inaccurate fire from a flank and I dived into a ditch. A grenade landed by me which I quickly picked up; the pin was still in position and the firing suddenly ceased. I looked at the grenade and to my surprise there was a label attached which read, 'How do you do Mr Calvert'!

There were some first class officers and soldiers in the regular battalions, but there were some disappointments despite this, due to the military attitude I mentioned earlier. I remember going on patrol with a company from the King's Own Yorkshire Light Infantry and the OC was a bloody good chap. We had got a group of guerrillas on the run and moving into our own ambushes. We'd already ambushed two or three parties and we were set to do more when the Officer Commanding came to see me and inform me that he now had to leave. I protested that we were set for more success and asked why he felt that he had to pull out. His staggering reply was that his Commanding Officer was holding a guest night in the Mess and that his orders were that all officers would attend! I have no doubt at all but that he wanted to stay and he was indeed doing a grand job. Harding was furious when I mentioned the incident to him later.

There was also the occasion when I was discussing the situation and possible tactics with a Commanding Officer of the Scots Guards. I was very impressed by that regiment on the whole; they tried exceedingly hard and were very energetic, but much of their navigation was done by compass bearing and systematically hacking a route through the jungle in platoon strengths. I made the suggestion that perhaps they should try using patrols of four men. My principle at that time was that four men would be a little more frightened – if they were more frightened they would make less noise – if they made less noise they would be more likely to make contact with the enemy when their superior training would pay off.

The reply of the CO was to the effect that his battalion shouldn't be in Malaya anyway. They were trained for Europe and that he wouldn't upset the battalion in order to chase 'bare-arsed niggers' around the jungle. I mentioned to Harding later that with these sorts of attitudes the case was hopeless and he asked me for the name of the CO. I refused to give it but I was eventually ordered to reveal the name in front of witnesses – I had no option. Harding's instructions were simple: 'Have that officer brought here tomorrow with a packed suitcase.'

You have to appreciate some of Harding's difficulties at that time. He was trying to find a way to enthuse his men – remember that many of them were still in a state of lethargy and acute weariness after a long war; many were ex-POWs and many of the civilian superstructure seemed to have lost the will to rule. One of the reasons for Ferret Force's inability to get on with the army and the police was that it was well known that some of the members personally knew Chin Peng and this was viewed with much distrust especially by the police.

There was the attitude of the Sultans who still behaved as if their ownership of Malaya was total; most of them were in fact descendants of the Celebes Islands conquerors who had imposed their rule on the indigenous Malay. The police at the time were very biased towards the Sultans in supporting only the Malays, with scant attention being paid to the Chinese settlers who had been there for some five to six hundred years.

The type of operation was really fringe work with air attacks and bombing raids being carried out in conjunction with some seaborne attacks up the rivers with a few police and Special Branch operations up on the Thai border. The interior was being ignored with the exception of Ferret Force's forays of the year before.

Calvert's report was succinct at this point. His recommendation was that a specially trained counter-insurgency force should be raised. it would infiltrate deep into the jungle and be prepared to operate for lengthy periods to harass the enemy and to win over the 'hearts and minds' of the aborigines on whom the CTs had such dependence – they must be isolated from the guerrillas. Interestingly it was this phrase, 'isolation from the guerrillas' which was to be picked-up on later as part of the Briggs Plan. Shortly after making his report to Harding, Calvert was sent to the UK to present his findings and recommendations and answer questions at War Office level.

In attendance at the subsequent meeting at the War Office was Oliver Lyttelton (later Lord Chandos). Calvert was asked to state his recommendations and began by saying that he had twelve points but, unless the first of these points was agreed, then the whole thing was best forgotten.

'What is this first point?'

'One plan; one man with the powers to carry it out,' was Calvert's brief retort.

'Who do you suggest?'

Calvert's first suggestion was Casey (later Lord Casey), then governor General of Australia. Casey had been Churchill's representative in the Middle East and Governor of Bengal during the 'frightful time of the insurgencies when hundreds of thousands were killed. He was a great man and often Australians will say things which the Brits can't or won't.'

Lyttelton then said quite categorically that the answer was negative; the incumbent would have to be a British serving officer and Calvert was again asked if he had any thoughts:

'If I was a guerrilla, the man I'd be most frightened of having against me because he is so very efficient, can be quite ruthless and at the same time has got great charm is General Templer.'

Calvert remarked that this was noted by Lyttelton, though he refrains from saying whether he thought that significant at the time. He had met Templer at various CIGS meetings with Montgomery and had been very impressed by his penetrating capacity to 'move into your mind'., He seemed quite ruthless in asking questions.

The upshot of the meeting was that Calvert was sent back to Malaya and by the time he reported back to Harding it had been decided that he should be the one to raise his special counter-insurgency force. By way of an identity Calvert naturally asked that SAS be used. When this was denied, he suggested that SAS could perhaps be used in conjunction with a name identifying it with its locality and under the overall status of a regiment. His initial suggestion was 'South Pacific Rangers (SAS)' as much wider troubles were being predicted in that area. This was vetoed because the feeling was that it was geographically imprecise for a volunteer force which was only to operate in Malaya. The decision was made to call the new unit the 'Malayan Scouts (SAS Regiment)'. All ranks were to wear their own regimental head-dress and insignia with the shoulder title of 'Malayan Scouts' on the standard olive green issue uniforms. The arm flash was a shield with 'The Malayan Scouts' scrolled at the top; a Malayan *kris* through a set of blue 'wings' below which was the abbreviation S.A.S. An important decision, in line with Stirling's earlier concept, was that the Malayan Scouts would be under the direct command of the GOC.

Calvert was now set to recruit. It is interesting that there were so many parallels with Stirling's commission to recruit 'L' Detachment back in 1941. That history was to repeat itself such a short time later was a great shame as a tremendous amount of unnecessary pressure was put directly onto the shoulders of Mike Calvert. He stipulated the need for a good Quartermaster – he didn't get one. He requested an Adjutant – he didn't get one. He bid for a Training Officer – he didn't get one. His request for an Operations and Intelligence Officer was similarly turned down. Calvert, like Stirling, was a one-man band.

> I was told that I could recruit my officers by personal interview but that all the men would be selected by individual Commanding Officers. Of course, they sent me their 'boxing teams' and worse. This was entirely the wrong principle if one wanted to attract intelligent guys. It had to be accepted at least in the beginning. I followed Orde Wingate's precept that stated that, 'any man can command good troops but it takes a real commander to train good troops', i.e., turn bad or indifferent troops into good soldiers. Many books on the SAS say in the first chapter something about the 'bad beginnings' but we had our problems as you see.

Calvert made the right decision in accepting the limitations on recruiting; after all he could always weed out the ineffectual and build on the worthy. He was wrong not to press more forcefully for personal support in his headquarters. The pressure on him in his one-man campaign undoubtedly exacerbated his illness and this was to leave him much less effective at a later critical stage of the 'Scouts' evolution. Consider that he was recruiting by interview; attending high level planning conferences; conducting pre-operational reconnaissances; overseeing training (he had one assistant in terms of explosive training in Captain Ted Peacock); effecting whatever regimental administration he had time for as well as the normal duties of a Commanding Officer. A lesser man would not have made it.

5

GROUNDSWELL

Calvert's recruiting methods were simple, indeed they were the only ones possible given the restrictions. He arranged for inserts into Malaya District Routine Orders which were sent to resident battalions proclaiming that volunteers were required for special operations with the Malayan Scouts (SAS) now in the process of being raised. These were followed up with personal talks to the interested parties grouped together at their bases. Often the numbers were very small and consisted of those soldiers that the respective Commanding Officers were most desirous of 'losing'. Outside those men, motivation was not particularly varied. For the main part the soldiers thought that 'special duties' would inevitably mean a protracted period of training which would take them away from the pain and boredom of 'jungle bashing'. After the training, if the job did not appeal to them, then they would simply 'de-volunteer' and return to their units having had a decent break. Some were curious and thought that they would just go along for a 'look-see', express disinterest and then have a couple of good nights out in Kuala Lumpur before rejoining their mates. Some, of course, though initially in a minority, were motivated by the idea of getting to grips with an elusive enemy. The recruitment of officers was a personal issue and Calvert 'interviewed' each applicant in a variety of environments; a walk by the river; a chat in the Mess and so on. Captain Patrick Winter (later Colonel Winter, OBE) remembers the situation well:

In a word the recruitment and selection procedures were typically a British Army amateurish approach. After all a similar approach had won the War – eventually! Everyone was in a hurry. Recruits were drawn from all over the Far East. The Korean War was well under way and COs, understandably, would not let their best men volunteer. Travel for the recruiters, which was basically Mike Calvert in the hunt for officers, was difficult and time-consuming. Regiments tended to do the same as they had during the war when confronted with supplying 'volunteers' to join new outfits such as the Commandos, Popski's Private Army, the SAS etc., etc., and unload their trouble-makers of whom there were very many in National Service days, onto new units with some alacrity.

I had been commissioned into the Scots Guards in March, 1944, and served with them in Belgium, Holland and Germany. I was wounded on 18 April, 1945, much to my annoyance as I missed all the legal loot available a few days later when the Battalion liberated the German Naval Base at Bremen/Cux-haven. After the War and a year or so on public duties at Windsor I went into Italy which was quite fun as we got involved with the Yugoslavs at Pola and Trieste on the Morgan Line but when the battalion was due to return to the boring prospect of public duties once more I volunteered for the Parachute Regiment which was great fun until I broke my leg playing rugby and had to leave them. I was then fortunate to be posted to Malaya with the 2nd Battalion, Scots Guards.

I soon discovered that, in my opinion at any rate, the Guards Brigade, brave and efficient though they had been during the War, had less taste for the type of irregular operations required by the nature of the conflict against the very experienced communist guerrillas in Malaya. It rapidly became clear that my opinion of the Brigade of Guards was almost as low as their opinion of me! My request to resign from the army was greeted with joy and was being processed with remarkable speed when, on a trip to Hong Kong, I became aware of the Malayan Scouts. I immediately applied to cancel my resignation and to transfer to this new Regiment. This application was allowed provided that I also transferred out of the Scots Guards and they never saw me again!

So, I was interviewed by Mike Calvert in July, 1950. Though

I was not to know it at the time, Mike Calvert's interview techniques were typical of his unorthodox approach to life.

We met in an office in HQ Malaya Command on a Saturday morning. After the initial introductions, he said, 'Come for a walk.'

So we ambled around the back of the HQ and eventually found a scruffy Chinese coffee shop – certainly not the sort of joint normally frequented by any sort of officer, let alone a Guards' Officer.

Calvert asked a few questions relating to my outlook on life (military that is). He expounded at some length his own military philosophy and asked for my own views. He pointed out forcibly that what he was offering would be very different from 'normal military operations'. (These consisted in the main in those days of platoons patrolling the fringes of the jungle for 5–7 days at a time. Air supply was in its infancy and little or no attempt was made to operate deep in the jungle. There is the celebrated story, apocryphal though it may be, of the young Grenadier subaltern who wrote home to his mother saying that the jungle was really very neat – all the trees were in straight lines! Obviously, he'd never been anywhere apart from the Rubber Estates.)

Calvert said he would be sending into the deep jungle squadrons of 70–80 men broken down into troops of 12–15. The whole idea would be to operate there relying on air supply for weeks at a time thus denying to the CTs their previous sanctuary, where they had operated with comparative immunity during the War, and where they considered, with some justification, that they would be safe from the 'Running Dogs' (National Servicemen). When asked how this operational concept struck me, I replied that it was certainly different from anything I'd done to date and thought that it would be interesting, if nothing else.

He then asked me if I drank. I was not then aware of his drinking habits (I found out later that when touring Malaya compiling his report for the C-in-C, he had left a trail of destruction the length and breadth of the country) so I was totally unprepared for this question and was considerably exercised as to what reply I should give. Senior officers tended to have funny ideas about consumption of the 'hard stuff' by young subalterns. As it happened, I was suffering from the mother and father of all hangovers at the time. So, in for a penny, in for a pound, and I replied accordingly. I expected the interview to be terminated then and there. To my surprise, he said, 'Good'.

It transpired that he believed that if you could do a proper full day's work whilst suffering from a nasty hangover, illnesses such as malaria, typhoid, etc., would be regarded as mere minor irritations not to be taken seriously. He had a point. I should add here that I never saw Mike incapacitated despite his reputation.

At the end of the interview we both got up to leave only to find that neither of us had enough money to pay the bill for the coffee. We turned out our pockets and thankfully, between us, found just sufficient to settle up without having to offer to do the washing up. We strolled back to the HQ with me wondering what the outcome of the interview was to be. Just as we arrived back at his office, Mike turned to me and said, 'Well, thank you for coming – you'll do. When can you join us?'

A selection process somewhat different from that of today! Probably just as well too. I'm still convinced that the only reason I was accepted was because I was in the Scots Guards and so would raise the 'social tone' of the new Regiment. He also had a soft spot for the Scots Guards, I believe, because in 1940 he had resigned his commission in order to join the 5th Battalion Scots Guards then being raised to fight in Finland.

I arrived on or about 15 August and was greeted by the second-in-command, Major John Harrington, MC. He was a regular officer in the Lancashire Fusiliers and had been with Calvert in the Chindits. Others who were either there already, or who joined shortly after, were Major Willie Wilson, MC, Mike Sinclair-Hill, Frank Ward, Mike Pearman (later to be killed by his own men when serving with the Aden Protectorate Levies), the late Ted Peacock, Douglas Manson, Wilf Batty (Royal Signals and known as 'Spanner' on account of his making a cock-up of most tasks). Colin Park was also a member as a 'Civilian Liaison Officer'. He had parachuted into Malaya as a member of Force 136 during the latter stages of the war and had been badly injured on landing. A terrific guy – son of Air Vice Marshal Keith Park of Battle of Britain fame.

A major acquisition Calvert (now a Lieutenant-Colonel) personally attracted to his initial corps of officers was then Captain John Woodhouse who was in the post of G3 Intelligence to 40th Infantry Division in Hong Kong. Woodhouse agreed to join Calvert on the strict proviso that he would be committed to operations as a troop or squadron commander and not intelligence. Wisely, in our opinion, Calvert saw fit, on Woodhouse's arrival, to make him the Intelligence Officer thus giving him an extremely effective officer exactly where he needed one in the very early stages. Woodhouse was later to become the keystone in turning the regiment into a force to be reckoned with and would be recognised, in the eyes of all ranks who served under him, one the best Commanding Officers 22 SAS Regiment ever had. Indeed David Stirling, when he officially opened Stirling Lines in Hereford, was to refer to Woodhouse as, 'One of my co-founders.'

Woodhouse was a particularly astute choice for many reasons. During the war he had seen service as a soldier with the Dorset Regiment before being commissioned (1942) into that regiment's 5th Battalion. The end of that year found him commanding a platoon of the 1st Battalion East Surreys as part of the 78th Infantry Division in Tunisia and later Sicily. He was put in command of a 'battle patrol unit' and gained hard experience in working a system of small groups which conducted operations as fighting patrols, reconnaissance patrols and prisoner 'snatch' operations. By the end of the Italian Campaign Woodhouse had taken part in many fierce, spirited actions and was truly 'battle-hardened'. Apart from this he had gained a wealth of knowledge in two areas which gave him a natural affinity with what Calvert was aiming to achieve with his Malayan Scouts. He was very experienced in small patrol work by day and night in hostile areas and he had, on a number of occasions, worked with civilians and recognized the enormous value of them under certain conditions. In short, Woodhouse was already on side long before Calvert interviewed him.

It is interesting to reflect on Woodhouse's memories of his early meeting with Calvert as his perceptions of the man show, without any doubt, the influence he (Calvert) had on the whole campaign in Malaya:

Colonel Calvert was well-known in the army because he had been a brigade commander in the Chindits and most people who'd served with them thought of him as the natural successor to Orde Wingate, although, of course, this did not happen. He was known as 'Mad Mike' in the army as well as in the press largely because he was always a bit larger than life, a tremendous personality, a tremendous exuberance. Ideas bubbled from him rather like water coming out of a fountain; you couldn't sit down with Calvert for half an hour without hearing ideas flow in a way which I had never heard from anyone else in the army. He was both a fascinating and infuriating man to work for and I remember my first interview in Malaya with him when I joined the regiment very well.

He sent for me and gave me what I think was a brilliant exposé of the whole Malayan position. He told me the military and political background and then he told me the part which he thought a special unit would play. He explained to me that in the deep jungles of Malaya there were quite large numbers of aborigines. They'd had almost no contact with anyone except the CTs. The CTs, of course, had been there since the Japanese war, knew them well and controlled them and therefore the task of a special unit was to win the deep jungle, while the rest of the army, the infantry of the army, fought the main battles along the edges of the jungle. He described the winning of the deep jungle rather in the terms used by Montgomery talking in Western Europe about winning the air battle before you won the ground battle; first win command of the air, and Calvert decribed deep jungle as the first battle we had to win; win the hearts and minds of the aborigines. Until we could break them from the communists we would never be able to break the communists themselves.

He saw all this with a really remarkable clarity and he was able to put it over in a way where his ideas became clear to me very quickly and clearly. He described the whole business of

1. Officers of the original 'M' Independent Squadron. *Left to right*: Jeff Douglas, Alistair McGregor, Tony Grevill-Bell, Jock Easton. Note wings on breasts of wartime SAS. (*A. McGregor*)

2. What the well-dressed Communist Terrorist wore: a police 'model' wearing a captured uniform. (*A. McGregor*)

3. What a Communist Terrorist was issued with. (*A. McGregor*)

4. Early tree-jumping rig: Alistair McGregor and Tommy Corps. (*A. McGregor*)

5. An early patrol 'takes five'. (*A. McGregor*)

6. Brigadier Michael Calvert, re-founder of the SAS.

7. Sergeant Danny Cross ponders the next move. *(A. McGregor)*

8. Carrying a casualty was far from easy. Peter Walter in foreground. *(A. McGregor)*

9. Awaiting the chopper. On the left Danny Cross; 3rd from left 'Rocky' Blake; on the right Peter Walter. (*A. McGregor*)

10. Preparing the casualty for evacuation. Peter Walter and Bob Lawson look on. (*A. McGregor*)

cordon and search where large numbers of troops and police were lined up and then tried to drive the CTs rather like game on a grouse moor into stops. He described to me how this simply could not work under Malayan conditions, and that the key to success was the hearts and minds of the civil population (this was mainly Chinese and Malay on the edges of the jungle) but it was aboriginal in the deep jungle and he described how it would be possible if the men were properly trained to let them work in patrols of three or four thereby covering much larger areas.

All the business of giving medical treatment to primitive people who obviously had no such thing themselves, he described all that long before I heard it from anybody else and the idea of the Malayan Scouts establishing bases in the deep jungle and then spreading out rather like the ripples when a stone is thrown into a pond, living there and staying there and he emphasised the *staying there*. He reminded me that the CTs had been in the jungle for five or six years at that time; they *lived* there, they grew their food there and he said we had got to do the same thing.

Now at the time there were theories particularly strongly held in the Royal Army Medical Corps that after two weeks in the jungle a soldier should come out because the stresses and strains were so bad for them. This, looking back on it now, seems to me quite extraordinary because there were large numbers of officers and soldiers who'd served in Burma in the war and knew that this was simply not true. Of course it could be unpleasant and, of course, disease happened in the jungle, but, rather like the Chindits had set the example for the 14th Army in Burma to show what British troops could do in the jungle, so in Malaya Calvert thought that the Malayan Scouts, simply as a result of these tactical operations, would also help to remind everyone in the army that the jungle was there to be used and not something which was very hostile.

A point has been raised here which is not generally recognized when people discuss the 'Briggs Plan' which is covered at a later point. Within Calvert's initial report were five major points which he reckoned were critical to success:

1. Effecting deep penetration patrols into the jungle.
2. The denial of theretofore 'safe' bases in the jungle for the CTs.
3. Winning over the indigenous Aborigines (Hearts and Minds) thus depriving the CTs of food and support.
4. Concentrating the Chinese squatters who inhabited, in a very haphazard way, the jungle fringes completely out of the reach of the protection of the security forces and thus an ideal source of food supply for the CTs, into controlled fortified villages.
5. The raising of a special force to operate for long periods in the interior to actively harry the enemy and cut him off from his main sources of food, support and rest.

Somehow, by mid-August, 1950, Calvert had succeeded in amassing sufficient officers and soldiers with which to form 'A' Squadron, Malayan Scouts (SAS). He was under tremendous pressure to get them into the jungle and operating along the lines he had described, but, at the same time, he was faced with the matter of establishing a regiment from scratch. He was very poorly served with the administrative staff of the regiment – they were too few and too ineffective. The accommodation which they were first given within which to make their base (at Dusan Tua) was dirty and dilapidated. Ablutions and other facilities were limited and in bad repair and there were few home comforts coming from the Quartermaster's Store. Small wonder that they were an unhappy crowd at first and strived to spend as much time as possible outside their barracks.

On top of this Calvert was faced with the small matter of training! In the first place not all his men were from the infantry – there was a broad scattering from all of the Corps. Many were National Servicemen who had been pushed through basic training at great speed. No doubt from amongst these he could have bolstered the efficiency of his as yet poor administrators, but, these men had joined him to fight – not to administer – that was exactly what a large number of them were trying to get away from and that was something with which Calvert could more than readily identify. It was also a fact that very few of this hard core had any jungle experience at all; it is true that some had fought in Burma but under vastly different conditions with totally different tactical aims.

Training facilities for the Scouts were scant; ranges had to be constructed on the fringes of the jungle and at their first usage it became apparent how deficient many of the soldiers were in basic weapon handling and marksmanship. Grenade ranges were effected simply by utilizing handy ditches or animal wallows. As an aside, Calvert's initial grenade training was realistic in the extreme. Two grenades would be thrown but the thrower could not take cover until he had seen the second grenade land. This only continued until the perhaps inevitable point when someone was severely injured (blinded by a piece of shrapnel from his first grenade). Fieldcraft training was occasionally served by the simple expedient of soldiers crawling towards each other's positions armed with air rifles and protected, in part, by fencing masks. Gradually, with practise, weapon training and fieldcraft improved through a series of short exercises in fringe jungle. There was little attempt at this stage to impose the jungle skills of tracking, anti-tracking and battle procedures which were to become so necessary. They were simply not thought about.

One of the more alarming shortfalls in training was perhaps the lack of navigational experience. In those days it was not uncommon for the map to be something of a mystery to any rank other than officers or the occasional platoon sergeant, simply because it was only to those ranks that maps were issued. This situation was not helped by the poor quality of mapping at that time and the fact that many areas were unmapped in any event. Most of the basic instruction was in the hands of the few original officers and whatever experienced senior NCOs had been attracted to the Scouts.

Much of the officer training was conducted by Calvert himself and took the shape of lengthy discourses as opposed to formal lectures. These, as often as not, took the form of his thoughts and ideas on guerrilla warfare and the overall situation in Malaya and would be interspersed by direct lessons learned with the Chindits in Burma or the Special Night Squads led by Orde Wingate in Palestine before the war. Although Calvert's tremendous expertise in the tactical and strategic sense showed through all this there was still an important shortfall for troops about to go into action for the first time in a new environment. There are a number of essentials to any soldiering in the form of battle procedures, contact drills, communications, air to ground liaison and a score or more mundane but vital ingredients to success.

So it was that in August, 1950, 'A' Squadron was despatched north to the State of Perak for its initial training operation under Calvert's personal direction. It was an operation of very limited success. To quote Patrick Winter, 'all the learning was done on the hoof.' Battle procedures were slack, litter discipline was non-existent, troops were very noisy and weapon handling was careless. It must have had some benefits, though those involved find them hard to remember except that navigation did improve; some outstanding characters began to develop the 'ground feel' which is so important in jungle operations and 'at least we learned how to erect rudimentary shelters and use the jungle's natural products to look to camp defences . . . on the rare occasions we thought that necessary!'

John Woodhouse considers the first operation to have been a failure. In recalling the situation he refers at first to the observation made earlier about navigation:

The first essential, of course, in any military operation is to know where you are and where you are going. That was an initial failure. The second set of failures which arose was as the result of the boredom of failing to make contact. [This was probably no bad thing on that first operation!] Unfortunately this, after a few weeks, led to a slackening of battle procedures and battle discipline and 'A' Squadron became extremely careless; they were very noisy and rather bored. Also, I think mainly through a lack of good communications between the Colonel and the then officer commanding the squadron, they rather fell apart.

At this point Woodhouse demonstrates another facet of his Commanding Officer's character. One of Calvert's favourite sayings was, 'You've got to be in my mind.' He did a lot of talking on this subject and stated that one of the reasons that officers talked endless 'shop' in the Mess was that it was the only way they could be 'in his mind'. He said that he considered it to be one of the essentials of operations that an officer must be in his commander's mind. He must know what the commander wanted just as the commander must be able to predict what sort of action the officer would take at any one time. This was good luck for Woodhouse. He must have been 'in Calvert's mind' as he was placed in temporary command of 'A' Squadron.

Many books about the early days of the regiment paint a quite horrifying picture of a bunch of ill-disciplined, drunken layabouts. Woodhouse ably defends against that view:

In thinking why things went wrong, I think the main reason was quite simply a lack of detailed training. It's true that the officers and men were not selected in the latter sense, they didn't go through a selection course; as far as the soldiers were concerned they were simply selected in the sense that vounteers volunteered and, as far as I know, all those who volunteered were accepted. That in itself meant that a certain number of the soldiers were undesirable characters who would never have been any use in probably any regiment; it was the usual army principle of getting rid of the bad hats. It's a bit unfair to brand 'A' Squadron as being just a bunch of buccaneers. There were many good soldiers in that squadron, in fact certainly a majority and the same was true of the early officers in the troops. I would say that certainly four out of five officers would have passed into the SAS at any time in later years, so the material was quite good.

What was really wrong was that it was untrained, and secondly that discipline was really non-existent. Why Colonel Calvert didn't clamp down hard I've never entirely understood. He was under tremendous pressure, he was often not in the camp and other officers including myself didn't take a firm line with the troops at that time. It was rather thought that because they'd been in the jungle for two or three months when they came out they should have a jolly good time in the sense of parties and drinking and all the rest of it. This led to some very silly escapades which really got out of control. The sort of escapade when the air transport company and RAF officers were invited to camp and then, after a very noisy and rowdy sort of curry lunch cum drinking session, quite suddenly we all piled into boats and went shooting down the local rapids with no sort of precautions. Rifles were not secured to the boats with the result that certainly one was lost. That sort of thing used to happen amongst other things.

Another thing which was quite foolish looking back was that men were allowed to grow beards in the jungle which was a sensible idea in that it did hide a white face in the undergrowth but unfortunately they were allowed to keep the beards when they came out. This was contrary to all sorts of military traditions and the sight of smelly, scruffy, bearded soldiers coming out of the jungle was one which caused apoplexy in the staff and derision amongst all the other units of the army; it was a very bad mistake.

On the question of beards in general it never struck me as important one way or another whilst on operations. I couldn't see that it mattered if a man was bearded or not in the jungle or for that matter in the desert; there were more practical reasons in the desert if water was very short and so on. The SAS in World War II in the desert had frequently been bearded and so I never saw the importance of shaving on operations, but I did recognize the importance of looking tidy when you were not on operations and within a base area.

Success or failure is a moot point at this time in history, but we cannot find it in ourselves, after talking to so many of those veterans, to accept that nothing was learned. Certainly one aspect to be considered is that at least deficiencies were recognized and though it may have been something of a slow haul into effectiveness, the foundations for Calvert's 'building site' had been excavated. Recruiting was gathering momentum, albeit initially from an unexpected source.

6

21 SAS (ARTISTS) REGIMENT TA
AND 'M' FORCE

A t this point some of Calvert's earlier efforts were revisited upon him. After the disbandment of 1st and 2nd SAS Regiments on the cessation of World War II hostilities Calvert and two other SAS stalwarts, Lieutenant-Colonel Brian Franks, DSO, MC, and Major L.E.O.T 'Leo' Hart, OBE, had risen to the challenge of a War Office enquiry into the use of SAS troops. They had analysed the subject in great detail, drawing on their own and others recent experience, and in particular on Calvert's own strategic farsightedness, and persuaded those in power at that point that the great wealth of wartime experience should not be obscured by the sands of time.

Whether the War Office had any regrets at the premature disbandment is not known but the recommendation to reform a regular unit was rejected; instead a Territorial Regiment was given official blessing. Named initially 21 SAS Regiment (a simple reversal of the digits of 1st and 2nd SAS; subsequent SAS Regiments [22 and 23] have continued numerically) it was eventually to find its happy (and still extant) affiliation with the Artists Rifles. That story is well known but what is particularly important in terms of the development of the SAS 'family' of regiments is that under the Corps Warrant, 21 SAS (Artists) Regiment TA became the Corps with the authority to raise, when required, other regiments for SAS employment. This was ratified in a Joint Staff Memorandum which dictated that if any special force was to be raised in the future then it would be provided from the SAS. Thus the unique situation was arrived at where a Territorial Regiment became senior to its regular counterpart.

In September, 1947, 21 SAS (Artists) began recruiting and was very quickly up to its allocated establishment. Brian Franks was given the first tour of command and he skilfully took advantage of the fact that so many officers in the War Office hierarchy knew little of SAS work. He and his officers became the authorities with all the benefits that fact can bestow on a new regiment. How was this to assist Calvert now struggling to solidify the Malayan Scouts in Malaya?

Some three months before 'A' Squadron's first tentative foray into deep jungle, troops of the North Korean Army had crossed the 39th Parallel to begin their push into South Korea. Their rapid advance towards Pusan was sufficient for General MacArthur US Army to request mobile SAS troops equipped similarly to the 1st and 2nd SAS Regiments' scale at the end of the war. A volunteer force under the auspices of the 'Z' Reserve was called for to serve in an SAS rôle in Korea. 'Z' Reservists were all ex-regular officers and soldiers who had opted to remain on the reserved list to be called into action in the event of a sudden need for well-trained troops as first line reinforcements. They had an obligation to undergo annual training in the same manner as the Territorial Army. The force, which was a composite of ex-SAS officers and soldiers with wartime experience and direct volunteers from the Territorial Army, was put together under the auspices of 21 SAS (Artists) from whose ranks the majority of the Territorials had volunteered. In command was Major Tony Greville-Bell, DSO, who had served with the SAS during the war. His recruitment of officers was somewhat akin to Calvert's style.

Captain Alistair MacGregor DSO, MC, (ex-SAS), on return from working with the Greek Commando, met Tony Greville-Bell who asked him if he would be interested in going to Korea with 'M' Squadron. His answer was an enthusiastic 'Yes'. MacGregor recalls:

Tony was a great fixer, one of the best, and I was on my way to 'M' Squadron. He had also 'fixed it' that under the sponsorship of 21 SAS at Duke's Road, we would be blistered onto the Airborne Forces Depot (AFD). I got there to find that Tony had recruited five subalterns back into the army. Some were, of course, old friends from the SAS; at the AFD I met Sandy

McKenzie who had gone into the wine business (very useful), Jock Easton (a great vehicle mechanic), Rupert France – who I think was half-way through college – and Tony Royle.*

At AFD our first job was to get some refresher training in while all the vehicles were being mustered, checked out and equipped. We were allocated about six months for this as far as I can remember. AFD was not a happy place to be, we were not Parachute Regiment, nobody really knew what we were up to and we were given the worst of everything.

Initially 'M' Squadron seems to have been part of 'K' Force, which made no impression on the Parachute Regiment landlords of AFD, then at Maida Barracks, Aldershot. Bombardier 'Bob' Bennett BEM, MM, and one of Stirling's original 'L' Detachment from the Western Desert takes up the story:

After leaving the Guards at the end of the war I soon decided to re-enlist but I couldn't face the Guards bullshit so I joined the Royal Artillery where they made me a Bombardier. I came home from Greece in 1949 and found myself based in Wales. I heard about 'M' Squadron and volunteered. I was given instructions to get myself down to Aldershot and on the railway platform I ran into Alistair McGregor, Tony Greville-Bell and Jock Easton, so, of course, we went straight to the pub. It was a lovely little reunion. Tony virtually made me SSM on the spot!

God, Maida Barracks was awful. We were hated by the Paras; if something needed painting, guarding or peeling then we painted, guarded and peeled! I'll give you an example. I got back from training one day to find myself put into open arrest and charged. When I was marched up in front of the CO (it was Pine-Coffin I think), Jock Easton was standing beside him and he gave me a great wink. I was charged with having explosives and detonators in my bunk. Well, of course I had. If we'd handed them over to the Paras we'd never have got them

---

* Royle was later stricken with polio from which he fought his way back to full health to become involved later with David Stirling in some of his post-war ventures in the Middle East.

back! Anyway I launched into my Guard's patter and said, 'Permission to speak, Sir.'

Then I got wound up and let go: 'I'm not stupid. We're training for Korea and how can we train without explosives? I know what I'm doing, I handled enough explosives during the bloody war. They're not detonators; they're copper sealing caps to stop the ends of the detonating cord getting damp.

Of course they **were** detonators, but I knew he wouldn't know the difference. Anyway he lost his temper and shouted at me to get out and put the bloody stuff into the guardroom for safe-keeping. So I got a truck and me and the lads took it to the guardroom and the RPs (Regimental Policemen) didn't want to know. I told them they were getting the stuff whether they wanted it or not – their CO had said put it in the guardroom and I was doing just that. Then one of the lads, who I'd briefed earlier, threw one of the boxes of plastic explosive off the truck at the feet of one of the RPs and he really shit himself. I tell you they were anti us all the way and that's the sort of silly stuff we had to put up with.

I think we were there about three months in all and then one day we were paraded by Tony Greville-Bell to be told that as the Yanks had now reached the 39th Parallel there was no job for us in Korea. The good news was that volunteers were wanted for Malaya where Mike Calvert had started up the Malayan Scouts and if enough volunteered then we would go out as a ready formed up squadron. The choice was simple; go out there or go back to our own units or back to civvy street in the case of the TA boys. Not everyone fancied Malaya, of course, but it would have been between thirty and forty who decided to go.

Both McGregor and Bennett were somewhat surprised to say the least when they arrived, as 'M' Independent Squadron, at the Malayan Scout camp at Dusan Tua and saw the bearded lackadaisical figures of the 'A' Squadron soldiers lying around the place.

'It was a hell of a problem,' said Bennett. 'We had a pretty good discipline in our Squadron and it made things difficult all round when I was making my guys shave and do all the normal things soldiers do in camp while 'A' Squadron seemed to just do as they pleased. Roadknight, the RSM, wasn't a lot of help in things like that. We soon heard the stories of Calvert's boozing and the wild parties that went on when the lads were out of the jungle. I remember one night when he [Calvert] booby-trapped the bogs at the Aussie RAF base. They got their own back though when they did a 'bombing' run over our camp and bombarded us with bog rolls.

There was one time when we were on the ranges, I think, and we were visited by an Indian General all dressed up in his spotless tropical white uniform. I can't remember why he was there but Mike Calvert pulled one of his tricks and threw a grenade into a pig wallow and you should have seen the expression on the Indian General's face when he stood up after throwing himself down in the mud and the pig shit. His uniform was ruined. It was all a bit daft really. There was no point to that sort of thing though everybody laughed at the time.

Anyway, we became 'B' Squadron and our first couple of small training operations were a bit of a farce. On the first one we were sent off to 'stonk' a grid reference with 3″ mortars and water-cooled Vickers, would you believe. God knows what was supposed to be there. I'm glad it wasn't me but we were getting a bit disillusioned then. The second consisted of us being sent off into a very swampy area for eight days or so and being told to make ourselves familiar with it. It was a pretty grotty area, as swamps are, and when we came out Calvert asked me what I thought. I said that we'd seen nothing and that it was a waste of time. He laughed and said that's what he thought but it was good training anyway.

This is a good point at which to dispel another myth: the Malayan Scouts were never disbanded even temporarily during these early 'teething problems'. Many books and many personal reminiscences give the myth credence; however, there is no supportive data to back it other than a suggestion that this may at one time have been an option. What is certain, though, is that internal differences of opinion regarding tactical deployment and, in particular, discipline created an atmosphere of uncertainty as individual actions were bolstered by rumour. Calvert, still very highly regarded by all his officers as a brilliant strategist, had not yet begun to get his administrative house in order. He readily admits that he was guilty of not pressing his case ardently enough with his superiors and he was still trying to command and administer as a one-man band. His approach to discipline was unusual and at this point, in mid-1951, he was plagued with illness which he tried to cure with the 'water of life' rather than those measures prescribed by the medical profession. Again John Woodhouse shows an interesting slant on Calvert's approach:

Of course people like myself, in particular a close friend of mine the Adjutant, Willy Wilson, who took over 'A' Squadron when I left it, discussed all these problems that we were having. We were both of us aware that discipline was not right, but Calvert dominated us in a way which is rather hard to explain now. I think with any other Commanding Officer we might have been more forceful in our personal representations to him. The sort of case which came up was when a sergeant in the regiment had struck an army medical officer in some heated argument and the sergeant was put on a charge in front of Calvert and the medical officer appeared as a witness. All that happened in that case was that Colonel Calvert told off the sergeant in severe terms and then turned round to the medical officer and said that these problems must be settled amicably, told them to shake hands and that would be the end of the matter.

There was a Polish soldier who misbehaved extremely badly and Colonel Calvert had him on a charge; the sort of thing which would normally have seen him go into detention. At the end of the hearing he was simply admonished for his bad behaviour. I remember asking the Colonel if he didn't think that that was rather a light punishment for such an offence. He replied, 'John, the Poles are a cross we have to bear. We betrayed them during the War and the fact that they misbehave now doesn't mean that the man isn't a good soldier.'

This to me was always Calvert's weakness, that he didn't seem to appreciate the importance of good discipline.

There is little doubt that the outbreaks of offences resulting from ill discipline can be laid at Calvert's door, but it is important to look to what he was trying to achieve and the effects of his own background in jungle warfare. In the matter of 'B' Squadron's unrest it must be remembered that they were all found from within a hardcore of ex-SAS soldiers of wartime proven experience or from within the ranks of 21 SAS which already had its own system of selection for recruits and thus that squadron was already practising a firm system of self-discipline which was to provide a clear distinction between it and the Malayan Scouts.

The Scouts, as dictated by Calvert, were following a doctrine propounded by his wartime Commander, General Wingate, i.e., that any properly trained infantryman could successfully undertake special operations if given extra training. It is interesting to note how this theory, correct when applied to such operations as those of the Chindits, broke down when used as a basis for very small parties.

In a Chindit Column, isolated as they were, the weak could yet find strength in the numbers around them and the knowledge that their units were large and fought as such. In a small one as was the Malayan Scouts, where squadrons operated independently for long periods, the stresses both internal and external were that much greater. There the emphasis was on the individual who, operating in a small party, experienced a sense of isolation and loneliness not met with in larger formations. The lack of any stringent personnel selection, previously found so necessary both by the SOE and the SAS, began to manifest itself both in a breakdown of military discipline and in a failure to utilize the well-tried and taught skills of the infantryman. Although doing little more than long-range patrolling on foot (the infantryman's birthright?), they ignored many of the lessons of the past.

This then was the situation when 'B' Squadron arrived to form the curious union of wartime SAS and the strange child of the Chindits. It was unsettled to say the least. 'B' Squadron, accustomed to the self-imposed discipline of 21 SAS, was horrified by much of what was commonplace in the other squadron; they, on their part, regarded 'B' Squadron as interlopers with scant knowledge of the jungle. It was an unhappy period both within the unit and in the effect it had on outside opinion; this is understandable; the reasons are clear to see, but the important thing is that it was not to last.

On Saturday 16 September, 1950, *The Rhodesia Herald* carried a small box article which was to have great significance to Calvert in his hunt for recruits:

RHODESIA OFFERS TOKEN FORCE FOR FAR EAST

The Prime Minister, Sir Godfrey Huggins, told a meeting of the United Party at Bulawayo, writes our Bulawayo correspondent:

'We have offered the United Kingdom a token force for the Far East and that is still under consideration.'

The meeting greeted the announcement with applause and cries of 'Hear, hear'.

Early conjecture by the politicians and military alike was that the force would comprise either a small infantry unit or a detachment of the Staff Corps. It was initially decided that the force would be known as the Southern Rhodesia Far East Volunteer Unit; volunteers to be attested as members of the Defence Force who may thereafter be attached or seconded to any of His Majesty's Forces. It is historically interesting to look at the Defence Notice asking for volunteers:

SOUTHERN RHODESIA DEFENCE FORCE

VOLUNTEERS ARE REQUIRED FOR SERVICE IN THE FAR EAST

1. Single men between the ages of 19 and 30 are required for enlistment in the Southern Rhodesia Forces for service with British Forces in the Far East.
2. Period of engagement will be for 2½ years from the date of attestation. It should be noted that service may be anywhere in the Far East.
3. In exceptional cases married men may be accepted.
4. Rates of pay are as follows:

	Per diem		
	£	S	D
Privates		10	9
Corporal		14	3
Sergeant	1	0	9
C/Sergeant	1	3	9
S/M (WO II)	1	5	9
S/M (WO I)	1	7	9
Lieutenant	1	6	6
Captain	1	16	0

NOTE: Whilst attached to a unit of the British Army a volunteer shall receive pay at the rates appropriate to that unit. Should this pay be lower than that provided by this Government, the difference will be paid to the volunteer's account in this Colony.

5. Dependant's allowances will be at a flat rate for all ranks and will include:

To a wife	£230 per annum
For the first child	£30 per annum
Each additional child	£24 per annum

(Plus cost of living allowance)

Bona fide dependants, other than those mentioned, will receive such allowances as may be approved by the Minister of Defence.

6. Pensions will be provided for.

7. Leave on full pay may be granted subject to the exigencies of the service as follows:

   (a) 5 days prior to embarkation.
   (b) 30 days per annum inclusive of any leave granted by the British Army.
   (c) 30 days on discharge, plus any annual leave as per (b) not taken.

Free Second Class rail travel will be provided for leave journeys *within the Colony* except that Warrant Officers Class I will receive First Class travel.

8. Volunteers will receive free medical and dental treatment.

Recognised dependants will receive free medical attention and hospitalisation in Government Hospitals, exclusive of dental and optical treatment and the cost of dentures.

9. Income Tax will be paid, where applicable, at Southern Rhodesian rates.

10. On return to Southern Rhodesia a gratuity will be paid at the rate of two and a half days' pay for each month or portion of a month's service outside the Colony.

11. Full details of conditions of service may be obtained from any Drill Hall or from Defence Headquarters.

12. Application forms, which may be obtained from all Drill Halls, must be sent direct to:

DEFENCE HEADQUARTERS,
P.O. Box 21, Causeway,
Salisbury.

It may seem strange today but these conditions of service were attractive and there was no shortage of volunteers from all corners of Southern Rhodesia. Stringent medical parameters were laid down for selection, but by the end of November, 1950, the unit was almost up to strength and training at King George VI Barracks at Salisbury. Calvert, on learning of this force, had not been idle. He had presented his case for their attachment to the Malayan Scouts and this had been accepted. In early January, 1951, Calvert journeyed to Salisbury via Cairo to speak to the new force and begin its formal training.

One newspaper reports him as saying:

'I have seen these Rhodesians at work and I am very much struck by them indeed . . . I feel that they will pay a very big dividend as compared with their actual numbers. What is required for the work we are doing is the individual who can look after himself, is full of keenness and drive, and does not lose those qualities when conditions are difficult . . . From what I have seen of them, these Rhodesians strike me as just that type . . . After basic shooting has been acquired what we need is the 'game' type of shooting – quick and on the mark as soon as a target is seen. These bandits are off like deer once they are spotted and you must get them at once . . . If for every bandit so far accounted for, we had been able to get two, this show would have been finished by now . . . This should suit the Rhodesians.

The Rhodesian contingent, to be known as 'C' Squadron (Rhodesia) Malayan Scouts (SAS), finally arrived in Singapore on 29 March, 1951, after a long trip on the MV *Tegelburg*, to get their first taste of what the Malayan Emergency was all about. Under the command of one Captain Peter Walls (later General and Commander of his country's Army) they were at full strength with eight officers and ninety-two men. Their planned trip by train to Kuala Lumpur was delayed whilst repairs were made to the track which the CTs had blown up the night before.

Rapidly following the Rhodesians came 'D' Squadron from England. This was another squadron of volunteers who had not been through any form of selection course other than the indignity of heaving wood and coal around the AFD Barracks at Aldershot. As with 'B' Squadron before them, however, these later two squadrons were well disciplined in themselves in contrast to the early, and still extant, 'A' Squadron. The situation was still fraught insofar as some key members were concerned.

Tony Greville-Bell, for example, felt that he could not tolerate the situation and made a direct representation to 21 SAS Headquarters in London expressing his feelings and suggesting that 'B' Squadron revert to its former title of 'M' Independent Squadron and be tasked separately. After having gone above his Commander's head and having received no acknowledgement of his suggestion, he chose to resign his command and signified this intention to HQ 21 SAS. An extract from a letter from Leo Hart to Greville-Bell goes some way towards explaining the situation:

Fm: Major L.E.O.T. Hart, MBE, Headquarters,
    The SAS Regiment. 21 SAS Regt (Artists) TA,
    17, Dukes Road, WC1.

Tel: EUSton 3677   2nd July 1951

Dear Tony,
    I was very glad to receive your letter of the 22nd June this morning but horrified when I realised that through our stupidity here, my letter to you in answer to your very bad news a month

ago had been sent off by surface mail so that you will, obviously, not get it for a long time to come. For what it is worth I send you another copy herewith but, of course, your news in your last letter puts a very different complexion on everything.

So far as the possibilities nearer home are concerned, the situation is completely vague and if you are coming home I am sure you will be back here before anything is decided. Meantime I shall be having lunch with someone tomorrow who may be able to help and shall discuss the employment of your squadron with him.

The position with regard to information you give is, of course, frightfully tricky. I know better than to let anybody have your letters again but, naturally, I can do nothing about the things you tell me, nor can I do what I want to do to help you without disclosing the information you give me.

However, I can assure you that I am not going to land you in the soup again and, in fact, would say that, on the whole, at the moment the situation is about as good as it could be. We have never been at all happy about the Regiment out there knowing so little about it apart from your own information and various rumours and, naturally, I think our first reaction if it were disbanded would be one of relief.

To sum up, I cannot say anything more today than that really if you can get home I am sure it would be the best thing; subject to your being able to arrange out there to revive the independent squadron as a sort of permanent Force in your Theatre for future eventualities even if not suitable for Malaya at present. Would it, for instance, be possible to sell the idea of attaching it to the French SAS in Indo China until it was wanted elsewhere in the Far East, e.g., if Korea doesn't end as it now appears likely to do? On the other hand my interview tomorrow may produce further ideas and if so I shall write straight away. (*The rest of the letter is personal*).

Yours,

(Sgd L. E. O. Turton Hart

It is unlikely that Greville-Bell's somewhat unconventional move had any direct bearing on the future of the SAS as things were rapidly improving beyond all measures. Nonetheless the SAS lost a very able officer. Much of the speed of improvement can be ascribed to John Woodhouse, ably assisted by Captain Ted Peacock and Sergeant Eddie Waters.

This team was attached to each squadron in turn to instil the basics of battle discipline and jungle warfare. Woodhouse, in typical fashion, makes light of his achievements:

When they arrived ('B' Squadron) there was still, of course, nobody competent to train them, there was only 'A' Squadron who were committed to operations anyway and 'B' went more or less willy-nilly into the jungle and since somebody with some sort of experience had to take them over, I was put in command of them very shortly after their arrival. Once again it was very difficult to train them for jungle operations when they were supposed to be actually on an operation. I was the only officer with experience in Malaya in that squadron, and in the three months I had with them, I think all I can say is that I perhaps did achieve was that I did establish the rudiments of battle discipline. We got away from the rather slap-happy way in which 'A' Squadron had gone around the jungle with big fires at night, dropping sweet papers or ration tins around the place and not hiding them, we did perhaps just begin to master that problem.

Now once 'B' Squadron had arrived, within a matter of two or three months came 'C' Squadron from Rhodesia who had been volunteered by the then Rhodesian Government to help in Malaya and the same procedures happened with them. They were given two or three weeks training in the jungle where an officer called Ted Peacock, a Sergeant Eddie Waters and myself were attached to them for this period, doing our best to give them some idea of what they should do; they were then let loose in the jungle after just that short period of elementary training.

Hot on their heels arrived 'D' Squadron from England; they had spent a few weeks at the AFD in Aldershot, not the best preparation for joining the Malayan Scouts. They arrived and I was put in command of that Squadron where I'm happy to say I stayed rather longer.

In between operations the soldiers continued to enjoy their leave periods. After a three-month sojourn in the jungle there was enough back pay to ensure a good time, but often this went all too quickly. Bob Bennett remembers one such occasion when he and Jock Easton, who had been wartime comrades, were feeling the pinch and decided to have a quiet few days on Changi beach. They scrounged as much as they could by way of rations from the cookhouse and took their tent intending to enjoy the sun and perhaps a spot of fishing:

We pretty soon got fed up with the fact that it was pretty boring just lying around in the sun with no cash for the odd beer in the midday heat. We were ambling along the beach when blow me if we didn't bump into Pat Riley. (Riley was another of the original 'L' Detachment warriors who had been commissioned during the war and had rejoined the army after a brief attempt at becoming a peacetime civilian.) He invited us to a dance at the Mess that evening with the promise of a good tuck in at the buffet.

Well it was alright for Jock, I mean he was an officer, but me – I was just a Sergeant Major! Anyway Pat said not to worry as he could fix me up with all the right gear and we went back to the Mess with him. He fixed us both up with smart tropical uniforms and I became a Colonel for the night. We had a good scoff and all was going well. I asked one of the ladies to have a whirl with me and we were getting on OK. She asked me what regiment I commanded and I said the SAS making a guess that she wouldn't even know what that was. I was right – she didn't. I have to tell you that I didn't make the mistake of trying to talk 'posh'. I'd come unstuck doing that before and then dropping my aitches all over the place. It was a damned good night – much better than the tent and nobody seemed any the wiser which was a good thing for Pat I reckon.

There were favourite haunts, of course, and one of these was 'Nanto's', a bar-cum-restaurant on the then Batu Road (now Jalan Tunku Abdul Rahman) in Kuala Lumpur and any time a squadron was in town between ops there would be a strong contingent present. On those nights the planters tended to give the place a wide berth. Maybe 'Paddy' Winters had something to do with this. Ian 'Biffo' Cartwright recalled a party when he was a Troop Captain:

The Squadron had been on ops over Christmas and the New Year, and therefore celebrated the festive season late. A Christmas meal and 'smoker' was laid on for all ranks in the cookhouse. At the back of the room there were crates of 'Emu' beer, which had been donated by the Australian Government so that every soldier in Malaya received one can. 'D' Squadron was the last squadron to celebrate Christmas, and the fact that all this free beer had been left untouched demonstrated the quality of it! We tried one or two cans but preferred to pay for the local brew – 'Tiger'.

The party was in full swing when there was a shout of, 'Look. He's stealing our beer.'

We turned round to see a young National Service driver who was attached to Transport Section helping himself to the free 'Emu' beer. He was immediately grabbed and brought across to the table I was sitting at. There was an immediate pronouncement of sentence from my Troop Sergeant, Paddy Winters, of 'Hang him.' The unfortunate lad was laid on a six foot folding table while an unsuccessful search was made to find a suitable rope. I thought they were joking. But I should have known Paddy Winters better. He was a veteran of 2 SAS in the Western Desert and Italy, and a renowned 'hanging man' in the Regiment.

On this occasion he was the Orderly Sergeant and was wearing his scarlet sash. He removed it, made a noose and tied the loose end to the top of the open window frame. The offender, still lying face down on the table, had the noose placed around his neck. Several hands then swung the table until it struck the lip of the window flinging the young driver through it. There was a tightening of the sash as the body disappeared. I suddenly thought that I had witnessed a murder – not only witnessed it but condoned it by my lack of action! I ran outside to find the young lad sitting on the ground sobbing, still attached to the sash. I was certainly relieved to find him alive. Some of the boys also arrived and invited him back in to join the party. He replied with some feeling that he did not want to drink with brutes like us and he disappeared into the night.

Paddy Winters hung a lot of people, but never actually killed anyone, either by luck or judgement. It was not unusual to go into Nanto's, a bar frequented by the SAS, and see one or two people hanging by their ties from hooks in the wall. You knew Paddy was present, and he objected to people wearing ties despite the fact that it was the accepted dress after dark.

Generally speaking, when chatting to soldiers about operations in Malaya some thirty odd years later, it is the moments of comedy and the good time which spring to mind. Perhaps this is nature's way of blocking out the distasteful but it is a fact that operational life was very demanding. Rations were totally unsuited to the work. At the beginning of an operation when maximum mobility was needed for the walk-in and initial deployment into an area there could be a requirement for a troop or squadron to be self-sufficient for up to three weeks. The ration in that case would probably be along the lines of half a tin of corned beef; 4 oz rice; a packet of chicken noodle soup; some dehydrated cabbage and sufficient 'makings' for three or four well-sugared brews per day. Obviously the shorter the walk-in the more the man could afford to supplement this meagre ration. Favourite additives were 'ikan bilis', (whitebait dried in the sun) which could be munched dry or added to any meal, dehydrated onions, curry powder and garlic. Despite the luxuries which arrived every air drop day it was the norm for men to lose a lot of body weight over the duration of a three-month operation and, over a year the body could become quite run down with a lowered resistance to disease.

Humour would out even under the strangest of situations. The story is often related about Eddie Waters, mentioned earlier but one of 'A' Squadron's earliest recruits under Calvert. Ex KSLI, he had been languishing in the Guard Room under sentence for assault when Calvert had winkled him out; he was a superb soldier though he could never refrain from lashing out in heated argument. On one operation Waters was acting as leading scout to a patrol when he spotted a CT camp; he half-turned to indicate the fact to his patrol when a hidden sentry fired at him with a

Thompson sub-machine gun. Waters was hit in the shoulder by three or four rounds and sent spinning backwards. He was thrown into the midst of the patrol at which point he was clearly heard to shout, 'Watch it, lads, they're firing live ammo'.

The bone structure of his shoulder was shattered and it never properly knitted together again. Nonetheless, such was the calibre of the man that he was allowed back to the Regiment and, as Squadron Sergeant Major to 'D' Squadron, he had special dispensation to have an aborigine porter to carry his rucksack on patrol. Of course, as well as humour, Waters could show compassion! Cartwright recollects:

Some years later, in June, 1958, I commanded 'D' Squadron in the Tasi Bras area while the Squadron Commander, Alan Julius, was away doing his Staff College exams. The mission was to establish whether there were any CTs remaining in the area before it was declared 'white' (terrorist free). It was a flat, low-lying area of filthy swamp which had been the scene of much action in the past. We found nothing to report, except debris of previous activity. Sickness was a real problem and after about six weeks I caught leptospirosis (for the second time). Initially I was too sick to evacuate and it was decided I should be held in base until my condition stabilised. While I was there, Eddie Waters took out a patrol. He returned the day I was due to be evacuated. I can remember lying on a stretcher completely enveloped in a parachute. He came into camp and I heard him ask, 'How's the Boss?' The next thing I was aware of was him standing over me mumbling some prayers. I removed the parachute from over my face, looked up and grinned at him. He showed his emotion by nearly kicking me off the stretcher. He seemed almost annoyed that he'd wasted a prayer!

7

THE APPOINTMENT OF BRIGGS

Though the infant Special Forces were having their teething problems in 1951, life was no easier for the more settled formations of the line battalions and it is important at this stage to look back briefly at the situation from the declaration of a State of Emergency to the point at which we left the Malayan Scouts.

During the first eighteen months after the declaration the initiative had rested with the CTs. There had been the occasional success for the security forces but in the early days it was very much a hit or miss affair. The lack of information on the CTs covered the complete spectrum of tactical intelligence on movements, strengths, organizations, tactics and personalities. From the declaration throughout the following year this was to prove more of a handicap than the shortage of men on the ground. Such information as was held by the police was not passed on to the army.

This desperate state of affairs is amply illustrated in a conversation at the end of July, 1948, between General Boucher and the British Administrator in Pahang* when the former stated that he had plenty of troops but not enough targets, partly because the police were 'reticent'.

The result of this lack of trust and liaison between the police and the army was that well into 1951 the majority of field patrols were 'blind' and contacts were accidental. Naturally, this was good news for the CTs who were relatively unhindered as they pursued their own tactics which involved attacks on the civilian population (as a form of coercive terrorism); economic warfare

* Ref CAB 103/532 120959 Appendix C

(the slashing of rubber trees so that they 'bled to death'); the destruction of mine machinery and attacking communications, ambushing trains and police stations, blowing up bridges, telegraph lines and railway tracks.

Most of the civilian casualties were Chinese which is one reason why the Emergency was not taken sufficiently seriously in Whitehall. But there were other factors which intruded into the Government thinking, not the least the international situation. In the same month as the Emergency was declared, the Russians blockaded West Berlin. The airlift was under way and US Air Force B-29 Superfortresses were deployed to Britain armed with nuclear bombs. War with Stalin's Russia seemed imminent.

In the Mediterranean Britain had retired ignominiously from Palestine and Arab and Jew were locked in deadly battle for possession of the Holy Land. In Greece the march of communism had reached its peak and controlled two-thirds of the country, and in Eastern Europe the Soviet writ held sway. The world to the east of Suez was in a mess. Despite the best intentions of a well-meaning Mountbatten as the last Viceroy, the partition of India had resulted in a bloody civil strife in which the casualty figures put most of those incurred in the Second World War into the shadow. And now India and Pakistan were fighting over Kashmir. The French were deep into the thick of things in Indo-China and the Dutch were having second thoughts about their possession of the East Indies. In Manchuria, Mao Tse Tung had launched the final offensive destined to expel Chiang Kai Shek from the mainland and there were rumblings in partitioned Korea.

At home there was rationing, unemployment on a grand scale, gloom and an economy that was too war weary to absorb the brave new world of socialism where nationalization was already proving to be a double-edged sword; the trains still didn't run on time and the coal mines were strike-bound.

Set against such a background, both at home and abroad, just how much time did Clement Attlee and his Labour Council devote to the problems of Malaya? How much of a case could be made for Malaya and Singapore by a government that had already incurred enormous debts by borrowing heavily from a United States which was, in any case, highly suspicious of Britain's imperial aspirations? Malaya had its rubber and tin, worthy items for the exchequer only so long as the profits were not eaten up by the costs of security, and though Singapore still had its base complex intact, its strategic importance depended upon the political perceptions of Britain's role in the world.

Thus the imperialist sentiment in the Conservative Party talked in terms of the 'gateway between East and West'. If Singapore was to fall to the communists, the strategic line of communication (SLOC) would be compromised and the integrity of Thailand, Indo-China and the Dutch East Indies would be placed in jeopardy. Nobody hated communism with greater vehemence than Ernest Bevin, Britain's Foreign Secretary, but Australia did not feature with any great significance, other than as a convenient destination for emigration so helping to relieve some of the burden at home.

So, in the global scheme of things, the Emergency in Malaya was small beer indeed. It was not until September, 1948, that Whitehall got around to appointing a successor to Gent. The gap was most ably filled by the Commissioner General. MacDonald had, in any case, played an extremely important part in the first weeks of the Emergency which has never really been acknowledged. His biggest single contribution was probably his insistence, at the crucial conferences of the first week, on the overriding importance of preserving the economic resources of the country by protecting the estates and mines which he had visited. This had much to do with keeping up the morale of the managers. He, in fact, overruled the High Commissioner and the GOC on the use of troops as static guards until Special Constables could be mobilized. He seems to have had a much better understanding than any of the others of the magnitude of the coming struggle.

The new High Commissioner, Sir Hugh Gurney, was to hold office for only two years before his tragic death. He was another career diplomat and administrator from the Colonial Office who found his way east of Suez after Palestine where he had been Chief Secretary and the last civil servant to leave. He cut an eccentric figure because of his ultra-orthodox appearance. Rarely without a trilby hat, the slightly built man of military bearing made no concession to the tropical climate but always wore a jacket and tie and was seldom seen without a cane. Local affectations such as the 'planter's rig' of shorts and open-necked shirt were alien in an upbringing which had stamped conformity on his personality from the beginning. One can imagine that as a child in prep school he slept at night with his hands outside the sheets and learned from an early age not to display emotions in public. But it was on men such as him in the twenty years following the ending of the Second World War that Britain depended to surrender the largest empire the world has ever witnessed with a modicum of fuss, little bloodshed and much good grace.

Gurney's rather severe and forbidding appearance, however, hid a lively mind and a clear perception of what the job in Malaya entailed. Even so, he and his advisors grossly underestimated the time it would take to master the communist insurrection. Policy was devised and directed in a time frame of months rather than years, but Gurney did get two things right. He recognized the primary importance of political and economic responses over a military solution; thus from the outset the principle was clearly established that the military were subordinate to the civil power. In turn this encouraged the search for a political solution to the crisis rather than a military victory. Secondly, he insisted on the primacy of the rule of law even though this placed what must at times have been regarded as intolerable constraints on operational demands by the army and the police.

Even while he settled into the appointment, Gurney would have appeared to have reached another conclusion. He must have realized that he had inherited a mediocre team and a faction-ridden, quarrelsome apparatus which had made little impression upon the counterinsurgency effort.

There was a new Commissioner of Police, Colonel William Nicol Gray, CMG, DSO, a distinguished veteran of the special forces. He commanded 45 (Royal Marine) Commando in Normandy and through to the end of the war. He was later to be the Inspector General of Police in Palestine where he knew Gurney. He was appointed to Malaya because he was available and had the right seniority and reputation as an expert on anti-terrorist operations.

The Malayan Police were short of manpower and Gray filled out the ranks for European inspectors with lots of his ex-colleagues. Several hundreds of ex-Palestine Police, neatly and uniformly dressed in Palestine Police club ties and blazers, descended upon Kuala Lumpur. There was an abundance of cynical comments about Malaya becoming a second Palestine, and to a faction-ridden Police Officer Corps, which was still feuding about the rights and wrongs of the Japanese occupation they were as welcome in the officer's mess as the Black and Tans had been to the Fenians in 1920. There was a drop in morale among the veteran British, Malay and Chinese policemen which grew to huge proportions as Gray's belief that the answer lay in aggressive patrolling resulted in increased casualties. This dissatisfaction was eventually to result in a Police Commission being sent out from the United Kingdom to examine the equality of treatment between the ethnic groups.

Whatever the arguments may be about Gray's style of leadership, he was a hands-on-copper and never the desk-bound executive. He ran things his own way, making his recommendations on priority areas and actions directly to the GOC (Boucher) who may or may not have agreed. If he disagreed then the matter was referred to Gurney for arbitration and the result would be an Operational Instruction distributed through the police and military chain of command. Generally speaking up until early 1951, Gray had things very much his own way.

Under the Emergency Powers Act there was ample scope for the 'carrot and stick' approach to the problem; some of the results of this were to affect SAS operations at a later date. The first set of Emergency Regulations contained four crucial provisions:

* Arrest and detention without trial; to counter the intimidation of witnesses.
* The right of search without warrant; to speed up operations.
* The registration of all the population and the issue of ID cards; to help in the identification of suspects.
* Strict control of firearms, including mandatory death sentence for their illegal possession.

In the face of these regulations the 'carrot' factor was twofold. Firstly there were generous surrender terms which amounted to an amnesty for all CTs except those who were found guilty of murder. In the early months this offer tempted a few hundred of the weaker brethren out of the jungle. Quite a number of these Surrendered Enemy Personnel (SEP) were to be allocated to the SAS as guides and tutors on CT tactics and in the early stages of this practice it was a nerve-wracking proposition to be a member of a patrol in the hands of an ex-CT not knowing whether he was bent on leading the party into a deliberate ambush.

Added to the amnesty was the system of lucrative cash rewards. Such a business is tricky to operate without the danger of corruption, but this was made difficult by the way it was structured. Post-war history shows that there are notable examples of success and embarrassing failures. In Italy the power of the Red Brigades in the later seventies was broken by the penitos; in Northern Ireland the supergrass proved a disaster. In Malaya, however, it was an early success and different to the other examples in that it was methodically applied throughout the twelve years of the Emergency. It is interesting to look at the graded scale of payments introduced in 1949:

★ Casual information	$50–$100**
★ Capture/killing of CTs	
Secretary General	$60,000
State/Town Committee Secretary	$30,000
Member	$20,000
District Committee Secretary	$14,000
Member	$10,000
or Coy Commander	$10,000
Plt Commander	$6,000
Sec Commander	$5,000
Cell Leader	$3,000
Others	$2,000

** Equating to the norm for a month's pay.

The main reason behind such a generous scale of payments was because it was felt that the informant would have to remove with his family to another district for fear of retribution. In the event there are few recorded cases of revenge which is remarkable given the manner of some of the betrayals. Once committed to such a scale of rewards the Government could not reduce it; indeed for some, particularly the more senior terrorist commanders, the rates were significantly increased during the course of the campaign.

The 'stick' side of the coin included the ultimate penalty of death for terrorists found guilty of murder (capital punishment still operated in the United Kingdom). In addition the Emergency Regulations in Malaya allowed for arrest and detention without trial followed by deportation. By the end of the Emergency some 14,907 detainees had been deported to Mainland China.

The military and the police were not communicating and Gray did not believe that this war should be run by the army. On the other hand that was precisely what General Boucher was about. He was never reticent in stating his firmly held view that it was unthinkable for 'a bunch of coppers to start telling generals what to do'. He was a firm advocate of the 'big battalions' argument. More troops were made available once Palestine had ceased to be a commitment; four battalions were despatched from Hong Kong in early August, 1948. A battalion of the Coldstream Guards arrived in the country exuding spit and polish as the advance party of the 2nd Guards Brigade. This was the first time the Brigade of Guards had served east of Suez since the Shanghai Crisis in the late twenties and not surprisingly it took them nine months to kill their first bandit.

The cavalry were also given their chance to play a part, albeit as dismounted troops. The 4th Hussars came from the United Kingdom, although initially without their armoured cars because some Staff Officer had got it into his mind that the road bridges in Malaya could not support their weight. The error was quickly recognized but it took longer to get the armoured cars to Malaya and into effective action.

One of the main reasons for the early squabbles and in-fighting among the Security Forces was that neither side was well served by the Intelligence Services; this simply added to the sense of frustration and a general feeling of inadequacy. This failure of the Intelligence Service is a confusing business over which the secondary accounts are contradictory. If we are to believe that the Malayan Communist Party had been penetrated and that Lai Tek was a British double agent, then how is it that despite the fact that the communist insurgents were active from the Thai border to the Strait of Johore, the only thing that Intelligence claimed it knew with any certainty was the identity of Chin Peng?

In the event the Intelligence function was passed to the Police Special Branch which had to start virtually from scratch. The task was clear. Special Branch had to find out all it could about the CT threat, the identity, strength, arms, deployments and, above all, the enemy intentions; there was equal priority for the same information regarding the Min Yuen. At the same time the Intelligence organization had to be expanded and its personnel trained in the new function.

Gurney had recognized the Intelligence failure early in his appointment. In a report to his masters in Whitehall he wrote:

> Unfortunately our Intelligence organization is our Achilles heel and inadequate for present conditions when it should be our first line of attack. We have not got an organization capable of sifting and distributing important information quickly.

The High Commissioner lost no time in trawling the available talent among the Malayan Colonial establishment in his search for an Intelligence co-ordinator in the Government Secretariat in Kuala Lumpur. He settled on Robert Thompson who had previously been a Chinese Affairs Officer to a state government. A fluent Mandarin speaker, Thompson had direct access to Gurney and his early position papers on the communist threat and appropriate countermeasures exerted an undoubted influence on future thinking: 'It's all very well having bombers, helicopters, fire power, but none of these will eliminate a communist cell in a high school which is producing fifty recruits a year for the insurgency movement.'

It was obvious that the communist threat to Malaya would never be eradicated unless the problems caused by the Chinese squatter community were addressed and resolved. This, coupled to the Chinese mentality, their own set of loyalties and the peculiar influence of family, presented a formidable obstacle to a political solution.

Neither had the position of the Chinese community, even the loyal and law-abiding members, been helped by the announcement on 1 November, 1949, of the creation of the People's Republic of China. This momentous event had sent shock waves rippling through the Chinese communities scattered across Asia. It was a boon to the Viet Minh in Indo-China, and as inspiring to the CTs as it was frightening to the thousands of Chinese in Malaya who were anti-communist, but were too frightened or cowed by reprisals to resist. Many must have anticipated invasion and few would have had any faith in the British military ability to repel such an attack in the light of their humiliation by the Japanese.

Hardly had Malaya absorbed the shock of the communist victory when they were forced to come to terms with the British Government's decision, announced in February, 1950, to recognize Peking. Diplomatic recognition was a standard practice based upon time-honoured standards of pragmatism and a major concern must have been not to antagonize the new regime of Peking lest it send its forces to complete the 'Long March' by taking Hong Kong. This decision did nothing to wean the Chinese in Malaya away from the communists. Instead the response of the vast majority of them (and probably a prudent move given their circumstances) was to sit on the fence and remain there until a winner could be detected.

The squatter areas were so widespread that, no matter the size of the security forces, adequate, leave alone complete, protection could never have been provided. The result was that the squatters in the jungle fringe and the Chinese in the towns and the larger settlements in the mine belt and rubber plantations were open to the CTs and collaboration was rife.

Insurgency does not, as is frequently presumed, need a vast and enthusiastic following and support; rather acquiescence, tolerance and passive support among a significant segment of the population will suffice to allow the terrorist to function. This is precisely what happened in Malaya. By the spring of 1950 the CTs, despite some significant losses, had pushed their insurgency to the threshold of a crisis that threatened to envelop the country. Both sides had made terrible blunders, but the CTs tended to recover from their mistakes more quickly. The level of incidence had reached that point where the nation's morale was undermined and the economy placed at risk. Despite strenuous Government

11. Colonel John Sloane visits McGregor and Cross. *(A. McGregor)*

12. An informal patrol briefing. *(A. McGregor)*

13. An early parachute course.

14. Colonel Sloane on a jungle course. *(A. McGregor)*

15. 'C' Squadron on training in Rhodesia. (*Ted Bates*)

16. 'C' Squadron relaxes under the eyes of the Brass: the three officers are Major Walls, Colonel Sloane and General Sir Charles Keightley. (*Ted Bates*)

17. On patrol: in the foreground Lawrence Smith, behind him Peter de la Billière, followed by Jim Peebles.

18. Dinner in the Mess: 2nd from left 'Lofty' Ross; 3rd from left 'Jesse' James.

efforts, communist cells were being formed at an increasing rate in the towns, villages and more especially the squatter encampments along the jungle fringe.

Gurney had very early on reached the conclusion that he needed a Director of Operations with military experience and sufficient clout to knock heads together and bring about a co-ordinated government, civil and military response and counter-insurgent strategy. He must also have been frustrated by the narrow and inflexible strategy pursued by General Boucher and by his not inconsiderable military forces.*

Boucher's lack of comprehension had been revealed as early as 1948 when he spelled out his objectives to the Legislative Council: 'To break up the insurgent concentrations, to bring them to battle before they are ready, and to drive them underground or into the jungle, and then to follow them there. I intend to keep them constantly moving, and deprive them of food and recruits.'†

Using these tactics, reminiscent of Custer's pursuit of the Sioux through the Dakotas, and just about as effective, Boucher unleashed a number of military sweeps through Johore, Selangor and Perak. They were all counter-productive and very costly in time, effort and resources. The full military orchestration included amphibious landings, Spitfires strafing the jungle to their heart's content and Staff Officers vaingloriously marking their maps in pretty colours to declare areas clear of CTs. Such strategies were totally unsuited against an enemy who would melt away rather than stand and fight and who was prepared to sit it out for years if necessary. Like Custer against the Sioux, the best they could do was to torch the occasional abandoned encampment.

Despite glaring evidence of failure, Whitehall procrastinated against Gurney's request for a Director of Operations for a host of reasons. There were more pressing problems both at home and abroad, and a General Election was due. The Civil Service was opposed to the appointment and in the period before an election,

* By early 1950 Boucher had received additional reinforcements: 26th Gurkha Bde (1 UK + 2 Gurkha battalions); 3rd Commando Bde; 13th/18th Hussars with armoured cars to assist 4th Hussars and additional RAF squadrons including 1 squadron of Lincoln Bombers from Australia.
† *The Communist Insurrection in Malaya 1948–60*. Anthony Short, pp. 136–7.

when inertia sets in, the Mandarins wield undue influence. The Colonial Office was horrified at the thought of surrendering executive powers to the military and the latter were equally aghast at the prospect of some civilian having a say in tactics.

Gurney persisted, and he did have increasingly depressing casualty figures to support his argument. There was no rush of candidates to fill a job which possessed every potential for a poisoned chalice and therefore something to be avoided like the plague for those still ambitious – civilian or military. Lieutenant-General Sir Harold Briggs was appointed in April, 1950. He agreed to do the job for a year, stayed for eighteen months and died very shortly afterwards. This was an interesting choice, one which employed all the elements of compromise for which the British establishment is renowned. He was fifty-five years of age and had already retired from the army to live in Cyprus. Briggs, as his rank reveals, had enjoyed a distinguished military career, including wartime high command fighting the Japanese in Burma; in fact it was Slim, his old wartime boss, who persuaded him to take the job. As a retired Lieutenant-General, Briggs arrived in Malaya as a civilian, which could cause offence to none of the factions.

As Director of Operations, Briggs's brief was: 'To plan, to co-ordinate and to direct the anti-bandit operations of the police and the fighting force.'

He ranked alongside the Police Commissioner and the Chief Secretary, but herein lay the essential element of compromise. He had 'Authority over all security, police, army and air force, and the power to co-ordinate actions of all civilian departments that affected the war.'

In practical or operational terms this meant that Briggs had no power over the police or the military; his was a co-ordinating role since he could initiate policy but the service chiefs had the right to appeal. The mental agility to create this form of wording assumed a man of enormous tact, patience, skill and quiet authority to orchestrate the disparate factions into a cohesive unit. Briggs was imaginative and incisive but also modest and tactful. It was these personal qualities which allowed him to achieve much of what was required, but at the price of his health and ultimately his life.

8

THE BRIGGS PLAN

The Briggs Plan as it was to become known was important to the evolution of the Malayan Scouts in that it gave greater importance to their deep penetration role; it is therefore worth examination in some detail.

By the time that Briggs arrived in Malaya in April, 1950, a great deal of the work which was later to form part of the plan to which he lent his name was already underway. Even so, the appointment of a Director of Operations by Sir Henry Gurney, and one, remember, made in the face of Whitehall doubt, was a very wise move.* There was a desperate need for someone of the right military background and experience to give his undivided attention to the problems of the Emergency, thereby leaving the High Commissioner free to concentrate on governing the colony.

Within a couple of weeks of his arrival Briggs submitted an appreciation of the situation via the High Commissioner for Cabinet consideration in London. He had recognized that the CTs' morale and the strength of their adherents increased in proportion to their success, to the influence of external events, and to their propaganda. The fighting strength of the CTs on the other hand was conditioned by the availability of weapons as well as by the squatters who provided food, recruits and information. The communists were winning the propaganda war because the Government was hamstrung by a shortage of Chinese speakers. This was a direct result of Gray's refusal to send any of his officers

---

* This chapter is compiled from the material held in the Public Records Office and relating to the Briggs Plan.

on Chinese language courses in Hong Kong – a position he was to hold to until such courses were eventually established at Berinchang in the Cameron Highlands. It is also a fact that the CTs were much more efficient at exploiting the fears and aspirations of the Chinese community than the Government were in protecting them.

The military were not winning the battle and even the occasional success against CT gangs was insufficient. If the Crown could win over the Chinese community, wrest their allegiance away from the terrorists and thereby isolate them from their constituents then success would follow. From the outset, however, Briggs stressed that it wasn't just a question of separation but the manner in which the Chinese populace were separated that was the key to the solution.

On 24 May, 1950, the précis of a plan, long, detailed but not at the time complete, was presented to the British Defence Co-ordination Committee, Far East. It was this précis which became known as the Briggs Plan. In truth Briggs gave his stamp of approval to a series of recommendations made by committees which had been formed by Gurney in December, 1949, and working since that time. We have already noted the input and contribution made by Calvert.

Briggs described the situation he found as follows:

The CTs are dependent on the Min Yuen for food, money, information and recruits. The support organizations operate wherever the Chinese population are to be found in significant numbers – towns and villages, small holdings, estate labour homes and, above all in the squatter areas along the jungle fringe and the impoverished estates.

The Min Yuen are able to function because the Chinese population are not convinced that the Government will win, and because they fear CT reprisals and punishment if they side with the authorities. The Min Yuen are also very difficult to penetrate because they operate a very tight cell system whereby one cell doesn't know what the next cell is doing or who is a member.

Military and police counter-intelligence is constrained because there are not enough Chinese or Chinese-speaking specialists available and in any case the Min Yuen depend upon the strength of the family as an added security precaution.

So the requirement is to restore security and confidence in the Chinese population and this can only be achieved by the British demonstrating their intention to fulfil all their obligations to defend Malaya from external and internal threats. This requires that the squatter population will have to be resettled into protected villages where all the benefits of local government and welfare will be available.

On the military front the intention is to clear the country step by step working south to northwards but first of all dominating the populated areas to encourage confidence amongst the local community. This will help to create a confident environment in which information will flow and thereby allow the security forces to break up the Min Yuen. Lastly, with the Min Yuen on the run the bandits will have to attempt to restore the initiative but this will require them to attack on ground of the Government's choosing thereby inviting their defeat.

There were three elements to the Briggs Plan. The first, and the key to success, lay with the manner of resettlement. This required a massive and intimidating troop presence on the ground to provide the logistic needs and the physical protection. The recent arrival of two additional infantry brigades made this easily possible and D Day was set for 1 June, 1950.

With terrorist incidents running at five times their 1949 level and the death toll, mostly Chinese, from CT attacks at the rate of over one hundred per month, a crash programme of resettlement was introduced. The extra troops made it feasible, whilst maintaining equivalent security in the northern half of Malaya, to concentrate the maximum forces in Johore on 1 June; in Negri Sembilan and Malacca on 1 August and in parts of south-west Pahang on 1 September. Whilst resettlement was to continue throughout the country concurrently, Briggs determined that priority of personnel and effort was to be given to these southern states to produce quicker initial results.

Convoys of heavily protected British Army three tonners arrived at various squatter camps in Johore and there the families and their possessions were gently but firmly loaded up and driven away to a new life. The innate gruff humour, patience and sympathy of the average British 'squaddie' must have been an added bonus in this most delicate of operations as people were coaxed and cajoled into the back of trucks and then unloaded at journey's end.

The intentions, in the words of the Briggs Plan, were to give the squatters 'a standard of local government and a degree of prosperity' they would not wish to exchange for the life that the communists had planned for them. It was a 'hearts and minds' campaign in its purest and most effective form, although nobody spoke of it in those terms at the time.

The lucky householder was taken to a new wood frame house for which he received a temporary title deed which included a plot of land upon which to grow vegetables etc; this act alone must have given them a new feeling of security and permanence. Secondly they were moved into villages which were already protected and fortified. The physical defence represented a twentieth century upgrade on a motte and bailey fortification using tropical materials, and the fertile imagination and ingenuity for which the British Sappers are renowned. Bamboo stakes, ditches and barbed wire provided an outer perimeter topped by watch towers and searchlights. The static defenders comprised police, regular and locally recruited reservists and, as time passed, a local defence volunteer unit. The provision of firearms for the latter, however, was a more difficult issue where the obvious dangers predicated a cautious and very conservative approach at first.

Some people were taken to brand new villages, others were moved into existing villages which had been specially enlarged, while still others were taken to labour lines on the big estates which had been rebuilt and fortified. The villages 'on offer' broadly fell into two categories; 'dormitory' for those who worked in the mines or on the plantations and 'agricultural' for those who were farmers and smallholders. Wherever they were taken there was the immediate offer of employment because of the growing demand, worldwide, for rubber.

Success at the outset came about for a number of reasons some of which we have already touched upon. But there were other factors which were major contributors. Briggs had recognized the competition for government but in the resettlement programme there was no competition. The CTs had no alternative plan to place before the Chinese people and in any case what could they have done? Moved the 500,000 squatters deep into the jungle? They did not have the means or resources and it would have defeated the object since they relied on the Min Yuen enough to disrupt or hamper the operation; the crushing military presence was a more than adequate deterrent.

The speed and success of the operation, in other words the ability to keep disruption and turmoil to a minimum, was largely the responsibility of the British Resettlement Supervisors who were assisted by 263 Chinese Assistant Resettlement Officers. These hard-pressed men arbitrated over disputes, allocated houses and completed their documentation which listed the names of every Chinese in each house (and thereby provided both the Intelligence services and the local police post with an accurate head count). But they were not tax collectors nor were they called upon to conduct other unpopular tasks and so were usually welcomed by the Chinese communities. Although some were targeted and assassinated, by and large they were left alone by the CTs; their relative popularity proved to be their best protection!

These measures were, if you wish, the passive side of the operation. However, the Briggs Plan also called for an active and vigorous pursuit of the CTs. In this, of course, the resettlement made an important contribution because the terrorists were immediately disadvantaged. Resettlement denied them ready access to the Min Yuen and, starved of resources, many of the groups had no option but to split into smaller units. This in turn meant that, when attacks were launched against the fortified villages, they were conducted by these smaller, weaker groups against which the garrisons were able to hold out without difficulty. As this pattern of events emerged the confidence of local defence forces grew. The lessons were not lost on the villagers and more of them climbed down off the fence.

The second active element lay in the use of military operations against terrorist gangs. The plan envisaged a military framework of protection – working in the jungle fringes with the aim of getting between the CTs and the Chinese population in the settled areas. If the army could dominate the jungle edges, get astride the bandit's lines of communications, then it could force the CTs to accept battle on their terms and their ground.

The major problem to overcome, however, was the attitude of the average British soldier to jungle warfare. A continuing weakness of the early years was the clumsiness of British Army units (with the possible exception of the Marine Commandos and the Gurkhas) in the first few months of jungle operations. As a generality, the army was not really effective in the jungle at that time, and some units (though by no means all), even after a few months in the country, never settled to the task. Early in his appointment Briggs identified this as a problem and raised the question at a lunch one day with General Harding, the Commander-in-Chief. Afterwards Harding summoned the GOC and gave an ultimatum that his troops must stay longer in the jungle than the four days prescribed by tradition.

Alongside the infantry battalions and dismounted gunners were the Police Jungle Squads. They figure very little in the documentation because they were not a statutory formation. It is disputed who raised the first squads, or where, but it was probably in the Kinta Valley in the first month of the Emergency. They were not a new idea; earlier squads had been deployed against the Kuomintang bandits in Upper Perak. The squads were ad hoc military units, they could be formed at any time by any officer down to Superintendent level, were of regular size and had any variety of equipment. Sometimes the same men composed the same squad for quite long periods; sometimes all the men on a station took it in turns. On occasions they would stay in the jungle for just 24 hours, on others for three weeks or more; sometimes they worked directly alongside regular units of the army.

Briggs was dissatisfied with the efforts of Special Branch in their quest to obtain and collate Intelligence; they were after all spawned by the CID which was designed for the detection of crime. He made what was an obvious decision and set out to recruit some experts in the Intelligence field. Sir William Jenkin was such a man; after long years of experience in India he was recruited as Director of Intelligence for Malaya. He brought out from London British Officers who had experience of Intelligence work in India and in other parts of the Empire. They were joined by army officers seconded from the Intelligence Corps.

Jenkin did not have a happy time in Malaya. The main obstacle was the opposition and obstructionist behaviour of Police Commissioner Gray. The latter was a typical product of that strand of the British military profession which had always regarded Intelligence with the utmost suspicion. It is pertinent to remember that the Intelligence Corps itself was not created until 1938 and so suspicion was then still fairly widespread. Gray viewed the appointment of Jenkin, his terms of reference and the size of his establishment, with ill-disguised hostility. When Jenkin recommended that Asians, and particularly Chinese, be recruited and trained to undertake the bulk of the field work, Gray refused to co-operate.

The scene was set for a battle royal between the two men but unfortunately, Jenkin lacked tact, patience and resilience. Exasperated beyond measure, he resigned after a year and headed home; he had enjoyed a long and distinguished career and he had no intention of being blighted by the likes of Gray. This was a great shame because later events were to prove that he was actually winning; the powers that be were listening to him with more than half an ear and Gray was increasingly isolated.

The pity of it is that Briggs did not see fit to support Jenkin at the time and it took the appointment of Templer, with the powers of supremo to cut through all the stuff and nonsense of colonial red tape and ordain that the Special Branch should be given the priority and resources to become a professional and independent arm of Intelligence. In that process Gray became the casualty and his career was to end in ignominy.

The third and final component of the Briggs Plan was the fusion of the separate strands of authority, the political, judicial, police and military into a co-ordinating body called the War Council. In essence this meant putting the Federation of Malaya onto a war footing. The work of the Legislature was largely curtailed and any political changes in the pipeline were put on ice. For the Colonial Civil Service in the Federation all home leave, retirements and resignations were cancelled for the duration of the Emergency. Briggs set in place a very cumbersome and overly bureaucratic command structure to oversee the counter-insurgency campaign. At the top a Federal War Council (FWC) was set up under the Chairmanship of the Director of Operations and included the Chief Secretary, the GOC Malaya, the AOC Malaya, the Commissioner of Police and the Secretary for Defence. The Council, which answered to the High Commissioner, was responsible for policy and the provision of resources to meet the needs of the Emergency.

The FWC was then mirrored through the various levels of the Colonial Administration with War Executive Committees (WEC) down to local level and these subsumed responsibility for all Emergency matters. The structure of the Briggs Plan can best be explained by the following family tree:

State (SWEC) and District (DWEC) Executive Committees

SWEC	DWEC	Responsibility
Civil		
State Prime Minister	District Officer	Local Government
Executive Secretary		Admin of Prime Minister's office
Information Officer	Information Officer	PR and Psywar
Police		
Chief Police Officer	Police Commander	Command all police
Head Special Branch	Special Branch	Police Intelligence
Military Intelligence Officer	Military Intelligence Officer	Assistance to Special Branch
Home Guard Officer	Home Guard Officer	Training/ administration of Home Guard
Military		
Brigade Commander	Battalion Commander	All troops under command Requests for air support

The pattern and formula were invariably the same. Whether it was the SWEC or the DWEC, the Chairman was the Senior Civil Adminstrator and the permanent members the Senior Police and Military Officers. Briggs also laid down that the commanders on the spot attended, not their representatives or their deputies. This meant that decisions could be taken at the meetings and put into operation with immediate effect.

The WECs also had specialists on call i.e., Propaganda, Air Force, Special Branch, Home Guard, Naval Liaison Officer and, under the plan, the Military Intelligence Officer at whatever level was responsible to the Police Special Branch and not the Senior Army Officer.

At State and District levels the committees tended to meet in full session on a weekly basis but every morning the triumvirate of Administrator, Police and Military met at what became known as 'morning prayers'. The WECs and Committees helped break down the barriers and the inhibitions which hitherto had resulted in people pulling in different directions. It was all to take time but in theory at least, soldiers and civilians were working towards a common, co-ordinated objective. Progress was patchy, however; Combined Operations Rooms were instituted but it was to take another two years before they were really effective.

If this was a slow, and at times uphill, struggle it was nevertheless by these means that the Briggs Plan clearly established the principle that the role of the military was in aid of the civil power. The effective welding together on the ground of the Police, Military and Civil Administration was one of the two main turning points or cardinal developments in counter-terrorist strategy. The second was a gradual realization (over a three-year period to 1952) that protection of the rural population had to come before compulsion; i.e., that no amount of regulations, threats or propaganda could wean them away from supporting the CT unless they were made reasonably safe both at work and in their homes.

This was an emergency which, through the enactment of special powers, restricted individual liberty; but it never superseded the supremacy of civilian control over martial law. Herein Briggs established the theory and laid the practical foundations for success, but to achieve the latter it would require the fallibility of human beings and the reduction of service and individual barriers. The Briggs Plan was, by its very nature, optimistic but it was a firm plan; this was essential for the morale of civilian and soldier alike. It held out the promise of a better future, and that was something the communists could not combat.

9

THE TRANSITION

Improvements in the Government's security plans also saw a change in fortune for the fledgling Special Forces. At the beginning of August, 1951, there came about a series of events which was to signal a new direction for the Malayan Scouts and to lay a foundation stone in the postwar history of the SAS. 'Mad' Mike Calvert was a sick man and, though it was the last thing he personally wanted, the tough determined warrior was obliged to hand over the reins of command. Suffering from an amazing combination of amoebic dysentery, leptospirosis, hookworm and recurring malaria and, no doubt (!), abject tiredness (in itself another similarity to the wartime SAS – Stirling was well below peak performance when he was captured and lost his command in North Africa) Calvert was invalided back to England.

Various military pundits claim that what happened thereafter was only as a result of Calvert's 'accidental' removal from the scene and that disbandment would have been a certainty for the Scouts. We are not convinced of this by any means. He had planted the seeds for a particular type of warfare, recruited some excellent dedicated officers and men and had begun to prove his point. The force he had recruited would have seen for themselves the need to exercise discipline; to improve tactics and drills and to prove themselves to higher command. Had he remained, it is more than likely that some aspects of regimental discipline would simply have been 'hidden' from Calvert and that squadrons would have exercised their own system of weeding out as their sense of pride and achievement grew. It is almost academic to discuss the matter, but it is unfair to paint Calvert with the brush of failure, for fail he emphatically did not. It is not the farmer's fault if drought causes the crop he planted to wither.

Lieutenant-Colonel John Sloane, Argyll and Sutherland High-landers, and fresh from Korea, was selected to take over command. Although he knew nothing of jungle warfare he was a very able officer and a remarkable leader; he arrived (27 July) as Commanding Officer after Calvert's departure and he took but a short time to assess the situation he found himself in and made a number of far-reaching decisions. His feelings and tentative ideas are shown in a letter he wrote soon after assuming command:

> Special Air Service Regiment,
> (The Malayan Scouts),
> c/o GPO, Kuala Lumpur,
> Malaya.

From: Lt. Col. J. B. M. Sloane 20 August 1951

Dear Hart,

I have recently taken over this Regiment, arriving after Mike Calvert had left, and amongst many other things, I am trying to make my number with everyone who has shown an interst and helped us in the past and, I hope, will assist us in the future. Hence my writing to you.

The past history of events I find most confusing and in many ways unfortunate but I have no intention of dwelling on them; rather do I regard them as lessons for the future. I think the best thing I can do is to tell you briefly what we are doing at present; this is, of course, confidential.

The main task is to endeavour to get the Regiment on a sound and lasting basis. To this end the whole of the administration is being overhauled and reorganized; this is a major task since for a large part of the unit's life it has been regarded as unnecessary; how wrong and how expensive this conception has proved to be.

Secondly, the whole of the Regiment's future is up for consideration. Later in September a committee of 'distinguished' soldiers is meeting to consider our future; we, of course, are the main 'witnesses'. My approach to this is that we must have stability and permanence, we must be given a much wider rôle, not tied to Malaya. A new War Office Establishment is also being submitted to rectify some of the more obvious errors in the present one. What success we shall have remains to be seen.

I must say I find myself in rather a peculiar position here, since I have had nothing whatsoever to do with SAS, or anything approaching it, during my service. I was also whisked into this job shortly after my battalion left Korea and am still in something of a daze.

We shall be concentrating in Singapore shortly for six weeks' rest and retraining, and I hope that this will do the Regiment a lot of good.

I would be most grateful if I knew we could count on your support and perhaps you could let me know how you feel about things.

Yours aye,
John Sloane

Major L. E. O. T. Hart, MBE.,
The SAS Regiment,
HQ 21 SAS Regt (Artists) TA.

Sloane may have thought himself to be in a daze but he clearly was in no such state; within this short letter he demonstrated that he had quickly recognized the weakness of his regiment and the scale of the administrative follies; he had spotted its value both within Malaya and in the wider scheme of things; he had appreciated that he was going to have to do battle with the higher command; he had shown his confidence and acted with speed. There is no doubt that he had become aware of the fact that Hart was ill at ease with the regiment (perhaps from earlier correspondence such as that with Greville-Bell); he was aware of the need for a 'key' player in Hart's position, one who could carry the battle to Whitehall if necessary and on one foolscap page he had secured that officer's support for evermore.

The six weeks rest and retraining in Singapore was a master stroke. The regiment was concentrated; officers and soldiers of different squadrons got to know each other and future leaders began to make their mark during the ardent training sessions.

Many of the welfare problems which had been dismissed through ignorance or lack of time and interest were sorted out and the skeleton of a regiment was put together. Many men were dismissed to return to their own units and many who had been hovering on the brink of doing this voluntarily were persuaded to remain. Not the least of the tactics used during this period was that learned by Calvert from the CTs – the system of self-criticism which still goes on in the SAS today.

The principle of this system is simple. Any mistakes made were picked apart in the most minute detail at sessions during which every man, regardless of rank and seniority, was encouraged to give voice. Successes were rarely analysed. It was those occasions when something went wrong where lessons were to be learned. It is a healthy system made the more effective when it is realized from what diverse backgrounds the members of the unit came. There were corps men, infanteers, armoured veterans, staff officers, national servicemen with civilian outlooks and many with direct battle experience from World War II and Korea. It was and is a most valuable tenet and in this case it was an important part of the process of adding muscle and sinew to the skeletal bones.

Before returning to the business of revitalized jungle operations it is necessary to look at some of the fruits of the labours of Sloane, Hart and other key officers in terms of securing the regiment's future. It is interesting to note that during the retraining phase, which Sloane also used as a study session, there are no recorded visits by him to the United Kingdom or by Hart to Malaya. This means that any communication had to be effected by mail or the military communications network. Considering the detail of the study it is remarkable that such completeness was achieved. On 22 December, 1951, a letter was despatched by GHQ Far East Land Forces (FARELF) to the War Office and copied to HQ 21 SAS. A copy of the letter was made available by the late Major Dare Newell, OBE, and it holds the key to further developments in the story:

To: The Under Secretary of State,
   The War Office,
   Whitehall, London, SW 1

Subject: **MALAYAN SCOUTS – SPECIAL AIR SER-
   VICE REGT.**

1. The employment of the Malayan Scouts (Special Air
   Service Regiment) has been under consideration at this
   HQ and the following conclusions have been reached.

ROLE

2. The role of the Malayan Scouts (Special Air Service
   Regiment) is to operate in the deep jungle areas not
   already covered by other Security Forces, with the object
   of destroying bandit forces, their camps and their sources
   of supply.

   No other units in Malaya are so suitably organized or
   equipped for this task which is vital in bringing the
   bandits to battle.

   The result is that the unit is becoming a 'Corps d'Elite'
   in deep jungle operations and is a most valuable component of our armed forces in Malaya.

ORGANIZATION

3. In order to increase the efficiency of the Special Air
   Service Regiment, certain changes are now considered
   necessary in the establishment, but these changes are
   largely on the administrative side, which has been the
   weak link in the past. The Regiment is now to be
   organized on a four-squadron basis as shown on the
   outline War Establishment, at Appendix 'A' attached.
   This reorganization shows a decrease of two British
   officers, but an increase of 52 British other ranks. However, certain of the administrative appointments can be
   suitably filled by National Servicemen, thereby econom-
   izing in the use of the more experienced volunteers.

TACTICAL OPERATIONS

4. The regiment is having increasing successes in their operations all the time.

Their initial operations involved many weeks of patrolling deep in the jungle, which had the effect of disturbing bandits in their camps and providing a great feeling of insecurity among them.

The next main operations the Regiment took part in were deep jungle penetrations in connection with other operations by Infantry battalions. These were very effective and provided many bandit kills.

The Regiment is at present taking part in a most difficult operation in North Malaya, from which valuable results are expected.

TERMS OF SERVICE

5. This paragraph is covered by Reference 'B', (*Author's note: this reference is omitted*) which in short recommends a two year tour, with the option of extending for a period of one year.

TRAINING

6. The unit is authorized to recruit a percentage of parachutists, as there is a role for them during the emergency in Malaya and in wartime in the Far East. With the longer tour it may be possible to retrain a number of volunteers as parachutists by arranging local refresher courses for them. This is now under investigation, but there is no intention of carrying out basic parachute training in this theatre.

TITLE

7. It is felt that the present title of the Regiment indicates that the unit will only operate in Malaya and that volunteers would be more attracted if the words 'Malayan Scouts' were deleted from the title and that the Regiment should be known as a Special Air Service Regiment, with a suitable number to be selected by the War Office. It is believed that '22nd Special Air Service Regiment' would

fit in with the present order of battle.

It is presumed that the Rhodesian Government should be consulted before the change of title is approved.

RECOMMENDATIONS

8. (a) That the Regiment, reorganized as on the attached outline War Establishment remains in this theatre during the emergency (Note: the revised complete War Establishment will be forwarded to the War Office in the normal way with the Minutes of the War Establishment Committee).

   (b) That the Regiment includes a proportion of National Servicemen in certain selected administrative appointments.

   (c) That the initial tour be increased from 18 months to 2 years.

   (d) That the title of the Regiment should be a 'Special Air Service Regiment', with a number selected by the War Office, and if this is approved, that action should be taken to inform the Rhodesian Government of its wider implications.

(Sgd)...............
for General,
Commander-in-Chief,

So it was that in late 1951 the designation 'Malayan Scouts' was dropped for all time and 22 SAS Regiment came into being albeit at this time the red beret of the Parachute Regiment (adopted with the SAS cap badge in March, 1951) was still being worn. Paragraph 4 of the document from GHQ FARELF plainly shows that the Regiment was held in higher regard than they themselves perhaps realized, for they were indeed pioneering a new type of warfare for the British Army; operations from which rapid results were not anticipated.

In the months that followed, the four squadrons of the SAS did begin to make a lot of progress in terms of efficiency. Much was learned from the now commonplace 'self-criticism' sessions and the tactical development is apparent from operational reports.

Malayan Scouts - Special Air Service Regiment
Outline Organization

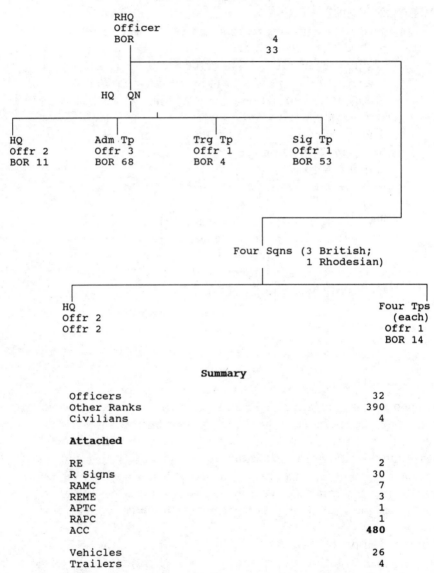

```
                RHQ
                Officer
                BOR                      4
                                        33
              ┌───────────────────────────────────────┐
              │
        HQ  QN
              │
   ┌──────────┬──────────────┬──────────────┐
   HQ         Adm Tp         Trg Tp         Sig Tp
   Offr 2     Offr 3         Offr 1         Offr 1
   BOR 11     BOR 68         BOR 4          BOR 53


                              ┌──────────────┐
                              │


              Four Sqns (3 British;
                         1 Rhodesian)

      ┌───────────────────────────────────────┐
      HQ                              Four Tps
      Offr 2                           (each)
      Offr 2                           Offr 1
                                       BOR 14
```

Summary

Officers	32
Other Ranks	390
Civilians	4

Attached

RE	2
R Signs	30
RAMC	7
REME	3
APTC	1
RAPC	1
ACC	**480**
Vehicles	26
Trailers	4

Patrolling was now a much quieter affair; navigation was improving in leaps and bounds and the arts of track concealment and physical tracking were starting to be accepted as important facets of life in the deep '*ulu*'. What is perhaps more important is that natural leaders were beginning to emerge as the men gained an understanding of, and an affinity with, jungle work. Some men were starting to learn the Malay language or at least a sort of 'lingua franca' which allowed them to conduct basic conversations with the aborigines who frequented many of the areas of tactical interest. Strangely, the importance of this was not recognized until a very late stage of the Emergency and then formal language training began.

The general pattern of life which was emerging was for a squadron to have up to three months in the jungle, followed by ten days of leave, then four weeks of retraining and preparation for the next operation. It was usual for a troop to move into its allocated area, establish a secure base and then patrol outwards in four-man strengths for periods of up to four or five days. Resupply was by air drop every two or three weeks and as the air drop was often the first indication the CTs had that a troop was in the area it was not unusual to move out to a new base in a more secure area after the resupply.

This simple statement of the routine belies the hard work required to achieve it! Entry into the area of operations was as varied as the country. It could be effected by march-in from an appropriate roadhead; by boat, later by helicopter and, on a few occasions, by parachute. Rarely, if ever, was the roadhead, boat disembarkation point or the helicopter landing zone (LZ) the point at which the troop base would be made. Invariably there would be a longish march of some days' duration before the tactical area was infiltrated.

The vegetation in the jungle is basically controlled by two factors; altitude and the results of man's interference with nature. Along the jungle fringes there would be rubber plantations – disciplined lines of trees with all undergrowth regularly cleared away thus allowing troops to march along at a cracking pace. In deeper areas, if man had cultivated large tracts for agriculture (ladangs), these patches once unattended became almost impenetrable thickets (known as 'belukar' or secondary jungle) as the vegetation engaged in a mad race to gain the necessary height to benefit from the sun. Belts of bamboo made for real pain; noisy to force a way through; irritating as the fine hairs of the plant wormed their way into sweating skin. Such areas were usually circumnavigated if possible – the problem being that their acreage could be quite considerable. Right into the interior and on the spurs and ridges would be found virgin jungle ('hutan rimba') reasonably clear of clinging undergrowth, criss-crossed with animal tracks and relatively pleasant to walk through. In most of these areas the unwary soldier could come across the 'wait-a-while'; a creeper with a mass of hooked thorns along the whole of the stem length. There was no point in trying to simply pull one's way out of it. It had to be patiently unhooked, hence the name given to it. Worst of all was the swamp. This could be a real nightmare; marching through the mangroves was a great test of endurance. Dirty brown, brackish water could be up to three or four feet deep and the art was to try to step from underground root to underground root by way of progress. The roots could not be seen through the filthy water and much of the marcher's time was spent trying to extricate himself from chest-high, muddy slime.

Take the different types of vegetation and it will be seen that an operation in the swamp was most unpopular. The average load on the initial march-in could well be in excess of sixty pounds in the rucksack alone then add the weight of the personal weapon and the ammunition, water and emergency rations on the belt and the difficulties can be only too easily imagined. Often soldiers would accept going light on rations during the first phase of an operation in an attempt to reduce the walk-in load as much as possible. Luxuries were non-existent and to the outsider it may seem that SAS soldiers went to ridiculous lengths to save on weight. Many soldiers carried only underpants instead of spare trousers. Half or a quarter of a towel would suffice as would half a toothbrush! They were in the right frame of mind to accept the adage 'the straw that broke the camel's back'.

The troop base became the 'home' where troops could, to a certain extent, relax between patrols. Air drop day was something of a holiday. On that occasion there would be at least one day's worth of fresh rations, mail, NAAFI supplies of cigarettes and the like, fresh clothing and even rum. This presupposed that all the 'chutes arrived intact; if they did not then it could well be a case of 'Hard Luck'. The first of the air drops would usually include those heavy items not carried on the march-in, such as extra explosives and trip flares etc., for LZ construction and camp defences. Provided that it was operationally acceptable then air drop day was a troop rest day.

By this stage the Standard Operating Procedures (SOPs) were developing as troops learned, and from the early days of large fires, much noise and litter being discarded freely, had evolved a certain discipline with regard to the siting and conduct applicable to troop bases. Such a base was treated as a 'hive' as opposed to a 'nest' and the site would be based primarily on five factors: secrecy; defence; suitability to radio communication; proximity to LZ facilities and access to water. Where possible natural defences such as cliff edges or steep spurs would be used to enhance security, but in any event it became the practice to evade detection by breaking the track some 3–400 yards from the base or making the final approach along a stream.

Camp routine would include the construction of personal stand-to positions within close proximity to each soldier's living area ('basha') with the emphasis being on tactical rather than comfortable siting. First and last light stand-to was practised if it was thought to be operationally sensible, otherwise it was the responsibility of each man to awaken himself before first light or risk punishment. Once away from the base camp and onto the 4 or 5 day patrols it was not the norm for soldiers to wash (at least not with soap); such smells lingered for a long time in the breeze-free jungle and many of the small waterways harboured the disease leptospirosis carried in the urine of rats. This could be contracted through the open sores left by leeches (or razor cuts) and would certainly lead to the need for casualty evacuation.

To get the flavour of a typical operation of late 1951, we can revert again to John Woodhouse's memoirs. He was planning an operation as the then Officer Commanding 'B' Squadron and there are a number of points of interest; the demonstration of a typical march-in; his deliberate decision to use booby traps as a main weapon and his experience of lone movement:

I picked a starting point, a few miles north of Chaah, for the squadron to enter the area. There we would cut a DZ and make a base. I would take a supply drop on the DZ sufficient to last the squadron for a month. Once this was done three out of my four troops would move out to far corners of our area to search for the enemy. We had been told that they were more likely to be near the edges than the centre. The fourth troop would stay at Squadron HQ ready to reinforce whichever of the other troops first found the enemy. When that happened its place would be taken by a troop from a quiet area . . . Good tracks which radiated outwards from Squadron HQ were carefully concealed so that they would not be spotted from existing tracks which may be used by the enemy.

My main weapon against the CTs was to be the booby trap. It had not been used before in Johore, and I intended to use it on the largest possible scale. I had been told by an SEP that the CTs often returned to their old camps, so I ordered any camp found unoccupied to be booby-trapped. I also decided to close all main tracks we found by putting trip wires across them attached to eight grenades. In the camps, we would bury mortar bombs, connecting them to small pressure switches which would detonate them if trodden on. Great care would have to be taken to avoid leaving any sign that we had visited the camps. Booby traps were to be inspected – from a safe distance, once in every ten to twenty days. However, in most cases I hoped that the explosion of one would be heard by the troop in the area. In that case they would at once rush to the scene. The troops were sufficiently far apart to make it impossible for one to walk by mistake into another's area.

The Rhodesians left at midnight on the 11th June, 'A' Squadron at 6.30 am on the 12th June. Wilson asked me what time 'B' Squadron were leaving. 'At 9.30 on 14th June after a late breakfast, Willie.' He laughed, 'My Christmas, isn't that just typical of the old men!'

We dropped off the trucks north of Chaah and scuffled away down a logging track. It was the end of a hot still day. After a mile through 'lalang' (long grass) we came to straggly jungle, with logging tracks branching off in all directions. I began to wonder if I was going to reach the stream I was making for before darkness stopped us. We left the logging track and struck off through jungle, having to cut occasionally. The ground was very flat. The light was beginning the rapid fade out which precedes darkness, when we felt the ground getting soggy under foot. A trickle only a few inches wide ran through the middle. Days of dry weather had already affected the stream. We made hasty *bashas*, or chanced the weather and made none at all. Water was slow collecting and most brews contained a good proportion of chocolate-coloured Malayan earth.

Next day we climbed into the hills which formed the centre of the Ma Okil Forest reserve. On the way up the column halted. If the man behind dropped out of sight, orders were to stop. This had happened. No one could see more than three or four men behind him before the jungle closed the view. I slipped my pack and walked down. I soon saw a slim white-faced soldier lying on his back, shivering and taking in great gulps of air. His troop officer and another soldier were leaning over him, giving him water. He was a signaller who had suffered from heat exhaustion on previous occasions in spite of every precaution. He was a great trier. I told him that we could give him five minutes, his pack was to be carried, but that was all that I could do for him. If he couldn't keep up he would have to walk out. These were unkind words, but ruthless determination to get on was an ever-present necessity in jungle marching. The conditions were hard enough to persuade the weak-willed to sit down or give up. I felt that at the first signs of leniency by me, one or two men feeling more exhausted than the rest, would sit down rather than force themselves on. He struggled on bravely though fainting again more than once. On top, however, he recovered.

We reached the site for the base camp on the third day. On two sides were banks six to twelve feet deep with a stream and river joining them. A good site for a DZ was next to the camp. We had recruited three aboriginal porters for each troop, and these now helped cutting the DZ. The supply drop arrived and the troops left, cutting tracks as they went.

Almost at once from the south-east came a signal from Teede, the troop commander. 'Camp for thirty found, good condition, recently abandoned.' As the details came in it was obvious that this would make an ideal place to try out our booby traps. I had got Sergeant Williams in to help and walked over with him to see Teede and the camp. It was sited round the head of a small stream at the foot of a very steep slope. The one entrance came in from below. Four or five bashas were spread around. Sergeant Williams sowed it with bombs, each one hidden with the greatest care, and replaced the leaves over the disturbed surface.

Meanwhile Jeff Douglas, commanding the troop moving north-east, had spent an unpleasant night in the middle of a swamp which had dried up in the drought. They were unable to get more than a mouthful of water even by digging. Once they had cut their way through they found freshly used tracks the other side. This area, therefore, also looked promising.

The troop in the south-west started operations uneventfully. In the squadron base was Sergeant Peter Walter. The latter began here to show the qualities which were to lead him in a few years to rise to the rank of Major and win the Military Cross with the Royal Lincolns in Perak.

I realized there would be occasions when only Squadron HQ, five men in all, would be in this base. It was impossible to know if the enemy knew we were here. In case they did I strengthened the defences in every way I could think of without keeping back men. Each of them was needed for offensive patrolling or ambushing. First we collected timber from the DZ and made bullet-proof cover for our stand-to positions. We laid out four 'nests' of grenades on the most likely approaches and connected them to four pull switches in my basha. Later I added a flame thrower to our armoury, thinking that this would have not only a tremendous surprise effect, but would help light things up at night. Finally I laid on through Brigade HQ an air strike which was pre-planned so that all I had to do was send the code word 'Blast'. Once these preparations were complete I waited hopefully for an attack. I thought of trying to pass them the news of our position and numerical weakness, but found no convincing way of doing so. At intervals we added refinements like low trip wires and sharpened bamboo stakes to our positions. I kept one sentry on by night.

Night sentry in jungle can be an eerie experience. Around

sunset there is a cacophony of sound, but this soon dies into comparative silence. On a dark night the darkness is absolute. The sentry can see nothing but must listen. There was slight danger on a night like this, since movement was almost impossible and certain to be noisy. But on clear nights with a moon, the jungle was dappled in silver and black. It was the black patches which drew the sentry's eyes. Little noises; a tree rat scurries over the ground; a dead branch falls; these would alert his wandering mind. All senses tense, he would stare until the shadows seemed to move. It needed a conscious effort to look away. It was comforting then to rub the smooth butt of a gun or carbine in hand. As tension departed he could look again at his watch, and glance back at the camp still in the silence of sleep, until the next imagined alert sharpened his senses once more.

If there was an alarm our orders were simple. Every man to jump to his stand-to position. At night, once in position, every man kept still and crouched low. No shooting was allowed until the enemy could be clearly seen. If they fired on us from a distance we should remain still. 'The answer to noise is silence,' Calvert had taught us. We would not give away our positions and strength by blind firing. Any man seen standing or moving could only be one of the enemy and would be shot.

Some people thought these defences over-elaborate. My arguments were that if the CTs did attack I had the means of destroying the maximum number with the minimum of risk. Moreover, these defences in no way interfered in putting out as many men as possible to hunt the enemy. Indeed, they reduced the need for men in base. Finally their cost in money or labour was small. Except for the flame thrower, I repeated this defence with many variations in nearly all my future base camps.'

John Woodhouse was to have a personal experience of the double-edged nature of booby traps on the same operation when he decided to visit one of his Troop Commanders, Jeff Douglas. One of Douglas' track booby traps had been heard to detonate and on visiting the scene the troop had found blood stains and a discarded communist cap complete with red star.

It was important for a Squadron Commander to see how his troops were getting on . . . On this, their first operation, it was essential . . . I had considered the question of escorts for myself in this area. If I had an escort it would mean either denuding the base to an extent which would involve unacceptable risks, or getting an extra three men from one of the troops. Even if I had three men as an escort, this would be of little value if I walked into an ambush or the sentry of an enemy patrol. Furthermore, I had been convinced that Colin Park (a civilian liaison officer) who always went alone, was right in saying that one man is quicker than three, and that you are much more likely to hear the enemy first if you are alone. I decided to find out what it was like to travel by myself.

By following the track the troop had cut I estimated that I could reach them by about one hour before dark if I started at dawn. I set off fast and at once noticed how much better I could listen with no distracting noise behind me. I carried a smoke grenade so that if I was fired on I could throw it and run away. If on the other hand I saw terrorists without being seen, there seemed no reason why I should not shoot one before escaping in the resulting confusion. I stopped only once in two or three hours, and hid well clear of the track. I came to the swamp where Douglas had spent the night without water. I was pleased to see his camp site so well cleaned up that it was hard to say whether it had been made by us or the enemy. I was grateful that I had not had to cut through the tangled denseness of the swamp. Then I got a shock. There was only three thousand yards to go to his position with three hours of daylight left – easy on a good track. But, there were two tracks diverging.

I chose the better one. After half an hour it ended. I decided against going back. I would make my own way to the troop. I had to cut but at last found my way out on to a newly felled clearing, obviously the troop DZ. I walked around until I picked up a worn track which must lead into his base. Knowing he could not be more than a hundred yards or so from the DZ, I went cheerfully down it. I was looking forward to an agreeable welcome and a mug of tea after a long day's march. Suddenly I stopped dead. Two or three inches in front of me, I caught, for a fraction of a second, the glint of very thin wire – trip wire –

across the track. I sensed the camp must be within yards so I called out 'SAS'. There was a scurry as men stood to. Then one of them having by then seen me called, 'Stand still'. He stood up. 'Walk back and round that side.' There was an urgency in his voice as he pointed the way. Very carefully I followed his instructions and went into the camp where I met Douglas.

Tea appeared with the startling rapidity which is one of the best outward signs of efficient soldiers that I know. Over it we discussed my nearly disastrous arrival.

'That was much too close for comfort, Jeff,' I said, 'lucky I saw it. What was on the end?'

'Only some gun cotton. We use it as a substitute for a day sentry,' Douglas said in his quiet, matter-of-fact voice, sipping his tea; he put it down. 'Could give you a nasty shock or even injury if you were too close to it though.'

I never saw Douglas perturbed. He could accurately be described as calmly confident in all he undertook, and it was always well founded confidence.

It was during the period of this operation that Sloane took over command of the SAS and he made an immediate impression on Woodhouse and his squadron. The operation taught the SAS a lot, not least about the dangers of booby trapping. Two of their explosive ambushes were triggered and blood stains, equipment and other battle debris were found on the sites, but there was no conclusive evidence as to how much the CTs may have suffered. One member of 'B' Squadron sustained minor injuries when setting up booby traps and a member of 'C' Squadron was wounded when he walked into one set up by another troop. This was sufficient to cause Sloane to put an embargo on all booby-trapping operations including those on enemy camps.

Woodhouse then handed over command of 'B' Squadron to Douglas and he was placed in temporary command of the newly arrived 'D' Squadron. The enforced rest and retraining session in Singapore gave him the chance to get to know his men before the advent of 'Operation Helsby'. This operation was to be mounted on the most reliable intelligence the Regiment had ever had and was designed to give it the opportunity to show what it really could do within the confines of the deep jungle. Before that, however, there is one more 'advance' that the Regiment was making which requires a mention.

During this period of late 1951 another similarity to the early desert days occurred in that it was an officer within the SAS rather than the commander who began to take an interest in parachuting as a means of entry into deep jungle. It is generally acknowledged that Major Freddie Templer (a cousin to General Templer) started the business along with Alistair MacGregor. Very much a hit and miss affair, the subject of dropping into trees was treated initially as being a possible misfortune which may befall a parachutist rather than a deliberate tactic and some strange 'tree lowering' harnesses were concocted by utilising the skills of a local furniture maker! MacGregor recalls that, though he was parachute-trained, all he could remember was a vague instruction that one should keep one's feet and knees together prior to landing. Nonetheless, between them the pair made some thirty descents over a period of a week.

A little later the interest was sufficient for a more formal trial to be conducted in the Betong Gap area of Selangor; to the team was added Johnny Cooper (one of Stirling's original 'L' Detachment), Sergeant 'Crash' Hannaway and Peter Walls of 'C' Squadron. The trials were not without mishap but at least a crude method of getting down from a tree-suspended parachute evolved.

Parachuting into trees became a recognized form of entry for the SAS and was used on a number of occasions. As time went on it was concluded that in fact it was safer deliberately to drop into good primary jungle than onto DZs which may have rocky river beds and bamboo in close proximity. The system which eventually evolved from the trials, though it was many months later, was the use of a webbing strap, some two hundred feet in length, which was threaded through a 'bikini' bottom and a steel suspension ring. The principle was that the free end could be attached either to the webbing of the parachute harness or a handy branch if such was in reach. From that point the parachutist was able to make a steady controlled descent to the ground.

There were many hazards to tree jumping though; if the chute just collapsed and did not snag then the parachutist could plunge two hundred feet or so through the trees, bouncing off branches as he fell. Often canopies behaved peculiarly due to the thermal updraughts which are ever-present in tropical, mountainous rain forests. Canopies could snag, appear to be secure and then slip away as the jumper began to shift his weight to fix his harness. There were other dangers not readily apparent such as hornets. The Malaysian hornet is quite a fearsome antagonist if it is disturbed and in swarms they will press home their attack with vigour. Deaths have occurred from hornet bites and many SAS men had very painful confrontations with the finger-thick, aggressive inhabitants of the trees.

The figures calculated as at May, 1955, show that there was a 74% chance of the parachutist becoming suspended on a tree drop and though the major injury rate was low (1.3%) those injuries tended to be sufficiently serious to call for speedy casualty evacuation. This led to an instruction that the strength for parachute entry should not be less than sixteen soldiers. The reason for this was to ensure that no operation was jeopardized by the delay caused by a major casualty i.e., it allowed a party of up to five to remain; construct the necessary LZ (or carry the casualty to a suitable point) whilst leaving sufficient men for a fighting patrol. Obviously this tactic also dictated the need for two signallers and two medics.

These newly acquired skills were to be put into effect first on Operation Helsby.

10

OPERATION HELSBY

Sloane's consolidation of the Regiment in Singapore was used to good effect as rumours of a commitment to a secret operation began to filter through in the inimitable way of the army. Training in earnest began with the corps men being taken in hand by the infantrymen to perfect their personal weapon-handling skills; tactics, contact and ambush drills were practised and practised again. Explosives training took place, mainly aimed at bridge demolition and perfecting techniques for quickly 'blowing' trees to construct emergency helicopter landing zones and a series of dummy raids on airfields and the like were carried out as part of the business of gelling troops and patrols together as working units. Parachute training began with serious intent (practically all of 'B' Squadron were already parachute trained) but no precise details of the operation were given out at this stage.

Eventually the Regiment was briefed in some secrecy on the outline plan for Operation Helsby. At a point some 20 miles south of Gunong Ulu Titi Basah which, at just under 5000', dominates the central portion of the Malay – Thai border, the thundering waters of the Sungei Perak divide to form two tributaries; the Sungei Belum, (it should be noted that on some maps the name Sungei Perak is maintained for the full length of what is referred to as the Belum) and the Sungei Singor. The Sungei Belum, the lowest line of communication of the Belum Valley, continues north to a point about 5 miles short of the border before swinging round to the east and roughly following the border line to the higher reaches of the mountains from which it is but a short hop over the border ridge to link up with the Sai Buri in Thailand. The Sungei Singor branches off to the north-

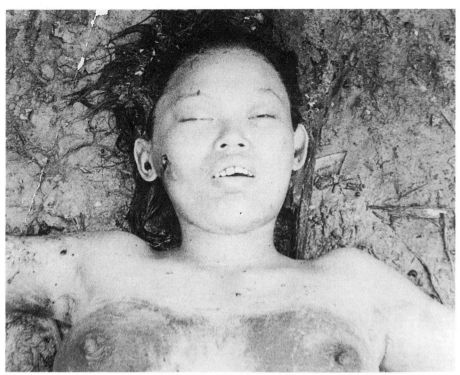

19. A woman terrorist killed in action by 4 Troop, 'A' Squadron on operation *Ash* in 1955.

20. Hostile aborigine killed in an 'A' Squadron ambush in Perak in 1956.

21. Bill Mundell tries an alternative mode of transport.

22. John Woodhouse talks to the 'Kiwi' Squadron at Coronation Park; Frank Rennie in the foreground.

23. Ricky Combe surveys the wreckage of a crashed aircraft.

24. Room to spare — not all LZs were as spacious as this!

25. The problems of moving through swampy country.

east before curving round north-west. Between the Belum and the Singor lies a steep, sharply crevassed land mass overlooked by Bukit Ulu Laha (4000'). This area, mainly the east-west portion of the Belum Valley, contained the targets for Helsby,

The word 'belum' can be literally translated from the Malay as 'not yet' but much of Malay translation depends on the mood and intention of the speaker at the time, hence 'belum' can also mean 'soon', 'perhaps later' or, as was explained to the troops at briefing, 'never-never'. The nature of the terrain is amongst some of the most difficult to be found on the Malayan Peninsula. The slopes of the spurs and ridges are very steep and the river, even in the upper reaches, is deep and can present a major obstacle. Alongside the river, though, are many flattened areas leading into the foothills lending themselves well to cultivation; in fact it was potentially one of the peninsula's most fertile areas. Growing in these clearings along the length of the valley were rice, tapioca, maize, coconuts and vegetables of all types in great profusion. In short a regular grocery store for the CTs.

The background briefing for Helsby seemed to promise the Regiment an exciting time! The intial intelligence, from four surrendered terrorists, purported that the HQ of XII Regiment was based in the valley, along with a company of approximately 100 soldiers. This group exercised total control of the valley and the lines of communication over the border into Thailand. It was strongly suspected at this stage that Chin Peng himself was based loosely in an area which straddled the border, and the Belum Valley was a distinct possibility. There were two main centres of indigenous Malays in the valley split fairly evenly between two kampongs, Belum in the west and Sepor to the east.

It was held that both villages were dominated by the CTs and that roll calls were held twice daily with the villagers being under threat of death should they leave the valley. This was certainly in accord with known CT tactics. They were not above executing a relative should a villager choose to escape. This was borne out by reports from Kampong Temengor, some 30 miles to the south, where villagers were reputed to be loyal to the Government, in that there were examples given of relatives who had not received expected visits from their kinfolk in Sepor and Belum for six months or more.

What is interesting to note about the background briefing is that there was no mention of the aborigines in the area. There is more to say about this in later chapters but it is a fact that there were known to be somewhere in the region of fifty Negrito aborigines along the flanks of the Belum Valley in early 1951. It was equally well known that the CTs in the more remote areas used the aborigines as their eyes and ears to provide an early warning of the presence of Security Forces.

At the end of January, 1952, the Regiment moved en masse to a new camp at Sungei Besi five miles south of Kuala Lumpur. Here the troops received their final orders. Three squadrons of SAS were to be used on the operation and their task was to locate the CT camps and destroy them and the occupants. In essence 'B' Squadron was to parachute into the western end of the valley onto wet padi fields bordered on the one side by the Sungei Belum and on the other by primary jungle. 'C' and 'D' Squadrons, under command of Woodhouse, were to penetrate by foot from the south-east in order to be prepared to search and ambush the valley tracks after 'B' Squadron had moved through the kampongs. This was an uncharacteristic use of the SAS in that they had never operated in such strengths before. It was considered that as the enemy numbers were uncertain (they could have been as strong as three hundred) there was a distinct possibility that they may be prepared to stand and fight their ground. There was some excitement (mainly outside the SAS) because this was to be the first parachute deployment of British troops since the Rhine Crossing in March, 1945.

The move in of 'C' and 'D' Squadrons was to be much harder than had been envisaged. On 1 February, 1952, both squadrons flew, aboard new Valetta aircraft, to Kota Bharu at the north-east corner of the Malayan Peninsula and approximately 15 miles from the Thai border. The rain which had fallen previously was unusually heavy even for Malaya and the force ran into problems when it tried to make the journey by truck from Kota Bharu to Batu Melintang well up into the foothills of the central mountain spine which they had to cross. The floods meant that they had to stop several miles short of their destination. Several miles in this case translates into two days' marching on open tracks in hot sun.

The canvas rubber-soled boots, reasonable when moving slowly over the soft jungle soil, were to leave many soldiers badly blistered during that initial long, hot march.

The force was resupplied at Batu Melintang and with seven days' rations per man (which brought the average load up to about seventy pounds) they left the town on 4 February to tackle the savage country between there and the Belum Valley. They were marching against the clock; the weather had robbed them of two days already and they were conscious that 'B' Squadron were scheduled to drop on 8 February by which time they must be in position. They had a native guide who was reputed to know the area well but such people are a mixed blessing. The questioner was never quite sure whether he was getting the answer that the guide thought he would like or whether or not he was being properly understood in the first place. On matters of distance the guides were vague – time meant little to them. The Regiment developed the technique of defining time by the 'cigarette'; the natives were inveterate smokers. If a native took five minutes to smoke a cigarette, ten smokes would define a journey of some fifty to sixty minutes. Hardly dead reckoning!

It must be remembered that the maps in use at the time were drafted from air photographs in the main and as such there was little ground detail, though rivers and bigger streams were, of course, accurately shown. Pinpoint navigation at that stage of the Emergency was difficult to say the least and a good idea of rates of progress under various conditions was essential to position reckoning.

The load could perhaps have been lightened but it would have meant taking a resupply as soon as the target was reached which in turn would have meant both a delay and a reduction in security. Woodhouse expected to have to follow up the enemy almost immediately on arrival in Belum. Conscious of the pressure of time he set a cracking pace with each squadron taking turns to lead. At the beginning the track was wide and good but even under these conditions those at the rear of a long straggling column have enormous difficulties keeping up. At each obstacle, no matter how small, there is a short delay as each man crosses. This brings those behind to a halt as the column 'concertinas'; as momentum is picked up it can leave the rear-enders almost running to make up the lost distance no matter how slowly and considerately the leading group moves.

The column kept going from 7.30 in the morning until 5.30 pm with no long halts for tea or cooking. Woodhouse, in his usual straightforward manner, had issued instructions that there would be no waiting for stragglers – those who could not keep up were on their own. This march exemplified the courage of one man in terms of his doggedness and tolerance of acute pain. The second day had brought about a distinct deterioration in the going; for four hours or more the column had to walk along a dried-up river bed with boots letting in sand to grind the skin off the feet and many men were suffering quite badly, but there was no letting up. L/Cpl Moseley reported that he was in a bad way. He showed Woodhouse his feet from which long strips of skin were peeled as he removed his socks. Woodhouse himself wondered how he had made it thus far. With two others in similar state Moseley was ordered to make his way slowly back to Batu Melintang.

Due to inaccurate advice from his guide, Woodhouse was obliged to stop early for the night as the next stage of the journey (his guide said) would take some six hours to complete with no access to water. His anger was severe the next day when the journey over the high ridge took only three hours – a distance he could easily have completed the day before. The column reached the turbulent barrier of a wide river. They were now little more than half way to the target with only two days left in which to cover the ground! Woodhouse decided to split his force and sent Walls and his 'C' Squadron to advance downriver and approach the target from the east while he would take 'D' Squadron over the mountains to arrive to the west of Kampong Sepor. The principle was that one of the squadrons should surely find a route in by the drop date.

It is a tribute to Woodhouse's leadership that he kept his squadron moving through what turned out to be very rough country in rapidly deteriorating weather. There was much cajoling of the tired, and the fittest men (Woodhouse included) carried two packs to allow men to recover their strength. In his own words:

I felt no tiredness, only a furious determination to reach the west of Kampong Sepor no matter what it cost us. There were no tracks. We spent all day doing one of four things. Climbing with hands and feet up hillsides which became mudslides after the first three or four men had passed; sliding down equally steep hillsides; stumbling and slipping up or down rocky stream beds; and cutting step by step through bamboo. Never before or afterwards did I find such hard going in Malaya.

Woodhouse's force had by now received the news that the 'B' Squadron drop was postponed due to the foul weather – it was resheduled for the 9th. A small enough respite! The 8th of February, after five successive days of hard jungle marching following the twenty tortuous, steaming miles of open country movement, found the tired column high on a mountain ridge still unsure of their precise position. The night before they had heard the news of the death of King George VI, which added to the sense of remoteness and isolation. On the morning of the 9th, the day of the drop, the force scrambled down the steep muddy slope. They were certain that the drop would not take place as the weather was, if anything, worse than the previous two days with a thick mist obscuring the hilltops. The drop, due at 9.00 am, had not taken place and the force was under orders not to close in on the target area until 'B' Squadron had landed. Woodhouse closed down his radio to conserve the precious batteries. However, quarter of an hour later the bedraggled soldiers were amazed to hear the noise of aircraft engines.

Adrenalin gave them a burst of energy and, hurriedly putting on packs, they forced a way through to the banks of the Sungei Belum where they stopped in horror. The rains had swollen the river to a massive forty-yard width well over six feet deep and it was a raging torrent. They had to cross. There was no handy tree to fell to make a bridge; at this point the river was flanked by bamboo thickets. Pearman made the courageous offer to swim across with a line while the rest constructed hasty bamboo rafts as a ferry system. Woodhouse later said:

It looked a very hazardous crossing but there was no alternative. With a line looped around his body he jumped in and seemed to me, holding the other end, to be torn straight down river. I decided to pull him in before he drowned. When at last I landed him like a monster fish, he was very angry:

'You bloody near drowned me hauling on the line like that!'

'I'm very sorry, Mike, but I thought you were going to drown if I left you.'

'No, but you bloody nearly drowned me yourself, I was quite alright until you pulled,' Pearman spluttered. 'Just let me go the next time. I have to go a long way downstream to cross.'

'Alright, Mike, say when you're ready.'

He went in again and this time reached the far bank. It was a dangerous crossing and it must have taken courage to try a second time. In an hour we were all across ferried over on two precarious bamboo rafts.'

To the great disappointment of 'D' Squadron, they had emerged from the jungle too far to the east of Kampong Sepor and they were quick to realize that they would play no part in any immediate action which may result from the drop. They pushed on west until night fell. They knew that the best they could hope for was to reach Sepor by late morning the next day.

Meanwhile, what of 'B' Squadron and the parachute insertion? Bad weather had caused the scheduled drop to be delayed until 9 February; the conditions on the 9th were scarcely better but there was a great determination to get the force on to the ground. The air support and transport came from the pooled resources of the RAF and the RAAF and the plan was to make three drops of paratroopers on to the designated DZ in the Belum Valley and to drop dummies' constructed of sandbags on parachutes some eight miles away to confuse the terrorists. The *Sunday Standard* of Singapore on 10 February gives a graphic account of the drop and the stresses it must have placed on those jumping. They had already got themselves mentally prepared for what could be a hazardous leap possibly into trees only to have this cancelled:

A reporter who flew aboard one of the formation of Dakotas says that the whole trip was a battle with threatening bad weather. The operation was planned to take place on Friday but had to be postponed until today because of bad weather reports. He says:

'Yesterday's drop was a race against time and shocking weather conditions. The drop should have taken place at nine in the morning. But a Brigand light bomber that made a weather reconnaissance of the DZ reported by radio that low clouds put it temporarily out of the question. While the Brigand investigated, our aircraft circled Grik for nearly half an hour waiting for the report.

'When it became known that the operation would have to be postponed, all aircraft were diverted to wait at the RAAF airfield at Butterworth, until the weather cleared . . . While we were feeding, the reconnaissance planes had been keeping the DZ area under observation . . . By one o'clock in the afternoon we were airborne again. As we flew towards the DZ, however, the weather steadily deteriorated and it became apparent that the operation would be touch and go.

'The DZ itself was a weird and tricky place from a flying point of view.

'A river, dotted with rapids, swung between the hills in the form of a letter 'U'. The inside of the 'U' was dotted with cultivated patches, some of them quite large, and with a few huts and houses. But, around the outside of the 'U' rose hills up to 500' high, with, in the background, mountains going up to 5000'.

'The DZ was complicated by the presence of a lone, small hill, like an inverted basin, directly in the line of the only possible approach route of the dropping aircraft.

'This means that they had to fly low and level to drop the airborne troops, then swoop suddenly up to avoid the hill, and come round again to drop the next batch of parachutists.

'As we arrived, a low cloud was beginning to spill over the tops of the five thousand foot hills, and rain squalls were sweeping the area.

'Each of the three troop-dropping aircraft made a dummy run across the selected DZ, an area under water-logged padi about six hundred yards by two hundred and fifty. On the dummy run each aircraft dropped parachutes carrying a weight equivalent to that of a man, to assess the direction of the wind.

'The wind direction was dead behind the only possible run-in, doubling the trickiness of the drop. The aircraft came round for the first run, and a stick of paratroopers, led by Major Alistair MacGregor, suddenly appeared in the sky, their khaki-coloured 'chutes blossoming above them.

'The strong wind carried them away from the centre of the DZ, and they landed amid small trees and scrub at the end of the area. One man's parachute tangled with a tall, dead tree, and presumably he had to slide to earth down the hundred foot rope each man carried against such a contingency.

'Now the aircraft began to come around regularly . . . After finishing the live drops, the Dakotas went round and round discharging parachute packs of supplies . . . all the while the Brigands droned high overhead awaiting a call to come down and smash any organised opposition on the ground.' As the reporter's aircraft turned away, he says, a line of twelve paratroopers could be seen advancing slowly and well apart towards the river. Others were rolling up their 'chutes and assembling the supply packs. Three parachutes were still to be seen hung up on the trees at the end of the DZ, but whether their wearers had by this time reached the ground could not be seen.'

(Yet another similarity with the conditions of Stirling's first drop in the Western Desert in 1941.)

The reality of the drop was a little different to the picture painted by the *Sunday Standard* reporter. The Dakotas had been on the point of returning to RAAF Butterworth when there was a sudden 'window' in the weather, provided that they got in fast, low and quickly. Under those conditions there could be no blame attached to the pilots that only four of the fifty four men actually landed on the DZ. A few of them narrowly missed the rocky river and most did in fact land in trees of varying height. All those who were caught up successfully lowered themselves to the ground with the crude rope systems they had adopted and only three men were slightly injured despite it being 'a pretty hair-raising experience'.

That there was enemy in the area is certain as 'C' Squadron had come under fire on their way to Kampong Sepor and when 'D'

Squadron married up with them they were busy sending out patrols in pursuit of the escaped terrorists. Whilst Woodhouse was planning the deployment of his squadron he got a mild shock when he heard a man walk up to his basha. On looking up he saw to his surprise that it was L/Cpl Moseley who he had ordered home all those days ago. The man had a slight smile on his face as he said: 'Reporting in, Sir.'

'Good God, Moseley, how the hell did you get here? Sit down.'

'Followed your tracks, all the time you had to cut we could follow quite easily, seemed to us we could make it, Sir, if we took it easy.'

'And what state are your feet in now?'

'Bit rough, but to tell you the truth I don't rightly know as I couldn't take my boots off. The other two are with me. They're a bit rough too.'

'Well, I'm bloody glad to see you. That's one sort of dis-obedience I don't mind. We'll get a basha up for you.'

'That's OK; it's going up now, Sir.'

Eventually when Moseley's feet were separated from the rem-nants of his boots and socks, Woodhouse confessed to being amazed at how he could have even stood up on the skinless, suppurating mess which had rubbed through to the bone. His two comrades were in little better condition and all were flown out by helicopter to make full recoveries.

The force was resupplied on 11 February and at the same time orders were given that they were to evacuate all civilians from the area (this in accordance with the Briggs Plan). While this was being done aggressive hunting patrols were still sent out covering as much of the area as possible. There were a number of contacts as the CTs tried ambushes, but there were, as far as we can ascertain, only two casualties. One CT was captured (by 'B' Squadron) but later died of his wounds and one SAS man ('D' Squadron) was shot in the buttocks while answering the call of nature. The captured CT turned out to have been a courier from Thailand, thus proving the theories of Intelligence about the area.

The evacuation of the civilians from the Belum Valley will long remain a moot point amongst those SAS men involved in Operation Helsby. It is true that after they were removed and the crops were burned to deny the CTs further succour the CTs lost a valuable base. But how much better would it have been to establish a permanent presence in the valley, turn the natives to the Government whilst sitting on the central span of a known terrorist supply and courier route? There was sorrow too in the knowledge that this beautiful, fertile valley would soon become a wilderness as nature took its course.

After the evacuation was organized, the walk-out took some four or five days and the troops were pensive during that phase. To their minds it was true that the CTs had, if only temporarily, lost a base, but the SAS seemed to have won little. A later reconnaisance, Operation Mustang, which took place between 11 July and 11 August 1953, showed conclusively that the CTs had indeed been using the area consistently, probably moving back into the valley within a month or two of Helsby.

The view of CHQ, FARELF was a little different to that of the SAS' own thinking. Helsby was taken as a success on a number of points. An administratively difficult operation had been undertaken smoothly, despite the bad weather. The parachuting concept had been proven and could be developed to the point when it was a deliberate decision to jump into trees. A major CT base had been disrupted and perhaps closed down and this would certainly have had a considerable effect upon the enemy's morale. Lastly, self-contained troops had covered some of the worst ground in the country, on schedule and with remarkably few casualties. Whatever else, Helsby served to heighten the appreciation of the SAS at an important stratum of the hierarchy.

The somewhat blasé statement regarding L/Cpl Moseley and his comrades, 'They were flown out by helicopter,' belies the facts. Helicopters were still very much in their infancy and, in fact, Malaya was the first major 'war' deployment of these wonderfully versatile machines. There could be no harder testing ground than flying to make casualty evacuation flights from tight, restricted jungle LZs often under severe weather conditions and we have met no veteran of Malaya who has not praised very highly the efforts of the Royal Air Force and Royal Navy and in particular the 'Cas-Evac Squadron'. An article only recently written for the 'Helicopter Operations (Malaya Emergency) Association' by Huw Griffiths perhaps serves to demonstrate the two sides to the coin:

It took a particular type of airman to fly the helicopters of 194 Squadron in Malaya. It takes a particular type of soldier to join the SAS. Perhaps it was the combination of their respective strengths that allowed two airmen and a Trooper to cheat the odds. Perhaps, in the words of the pilot, it was 'the Old Boy Upstairs'. This is their story:

194 Sqn (Helicopters) was based at Kuala Lumpur. Their primary function was 'CASEVAC'; flying casualties from the jungle, but they also made supply drops, search and surveillance operations, and anything else that required a chopper. Flexibility was the name of the game.

They were pioneers. They tested both their machines and aviation techniques to the limits. It was during this Emergency, in the fifties, that Westland choppers paved the way for helicopter outfits of the future. The conditions were hostile, and the climate both tropical and unpredictable. And above all their aircraft were untested – range, metal fatigue, durability, and performance levels were all unknown quantities. It took, of course, courage to get into a chopper and see if theory converted into practice. Sadly it sometimes did not.

The 3rd of March, 1956, started routinely enough for Sqn. Ldr. Cyril Turner, CO of 194 Sqn. A call from 'Ops'. his mission – to locate a missing Valetta supply drop aircraft.

The Valetta had crashed in a mountainous area of central Malaya, not far from the scene of a similar incident a few weeks earlier. Two men had survived this first crash, only to die afterwards in the jungle. So, along with Crewman Pat Lumb, Sqn. Ldr. Turner boarded a Dragonfly 255 and headed for Fort Brooke, via Ipoh, to set up his search programme. In fact the crashed aircraft was located by F/Sgt Shuvalski (194 Sqn) who returned to base to take Sqn. Ldr. Turner to inspect and assess the site.

As they circled the crash zone it was clear that there was no hope of a successful outcome. The weather was cloudy and not predictable. The terrain was hostile and quite unsuitable for either a landing or a parachute drop. All they could do was make a report and head for home.

It was as Turner was about to take off from Fort Brooke that the 'CASEVAC' call came in. This was always given priority, so they sped off at once to an SAS base deep in the jungle. It was called Paddy's Ladang. The casualty was not a victim of the CTs, but a trooper with a bad bout of malaria.

Paddy's Ladang was situated in primary jungle. This consists of dense undergrowth and trees, up to two hundred feet high, which are covered by a thick canopy of growth. At ground level it is a warren of dark tunnels and from the air a blanket of green. Getting there was one thing; actually landing was something else. First of all a hole must be cut in the jungle. For the chopper to keep its downdraught the landing area itself must be as flat as possible – losing downdraught would mean getting 'sucked' into the hole and smashed to bits. If the ground was too stumpy or insufficiently sound the chopper could get into the hole, but would have to hover as close to the earth as possible without actually landing. Paddy's Ladang, a recognized LZ, was such a place.

Turner held the chopper steady just a couple of feet above the ground. The clearing was narrow and it wasn't easy to get the casualty aboard. But between them the SAS lads and Lumb secured the stretcher to the aircraft, with Trooper Watkins' feet protruding from the aircraft on a specially fitted fuselage box. He was in a bad way. His temperature was high and he was semi-delirious. So it was a relief to everyone when the pilot carefully lifted his machine out of the clearing and headed for Ipoh. The tricky bit was over.

About ten minutes into the flight the helicopter seemed to lose power. The pilot headed for the river – the only line of communication in the jungle. Then, while still about five hundred feet up, the engine cut completely. In the words of Turner:

'Trying not to panic the two lads behind, I instructed them as casually as I was able to hold tight. We were going down. The helicopter was descending in auto-rotation (spinning on its own axis). I aimed for the brighter green foliage of some bamboo – the soft option! But to my horror a much higher tree loomed up out of nowhere between the chopper and the bamboo! Since we were descending at a very rapid rate I had no option but to 'flare' the aircraft to alight on the top of this tree. It literally skewered the chopper, the main trunk of the tree breaking through between my legs. It tore into my right arm and hammered into my chest and head – after which, needless to say, as far as I was concerned there was oblivion.'

And that, by the law of averages, should have been that. If they did not die on impact the chopper should have blown up. But it didn't and they survived. The first to come to was Lumb. His injuries were, in his own words: 'a broken arm, bruising and cuts. On recovering consciousness I found that I was lying under the aircraft equipment, and Watkins was on top of me. I struggled out of the chopper and fell into the river, which at this point was shallow, and made it to the bank. Shortly afterwards Watkins joined me.'

Though badly bruised Watkins of the SAS was relatively unscathed. He was an accustomed jungle fighter and the first thing he did on recovering consciousness was to find his gun. It was one thing to survive the crash; now they had to get out of the jungle – preferably alive. To make matters worse they were in the middle of a 'red' area – that is territory under partial control of the CTs. These people would shoot them on sight if they were lucky – to be taken alive was a worse fate.

On the river bank Watkins took control. He was anxious to get under way before he became delirious again. The first thing to do was to retrieve any on board weapons and the pilot, in that order.

Turner was in a bad way and takes up the story himself: 'I was hanging upside down, still strapped in. They rushed over and got me down, breaking my fall as best they could, and got me to the river bank. I became aware that the water around my feet was red and to my horror saw blood gushing out of my right arm. I flapped hanging flesh back and put pressure on the brachial artery. At this point I remember Pat and Fred rummaging about in the wrecked aircraft which was now inverted near the river bank. At this time I ordered Fred to take control of the situation, as he was the one with experience of the jungle, and this he did.'

Watkins knew they had to get away from the crash site as soon as possible. The CTs would almost certainly have seen or heard the crash and would be heading their way. They quickly dressed the pilot's arm with the shell dressing that all SAS men carried, though unfortunately the morphine that went with it was missing. Watkins then loaded Lumb's rifle, which he had never had cause to use before, and they were ready to head off.

Their plan, in Watkins' own words, was: 'before I got too ill to do anything, follow the river down until it got deeper and then make a raft of bamboo. Then it was go down river and hope for the best.'

With his rifle butt tucked under the pilot's left arm Watkins could just about keep him upright, dragging him along behind him. With his parang in his other hand he cut a path through the jungle. Lumb followed behind with their survival pack on his back. They tracked the river as best they could, though it was rough. At times they came perilously close to being swept away. The water was shallow but fast; they had to hack inland before rejoining the river further downstream. It was not easy for any of them, especially the pilot who was in terrible pain and progress was slow. Watkins was in and out of delirium. At one point he fell and vomited, and only the pilot, with his one good hand, saved him from choking by scooping the sick from his mouth. Only Lumb at this stage was with it the whole time, though his broken arm was giving him much distress.

They were making their slow way along the river with frequent halts to adjust Turner's dressing when Watkin's spotted movement ahead: 'I got ready for a shoot out but when I got nearer I saw that it was a family of aborigines. Usually they were friendly but there were two I didn't like the look of so I kept them covered. I asked them if there were any white men around and they said that there were. Keeping the two I was suspicious of, I asked the rest to go ahead and get help. This they did. I decided against shooting the other two but I kept them covered while they carried all the equipment; meantime Pat helped the pilot.'

In this way the party continued until they met up with the SAS patrol and the aborigines and soon they were back at Paddy's Ladang where Turner was at long last given morphine. He had not uttered a sound during the whole of his agonizing walk. By chance a helicopter was in the area and the whole party was taken off to Ipoh and thence to Kuala Lumpur and hospital.'

Although a great deal of luck was involved, the survival of the party was something of a minor epic of endurance and professionalism. The pilot's skill in 'skewering' the chopper was tremendous; Watkins' determination and resoluteness was in keeping with the best traditions of the SAS and Lumb kept a cool head throughout despite his own very painful injury.

Interestingly, Watkins' suspicions regarding the two aborigines were well founded. A later search of the area where the party had first made contact revealed two shotguns which had been hastily hidden.

As the size of helicopters increased to troop-carrying proportions so the SAS was to make greater and greater use of these flexible 'work-horses' and eventually they took over more or less completely from parachuting as a means of entry.

11

THE LOW POINT

S ure enough the SAS was bedding into its deep jungle role and
by this time the gospel was just beginning to spread; recruits
were in good supply as stories of the Regiment's interesting role
reached the rank and file. In understanding what sort of men were
volunteering it is necessary to take a look at the background to
the tasks of the line battalions and some of the problems they
faced. Chasing the elusive CT bands in the Malayan jungle was
to prove a wearisome business for special forces and line battalions
alike and in such a war of attrition there could be no expectations
of a quick victory.

In one of his reports Briggs was to write that:

> In a counter-insurgency, where pitched battles between organ-
> ized armies do not occur, and where success depends on the
> morale of and the help given by the population, and the
> breaking of Communist morale and organizations, one is left to
> judge the situation by a combination of factors.
>
> Perhaps the greatest weight can be given to the factors of
> communist surrenders and of the information and assistance
> forthcoming from the Chinese population as a result of their
> coming 'off the fence'. Other factors include the number of
> communist casualties and arrests, battle contests by our troops
> and the successful prevention of supplies, arms and ammu-
> nition, reaching the enemy.

Despite Briggs's early recognition of the dominant factors, it was
to take the British and Commonwealth units constituting the

security forces a long time to come to terms with waging a counter-insurgency campaign in jungle terrain.

The Malayan Emergency demonstrated a classic lesson of military history, namely the importance of retaining and practising all the military skills and abilities learnt in earlier campaigns. By 1945, the British Army had, through the Burma Campaign, become skilled in jungle warfare; yet the moment the war was over these skills ceased to be exercised. Thus, three years later, when the army was once again called upon to fight in the jungle, the collective wisdom and expertise had been dissipated, lost, or on occasion misapplied. Why was this? The uprising in Malaya not only caught the British Army on the hop, but also in the throes of the biggest rationalization in its 250-year history (even in those days 'rationalization' was recognized as a euphemism for 'reduction'), while newly formed units were learning to fight for a war which was totally divorced from Malaya. Before looking at the British units it is worth examining one link with the imperial past.

On 1 January, 1948, four Rifle Regiments of Gurkhas,* then each of two battalions, together with supporting elements of Engineers, Signals and Transport, were transferred to the Regular Army as the Brigade of Gurkhas. This was a wise and imaginative decision, but in June, 1948, the Gurkha battalions in Malaya were nowhere near ready for operational duties. The 2nd/6th could barely put a single rifle company into the field, while the 2nd/7th had only sixty men ready to deploy. Most of the Gurkhas were not veterans who had transferred from other regiments slotted for service with the Indian or Pakistani Armies, but raw young recruits still undergoing basic training and, of course, totally inexperienced and untrained in jungle warfare.

What made matters worse was that 2nd/7th Gurkhas had been intended as an Artillery regiment. The result was that they formed in Malaya with Gunner officers who had little understanding of Gurkhas or their language and when the battalion was despatched into the jungle those officers had no experience of infantry tactics.

* 2nd King Edward VII's Own Gurkha Rifles
  6th Queen Elizabeth's Own Gurkha Rifles
  7th Duke of Edinburgh's Own Gurkha Rifles
  10th Princess Mary's Own Gurkha Rifles

The Gurkha is an excellent soldier provided he knows precisely what is expected of him and he is rehearsed in the skills required, but if his leaders are also raw then the result is less than satisfactory.

It is hardly surprising that the Gurkhas began the war badly. But the battalions stayed in Malaya throughout the Emergency and over time their riflemen became superb fighting machines, the collective skills and wisdom passed down to each new member, officer or rifleman with a continuity which was unbroken.

Every time a British officer walked with us in the jungle at night, I saw that they believed in the eye. I believe in my feet and my hands, and I feel first, but they believe in their eyes, so they just walk and fall down. Anyone who lives in an advanced country, who has a car, metalled roads, electric lights, from the beginning, finds it very difficult in the jungle without washing, without shaving, without lights, without making a noise. Living in a village in Nepal is like a jungle, so we have early practice in walking up and down in the jungle and living without lights or running water. In Malaya I enjoyed the jungle because it reminded me of home.*

There were other difficulties which were largely the result of human error and a failure to anticipate future needs. Singapore was both the headquarters and supply depot of FARELF and its huge storage facilities were filled to capacity with arms and ammunition of all types. But in 1948 there were no emergency stores of combat rations, not a single tin of the dreaded 'compo' (composite ration) was to be found in the Federation or Singapore and neither were there any of the hexamine (solid fuel) stoves which came as part of the rations. This meant that, in the early months at least, the army units patrolled the jungle carrying fresh meat and rations, jam sandwiches, kettles and using wood fires to heat their food and drink. Under these conditions even the most

Purna Bahadur Gurung, quoted in *The Savage Wars of Peace*, p. 13, Charles Allen, Michael Joseph.

determined and resolute of men had to come out after three days in the jungle.

It is all very well to criticize line battalion and company commanders and their men for being out of touch with reality, but surely the senior commanders, those responsible for the direction of the effort, must be culpable in the first instance. We must accept that the security forces were up against a tough and resilient opponent who had years of experience in how to live and to fight in the jungle. By late 1951/early 1952, the terrorists had become more daring and this because they had learned their mistakes, one of which had been to overestimate the security forces. In those early years army units were consistently out-classed, but their commanders continued to commit the blunder of under-rating the enemy. Small wonder though if we look to the commanders at the beginning and what they bequeathed to their successors.

Major General Boucher, Commander Land Forces at the out-break, as we have already noted, considered himself an expert, having fought the Greek Communists and compared to whom he dismissed Chin Peng and his guerrillas as mere amateurs.

Then General Ritchie, who had already cried 'foul' because of the failure of intelligence to predict the trouble, was equally dismissive. He regarded the CT fighting qualities as not in the same league as the Pathans of the North-West Frontier of India, instead classing them as being of the same calibre as the Palestinian Arabs in the 1938–39 rebellion. Hardly surprising then, that faced with such racially biased and disturbingly inaccurate advice, the War Office was slow in coming to terms with the needs of counter-insurgency.

Ritchie was a Sepoy General, one whose horizons had been set by service in the Indian Army. In the Second World War he had proved an excellent staff officer, disastrous as an Army Com-mander in the Western Desert, but had recovered to finish the war as a competent Corps Commander in North-West Europe. He was nobody's fool and belied the 'Colonel Blimp' image which he tended to present to others. In what he described as the 'Communist Technique of Cold War', he correctly assessed the guerrilla tactics which have been described earlier and as laid down by Mao's theory of the prolonged war. In essence he outlined the classic communist approach to subversion, what the Americans had already dubbed salami tactics, but with a rural application. Nevertheless, in advance of the publication and dissemination of Mao's 'Little Red Book', this was a reasonably accurate assessment of enemy aims and objectives. The problems came with Ritchie's methods to counter the 'Cold War' technique. As he put it:

> For success this Communist 'Cold War' technique requires relatively static conditions if it is to thrive.
>
> Any form of defensive security-minded policy adopted as a counter to it is predoomed to failure. It is therefore essential, however meagre is the information available, to adopt an offensive military policy. Never leave the enemy alone, continually harry him, and keep him on the move. Disrupt his training and his organization into large bodies.
>
> While it is true that without really good information such action does not produce spectacular results, its adoption is nonetheless necessary if the enemy is to be prevented from organizing himself into relatively large bodies which can be concentrated as, when, and where necessary, and so gain for him the initiative.

In dealing with the communist threat the British High Command took the events of the Chinese Civil War as their model and precedent. Ritchie himself wrote:

> We have seen what has occurred in China. There the nationalists pursued a non-aggressive, defensive attitude with a great proportion of their military resources locked up in small packets. The result has been their loss of the initiative, which has in due course, led to the loss of most of China to the communists.

This was a very simplistic interpretation of the mistakes made by the Kuomintang. In Malaya, however, Ritchie was correct in one thing. Insofar as they were following Marxist warfare theory, the MRLA intention was to drive the security forces out of the countryside and into the towns. This was rigorously combated by the military which carried out intensive patrol activity and frequent sweeps through the jungle fringes, sometimes committing a brigade or more of troops. Such operations were initially of little effect based as they were on scant and untrustworthy Intelligence. If an enemy force, a camp or supply dump was encountered this was random good fortune, though even then the military very often failed. In the words of Ritchie the greatest shortcoming was,

> poor marksmanship, and a large number of bandits here escaped our clutches on this account. This is, I believe, due to the attainment of an indifferent standard in basic weapon training, a deficit which it is difficult and takes some time to remedy in conditions prevailing in Malaya today.

Although this lack of battlefield marksmanship was a factor, it is unfair on the British soldier to assume this as his greatest weakness. In many areas Ritchie was strategically correct in his attempts to harry the CT and deny him the ability to operate in strength. The tactics and the training, however, were wrong. At the lower levels morale was weakened in the early stages through the fact that almost every operation was labelled a success, proclaimed as such in the press and on the radio and, often, the medals were dished out accordingly. The poor bloody infantryman who had spent a fruitless couple of days crashing along trails supposedly left by a retreating enemy, who in such dense foliage was invisible at three feet, would tell a different story. Young, sweating conscripts, many scarcely out of their teens, were often frightened out of their wits; they knew the truth and so dismissed such fictitious results which ended with neither kill nor capture with cynical indifference or total disregard.

Troops earmarked to serve in Malaya were still being trained on Salisbury Plain in the mopping up operations such as had been employed by their instructors at the latter end of the Second World War against pockets of German or Japanese resistance. The CTs were not unaware of the fact that units did improve as their tour progressed and made a point, whenever possible, of targeting the units which had recently arrived. An excellent example of the effectiveness of this strategy is that of the 4th Hussars who, when only two weeks into their tour, drove their armoured cars into an ambush which killed the Commanding Officer and a dozen men. It is probable, however, that the greatest (and most personal) problem remained the arena of warfare – the jungle – which has been described earlier in terms of the fears it initially engendered.

The CTs were quick also to note the psychological effect of the home-made booby trap in a jungle environment. They were adepts at utilizing the skills of the aborigine in animal trapping and modifying the techniques to make man traps. They had their favourites, of course; one of these was the 'venus fly trap' which consisted of a carefully camouflaged pit lined with sharpened bamboo spikes which were often smeared with excreta to ensure infection. A second device consisted of a sack filled with about fifty pounds weight of sand into which iron or bamboo spikes had been embedded. The sack would be held in place by a trip wire; the first man through would trigger the device and the second man would get the benefit of the spikes. An adaptation of the pig trap was common in which a sharpened bamboo stake would be lashed to a bent sapling under tension. If the trip was triggered then the stake would crash forward into the hapless victim. At least two SAS men fell foul of the latter device in the early days.

Quite often it was fear and inexperience which created excesses. An incident which is mentioned even today is the Batang Kali operation of December, 1948, when a 14-man patrol from 2nd Battalion, the Scots Guards were accused of killing some 25 Chinese who were reportedly fleeing the village. Not unreasonably, questions were asked but the result at the time was a cover up – Like Vietnam, Malaya had its Mai Lai's.

So the British Army once more entered a war using the tactics developed at the end of the previous conflict and it was bound to take some while to put the balance right, retain and recapture the initiative.

But ignorance and incompetence can be eradicated by a combination of good leadership and training. Most battalions were to benefit from the experiences of Lieutenant-Colonel Walter Walker who had moved to Malaya to take command of the 1st/6th Gurkha Rifles. Walker was something of a firebrand and an expert in counter-guerrilla tactics. He applied the lessons he had learned during the inter-war years on the North-West Frontier and later fighting the Japanese in Burma. He was a skilled exponent of the ambush:

> I therefore laid down the technique of how an ambush should be laid, so that you didn't fire until the enemy had entered your ambush, and that one had stops to get the people who might not have been immediately in the ambush, and stops to make certain that those who retreated from the ambush were also killed. And this technique, which I learned in Burma, I carried forward to the Malayan Emergency.★

Walker's effect on the Gurkhas was dramatic and he was tasked by Ritchie to set up a Jungle Warfare Training School where some of the finest instructors of the time were Australian veterans who had fought the Japanese in New Guinea.

Briggs too was guilty of misdirecting the energies of his forces. Early in his tenure he proposed 'Operation Roll-Up'. The objective was to roll-up the MRLA regiments from the far south of Johore all the way to the northern state of Kedah. What was not fully appreciated at the time was that the best of the MRLA were to be found in Johore. This meant that the army had to take on the fiercest opponents first. More than two-thirds of the security force's fighting strength, together with considerable numbers of police, tackled the CTs in Johore – and failed. Once started there was no way in which the operation could be stopped immediately without a tremendous loss of face and the risk of repercussions to the Briggs Plan itself. After Briggs departed the scene, however, 'Operation Roll-Up' was quietly rolled down and eventually shelved; even so it was an expensive mistake.

It may seem that an unfair picture has been painted of the line troops; the fault was not theirs and once into 1951, the development into becoming effective jungle fighters was quite rapid. Some battalions were better than others; research would indicate that those with a systematic form of selection like the Commandos with their added emphasis on adaptability had a head start. Regiments which recruited from rural areas also stood out; the Suffolk Regiment, for example, is often cited as the best

★ *The Savage Wars of Peace*, p. 11.

British Battalion in Malaya. They ended a three and a half year tour with 200 recorded kills – more than any other battalion. In 1957 a member of the Malayan Administration in Johore wrote:

> The Rifle Brigade was far and away the best. Their operations were more carefully planned, they were better led, they shot straight, they patrolled more quietly and they hung on more tenaciously than anyone else.*

Of course things did improve. Training became more sophisticated and Briggs put a new emphasis on the jungle fringe and the plantations as sites for ambush rather than committing companies to futile jungle chases, but it was troops who were still at the start of the learning curve who were to put the Briggs Plan into action.

Though it is true that Briggs did not expect immediate results from the Plan, he did think that within two or three months of 'D' Day (1 June, 1950) he would begin to see tangible evidence of the success to come. What then went wrong? In part it was simply a factor of time. The main thrust of the Plan was in the imposition of economic sanctions against the CTs. Economic sanctions, as has been demonstrated frequently since, are an imprecise instrument of government, but which, in any case, always takes much longer to bite than is generally assumed. This factor is, of course, exacerbated by the impatience felt by the imposer for signs of an early success; the imposition of UN sanctions on Saddam Hussein is a case in point.

Terrorists and guerrilla groups also have an organizational momentum which works in their favour in the face of government countermeasures. They tend to plan well ahead, conduct detailed reconnaissance and have the forces deployed for operations which will often carry them through a period of enhanced activity. It is a war of attrition and only after time and multiple demonstrations of countermeasures will the insurgents give ground. There were also a number of contributing factors peculiar to the Malayan scene which Briggs readily identified as having an important bearing on their apparent lack of success.

Finance, as always, was a stumbling block. But in this instance

---

* *Jackets of Green*, Arthur Bryant, Collins, p. 435.

it was not so much the absence of funds which caused the problem but the bureaucratic and time-consuming delays to produce the money and pay the bills. The Emergency measures were largely self-financing from the increased demand for rubber and tin. But the Federation Government was handicapped in its planning through lack of any prior guarantee that Whitehall would help out financially, in proportion to its expenditure, for the full prosecution of the Emergency.

Programmes could, therefore, only proceed when the funds were physically made available and this process was sufficiently cumbersome to result in essential schemes, such as the purchase of the timber for new settlements, to be seriously retarded.

The main problem, however, lay in the shortage of trained civil servants on the ground. The reinforcements which had been requested from home arrived piecemeal and with no sense of urgency. In the early 50's the preferred method of travel was by steamship and a voyage which took anything up to nine weeks or more. Those who were despatched were young, untrained officers recruited straight from school, university or after national service. In any case it must have been an uphill task to persuade civil servants to opt for Malaya at that time. Postings were voluntary rather than enforced and there was ample choice in the still very extensive Empire and Commonwealth and without the risk of being shot at by terrorists.

The manpower problem was exacerbated because, when it came to leave, the Federation still operated on a peacetime basis. Civil servants in key appointments continued to depart for the UK on long leave when their time was due, whilst others were permitted to retire. Locally the problem was one of enticing civil servants out of the Federal offices and onto the ground where life was more dangerous and consequently less appealing. There were those at various technical grades who did answer the call and, heedless of risk, went out into the field and some paid the ultimate price; but there were, equally, many who found excellent reasons for their continued presence in Kuala Lumpur or Singapore. These remarks do not apply to those whose duties were in the field, including the District and Administrative Officers, whose work was charaterized by enthusiasm, considerable flair and ingenuity and, at times, the ability to rise to an occasion which was truly magnificent. But then these were the very qualities which had helped win and secure the Empire in the first instance; it is hardly surprising that they should be called upon in equal measures to propel its dismemberment.

The less savoury aspect was the racial overtone which accompanied the whole process and the price that had to be paid as a consequence. Indeed, in the case of Malaya, the irony was that the shortfall, especially in the technical field and executive appointments, could easily have been made good from the Chinese community. But such efforts were handicapped on two further counts. First by political reluctance and slowness of State Government to appoint officers other than Malays; and by the unwillingness of the Chinese community to climb off the fence in sufficient numbers and throw in their lot with the Federal Government.

Briggs was also disappointed by the reluctance of the authorities to enforce fully, and expand, the powers in the Banishment Act. He was convinced of the vital need for the deportation of detainee communists from Malaya which, alone of any measure, could have had the biggest effect on public morale, particularly Chinese and Malay. Although a number of alternative proposals had been discussed, none found acceptance. Briggs was convinced that if the Chinese community, which after all was the main breeding ground for communism, was left under no illusion that to aid the communists meant deportation from Malaya, then an immediate improvement in the situation would have been the result.

This was too strong a brew for Whitehall's palate, although Briggs was convinced that it would have had the support of the Malay and loyal Chinese population. By the same token there was the difficulty of getting Malay bandits (as opposed to Chinese) hanged after conviction, owing to the Malay preponderance on the Executive War Council which had the responsibility for confirming a death sentence. This was a cause for further alienation of the Chinese populace.

Despite an enhanced military presence it was the Police Force that carried the main burden for internal security; but there was still a lot that was wrong with them. By the autumn of 1950 the Federation Police Force had been increased from 9,000 officers and men to 100,000 of various grades, with all the consequences on quality that accompanies too rapid an expansion. There was a serious shortfall in officers; a great lack of experience; a sad deficiency in language ability, and the lack of response from London to the urgent requests for experienced CID and Special Branch officers resulted in a Police Force ill-equipped for the job in hand.

Briggs and Gray continued to clash at the top level. Gray, in the traditions of his Commando background, centred his interests on his jungle companies and totally ignored the need to deploy some of his better officers to the necessary run of the mill policing which Briggs saw as the priority. On top of this, of course, the police were heavily targeted by the CTs. The MCP consistently attempted to subvert the Special Constabulary by propaganda, by bribery and intimidation to the point where there were a number of cases of treachery by Special Constables, and other incidents reveal a live-and-let-live understanding with the local banditry.

All in all the picture was bleak in the early months of the Briggs Plan, but progress was steady thereafter. Much depended upon the quality of the local security forces and the backup provided by the army. But, despite the setbacks, things were beginning to come together in a more encouraging fashion. Co-ordination between the Police and the Military improved with time and the strategies agreed seemed to be the correct ones. The task of the Army was defined as an interception, ambush and patrolling role in the jungle fringes and the Police provided local security for the population and set about breaking up the Min Yuen cells. An awareness that the concentration of the Chinese squatters into the new villages resulted in an immediate improvement was increasingly supported by the comments made by SEPs under interrogation.

Throughout 1951 Chin Peng kept up the pressure. An MCP document was captured which declared that the MRLA was on the point of advancing to Phase Two of the guerrilla war strategy. The paper was carefully studied by the Army's experts in psychological warfare who pronounced it to be a propaganda document aimed at sustaining the morale of the fighters and the Min Yuen. Chin Peng increased the size of his army and also armed a large number of the Min Yuen for acts of urban terrorism. The importance of the security force's campaign against the Min Yuen is brought out in a Communist document consisting of directives on various matters. One extract is worth quoting:

> The Revolution now centres around our Min Yuen activities. All other activities are subordinate to this work. Only by expanding our Min Yuen foundation can the Army hope to continue to exist and expand . . . the utmost support for the Min Yuen is at the moment an important duty of the Army.

The second half of 1951 was the nadir for the security forces. The High Command of Gurney, Briggs and Gray seemed to be stuck. They were tired and unreceptive to new ideas, bogged down in endless arguments, especially over matters of Police training and deployment. But things were to change.

In October, 1951, the CTs killed Sir Henry Gurney. There are many conflicting reports of the incident but it would appear that he was not the intended victim of the ambush which claimed his life along with five police officers. This was probably the low point of the campaign. The shock of Gurney's death was deeply felt throughout Malaya, mainly because people thought that, as he represented the Crown, the High Commissioner was somehow 'above the battle'. If he could be killed in this fashion then nobody felt safe and morale hit rock bottom. News of Gurney's death reached London when the UK was in the middle of a general election campaign. There were similar sentiments in the UK and Gurney's death brought the nature of the Emergency home to the British people who, on 25 October, returned Winston Churchill to Westminster as Prime Minister.

12

THE PLAN AND THE MAN

When the Conservative Party was returned to Westminster it was with a majority of just seventeen seats. Nonetheless, among the British, Malays and the loyal Chinese there was something to cheer at last, for the new Prime Minister was seen as a man of action and decision who would provide the leadership and the means to see off the Communist menace.

The international scene was pretty dismal in that autumn of 1951 and the threat to Western interests was laid at the door of a communist conspiracy. In Europe, the then twelve-member North Atlantic Alliance partners were deep into a massive conventional rearmament programme to counter the threat posed by 140 divisions of the Soviet Red Army. But it was to the crisis in Asia that most attention was focused.

The Korean War had ground to a halt, but 800,000 UN troops were confronted by the Chinese Red Army and its North Korean allies. In Indo-China the French had 100,000 men combating the Viet Minh who were supported by Peking. While in Malaya 40,000 British and Commonwealth troops and 75,000 police were losing ground to Chin Peng and the Malayan Races Liberation Army.

From the moment he took office Churchill was convinced that Malaya was the critical area which should have the first priority for resources. First the Government needed to know what was going wrong in the country and why it was that the guerrillas were not being defeated. He had appointed as his Colonial Secretary, Sir Oliver Lyttelton, a good natured 58-year-old member of the minor aristocracy who, with a background of Eton, Cambridge and the Guards Brigade, was a typical Shire Tory.

Lyttelton had a short talk with his predecessor at the Colonial

Office, James Griffiths, who had confessed that the previous Government were baffled by Malaya. Sadly he said, 'At this stage Malaya has become a military problem to which we have not been able to find the answer.' Briggs was in the process of writing his final report, but he was known to be particularly critical of the police in general and especially of Nicol Gray's methods and leadership.

The new Colonial Secretary proposed that he should go to Malaya on a fact-finding mission before any remedial action could be implemented. Churchill agreed with reluctance because of the party's precarious majority. However, the Prime Minister had placed Malaya within the Asian strategic context and was already on record as saying that: 'If Malaya goes, all the Far East goes.' He instructed Lyttelton to come back with a firm proposal for revitalizing the political and military effort.

Lyttelton was away for about three weeks. There was nothing secret about his visit, neither could there be as Colonial Secretary and indeed, he held a number of press conferences while in the Far East. After the death of Gurney security was very tight. There were 2,000 police and troops guarding the airport upon arrival and Lyttleton travelled everywhere in a convoy of armoured cars and motor cycle outriders. He was less than happy with arrangements which had him frequently moving about the country 'canned like a sardine in an armoured car'. On one occasion he flew to Pahang in an RAF Valetta. Coming in to land the pilot, intending to use every inch of the runway, made a minute error of judgement and struck the drainage ditch at the edge of the tarmac. The plane careered off the runway, took to the padi fields and caught fire. The aircraft was a write-off but the Colonial Secretary and his party, though shaken by the experience, were otherwise unhurt.

In his memoirs, Lyttelton provides a damning indictment of what he found in Malaya:*

The situation was far worse than I had imagined: it was appalling. From a long life spent in administration I could draw no parallel. I have had experience of the Brigade of Guards, the

* *The Memoirs of Lord Chandos*, Bodley Head, London, 1962, p. 366.

most highly perfected and disciplined human organisation of which I can think, great joint stock companies and Government Departments, all faced at times with dangers and difficulties in their various spheres, but I had never seen such a tangle as that presented by the Government of Malaya. The last High Commissioner had been murdered five weeks before my arrival. No successor had been appointed. There was divided and often opposed control at the top. Civil affairs rested in the hands of the Acting High Commissioner, military and paramilitary in those of Lieutenant-General Sir Harold Briggs. The two authorities were apparently co-equal, neither could overrule the other outside his own sphere. But what was each sphere? The frontiers between their responsibilities had not been clearly defined, indeed they were indefinable, because no line could be drawn to show where politics, civil administration, police action, administration of justice and the like end, and where paramilitary or military operations begin.

The civil administration moved at a leisurely peace-time pace. A rough estimate put the police at 60,000 and that in a country the size of Wales with 5,000,000 inhabitants, but no one could tell me how they were disposed. The reason for this extraordinary fact was that the police force had been partially decentralised. There was no central roll and each state had posted and used its officers according to its own ideas.

The police itself was divided by a great schism between the Commissioner of Police and the Head of the Special Branch. Intelligence was scanty and unco-ordinated between the military and the civil authorities. Our weapons were not fitted to the task; there was a serious shortage of armoured or protected cars. Morale amongst planters, tin miners, and amongst Chinese loyalists and Malays was at its lowest. The grip of the terrorists was tightening and the feelings of the loyalists could be summed up in one word, despair.

Lyttelton was more than a little perturbed at the numbers held in prison without trial. The Government had wide Emergency Powers of mass arrest and detention without trial. It was estimated that perhaps 200,000 people had been detained for less than 28 days; it was known that 25,000 had been detained for 28 days or more; of those, less than 800 had been prosecuted. Even after deducting the numbers of those who had been released or deported to China, there were, at the time of the visit, still 6,000 people detained without trial. The Colonial Secretary believed that the fault for these unacceptably high figures lay with a poorly trained and largely ineffective police force.

At the end of a ten-day tour, Lyttelton had made up his mind on the main things to be done and how to do them. He held out the carrot of independence to Malaya, but made it abundantly clear that it was something which had to be earned through a concerted effort to deflect the insurgency and that it would be given to a united multi-racial country.

In private meetings with Malcolm MacDonald they both agreed that in this deeply depressing situation there could only be one solution and that was for a single leader in overall control of both the civil administration and military affairs.

This need was further underlined by the desperate situation he found with the police. By this stage Nicol Gray as Commissioner of Police and Sir William Jenkin as Head of Special Branch were not on speaking terms. Lyttelton was outraged that such prima donna behaviour should continue. He dismissed them both: Gray, because though 'a gallant officer but not a professional policeman', and Jenkin because 'intelligence was scanty and unco-ordinated'. Jenkin had been able to effect some improvements in the Special Branch, but these had still failed to get the organization right. He had set up a Special Branch Training Centre and an Interrogation Centre; but his bad relations with Gray were ruinous.

Gray left the country so quietly that nobody knew he had gone and his resignation was not made public until later. The *Straits Times* lambasted this high-handed approach in an editorial which stated:

It doesn't seem to be realized in official circles how much harm has been done to public morale and public confidence by the steadfast refusal to reveal even an outline of the facts. For more than two years the Federation has been buzzing with rumours about dissension in the Police.

When it came to the business of a new leader, Lyttelton favoured a general for the job. MacDonald was vehemently opposed; such

26. A troop base — Mick Reeves administers an antibiotic jab to Ralph Mason.

27. The troop takes a break — Bob Turnbull centre front with Bren gun.

28. An unsuccessful trial was carried out in 1957 using elephants as a means of carrying initial stores.

29. An unpleasant view for the 'Tail-End Charlie'.

30. Rafting along the Sungei Perak.

31. John Dearden meets the AOC Malaya at Coronation Park.

32. Colonel Sloane inspects a Maori Secret weapon.

33. News from home.

34. Fort Brooke.

an appointment smacked of a 'generalissimo' and broke the cardinal rule that the military should be servant of a political master. MacDonald's socialist principles were outraged at what he saw as a potentially dangerous abuse of power; he feared a military dictatorship. He, in fairness, was discreet but word that Lyttelton was to recommend a Supremo for Malaya who would be a military man, and that MacDonald was opposed, did leak out.

Lyttelton was under no illusions. He returned convinced that, unless something pretty drastic was done, the British would lose control of the situation in Malaya, and soon. He arrived home on Thursday 21 December and Churchill invited him to lunch at Chartwell for the Saturday. Field-Marshal Montgomery, who had recently handed over as Chief of the Imperial General Staff to Slim, was also invited. The press, who were playing 'Spot the Supremo', had Montgomery down for the job. The story was picked up in Singapore where the *Straits Times* made its position quite clear:

> Mr Churchill could make no bigger blunder than by sending Field-Marshal Montgomery to Malaya. Montgomery's appointment would be regarded as disastrous. We believe, without any qualification whatsoever, that Field-Marshal Montgomery could lose Malaya as surely and quickly as he had won North Africa.

The good Field-Marshal claimed that he was offered the appointment but declined. Lyttelton had no such recollection, though the plan for a military supremo was discussed over lunch and Montgomery's advice invited. Indeed, that very evening, Montgomery penned a brief memo to Lyttelton:

Dear Lyttelton,

Malaya

We must have a plan.
Secondly we must have a man.
When we have a plan and a man, we shall succeed: not otherwise.
>   Yours sincerely,
>   Montgomery (FM)

'I may, perhaps without undue conceit,' commented Lyttelton, 'say that this had occurred to me.'*†

Lyttelton had identified the three key appointments in Malaya:

* The High Commissioner
* The Director of Operations
* The Commissioner of Police

He proposed to combine the first two and find a senior policeman from the UK to fill the third, on secondment, until a home grown product could be identified. In addition, since the first was to be a military man, Lyttelton proposed creating a position new to the Colonial Civil Service, namely that of Deputy High Commissioner. This, he believed, should be a senior career civil servant who would be responsible for the day-to-day administration of the Federation.

In the end the policeman's post proved to be a relatively straightforward appointment. The choice was Colonel Arthur Young, then Commissioner of the City of London Police. Despite his military rank, gained through war service, Young was both highly regarded and seen as a 'Copper's copper', a policeman through and through. He was, above all, a professional and that was sorely needed. He was, at 44 years of age, initially reluctant to take the job. There was possible further advancement to come in his career, all of which could be irreparably damaged by the Malayan 'bed of nails'. After a meeting with Lyttelton, he agreed to take the position provided that he was seconded from the City of London Police and that the tour would be for one year. As Lyttelton demurred, Young pointed out that if he couldn't do the job in a year then he doubted whether he could do it at all. Lyttelton agreed.

Donald MacGillivray was brought across from the West Indies where he was the Colonial Secretary in Jamaica and the best man in his rank in the service for the post of Deputy High Commissioner. The problem Lyttelton was faced with was to find a

* *Memoirs of Lord Chandos*, p. 379
† See Chapter 4 for Calvert's mention of 'the plan and the man'.

suitable officer to be the High Commissioner. A number of men were approached.

Field–Marshal Lord Slim with his experience in Burma was an obvious choice but he felt that he was too old to go jungle-hopping in an Auster again. A more obvious choice was General Sir Brian Robertson who was then serving in the Canal Zone as Commander-in-Chief Land Forces Middle East. He was a soldier with an intimate knowledge of politics and experience of military government in unusual circumstances, notably Italy and Germany in the immediate post-war period. Robertson also enjoyed a reputation as a brilliant administrator which dated back to his service under Alexander in Italy. Lyttelton considered him to be a man of: 'acute intelligence, a character of the highest integrity and calm resolution, qualities which on any score would have numbered him amongst the great soldier-administrators of our times.'

Churchill agreed with Lyttelton's recommendations and Robertson flew home for consultations. The Prime Minister told Lyttelton that he first wanted fifteen minutes alone with Robertson. By the time Lyttelton entered the room Robertson had turned the job down flat. There had been no secret over the reason for Robertson's recall to London and so it was necessary to give an explanation. The press were told that General Robertson had spent twenty-eight of his thirty years of military service overseas and wanted a final tour at home; it seems a pretty lame excuse.

Templer was fifth in seniority in the Army List and at least third in the choice for Malaya. At 53 years of age he was really marking time for a couple of years, before he was to be considered for the post of CIGS. Anthony Head, the Secretary of State for War, recommended to Lyttelton that Templer was ideally suited for the job.*

At the time Templer was C-in-C, Eastern Command, having been Vice Chief of the Imperial General Staff and head of Military Intelligence. In the war he had briefly been the Army's youngest Lieutenant-General in the Anzio Beachhead, was badly wounded below Florence and finished the war on Montgomery's staff. Later he went on to command the British Military Sector in Occupied Germany where among his many achievements was a

---

* See Chapter 4 for Calvert's statement on Templer's appointment.

famous incident when he sacked the Burgomaster of Cologne for being inefficient and obstructionist. It was Konrad Adenaeur!

Lyttelton was convinced that Templer was the man to go with the plan, but, though he could recommend the appointment, it had to be approved by Churchill before it was submitted to the King. This was normally a formality but on this occasion Churchill had taken a personal interest and so he 'interviewed' Templer twice, once in London before Christmas and the second time in Ottawa in the New Year. By this time the press in England and Malaya were full of speculation over the deal and Templer's name had already been linked with the post of High Commissioner. He took the job on 7 February, 1952, and three weeks later arrived in Kuala Lumpur. He did not relish the task but he took it, not because he thought there was a choice, but because he understood it was an order from the Prime Minister. Templer had a high sense of duty and patriotism.

Templer was to be High Commissioner for two and a half years and nothing in Malaya was to be the same again. Love him or hate him, and there were plenty who had cause for the latter, nobody who came into contact with Gerald Templer could walk by on the other side. His detractors claim that he simply built upon the foundations of the success laid by others and that his motivational skills were those of the bully. The same critics describe him as a martinet who modelled himself on his hero, Montgomery, and just breathed fire into an administration that had become tired and listless. He came into the country, they said, in the American manner, 'to kick ass', and left when he had had enough, for pastures new.

We would reject these critics out of hand; though like Montgomery at El Alamein, Templer was fortunate in the timing of his appointment to fame, and he did arrive in-country with a brief which amounted to a blank cheque in both political and financial terms, this doesn't detract from the measure of his achievements. There are other parallels which can be drawn, not the least the contributions made by people like Gurney and Briggs, although, unlike his old boss, Templer was not in the least parsimonious when it came to praising the efforts of others. Lyttelton, who was mauled on a number of occasions in Parliament by the Labour opposition for some of Templer's wilder indiscretions, neverthe-less summed up his achievements as follows:

> Templer soon penetrated to the heart of the political tangle, and with the racial balance so delicately poised, nevertheless gained the confidence of all the races. He recast the military plan, and knit the police into it. He made some wide constitutional changes: he reorganised the intelligence: he travelled tirelessly and visited every part of the country.*

Templer seized and held the initiative as Director of Operations and High Commissioner and took upon himself the task of putting the plans of Briggs and Gurney into effect. In the process of translating the plans into positive action he introduced a broad sweep of new measures and programmes thereby laying the foundation for independence and the defeat of the communist insurgency. He also hired and fired as he saw fit. There is the famous incident of one high-ranking but obstructive police officer called Masterson, who was persuaded to take early retirement. Templer sent for him; as soon as Masterson entered the room, the General came out from behind his desk, reached forwards, shook him by the hand and said, 'Masterson, you've been a difficult and awkward bugger, but you've been a man.'

From the outset Templer built on the two messages that Lyttelton had emphasized during his visit. He reinforced the fact that Malaya would be granted independence; it was not a colonial or imperial war – independence had to be earned. Lyttelton had also used the expression 'Hearts and Minds', as had Briggs, who had in turn borrowed it from Mao Tse Tung. Templer turned the phrase into a household term when he emphasized time and again that the battle had to be won 'in the hearts and minds of the people'.

In the defeat of communist insurgency, Templer eradicated the myth that fighting the war and running the country were two distinct functions. While he was happy to leave the chore of day-to-day government in the more than capable executive hands of

---

* *Memoirs of Lord Chandos*, p. 382.

Donald MacGillivray, and would welcome his advice, nobody was under any illusions that policy, high strategy and the direction of operations were in his domain. He tightened the command system by welding the government and the war fighting effort into a cohesive whole. He amalgamated the Federal War Council with the Executive Council and kept a tight grip of the prosecution of the counter-insurgency war by having General Robert Lockhart demoted to Deputy Director of Operations. Of Lockhart, Templer wrote to Lyttelton:

> He is all I knew he would be, loyal, decent and honest in every way. But he is not my cup of tea for that appointment and in the way in which I propose to use him i.e., as Chief of Staff. I have given the matter a great deal of thought and I am quite sure in my own mind that it would be a very great mistake to get rid of him. It would make everyone think that I considered everything that had been done on the operations side recently was wrong, and would sort of be an expression of no confidence. I must therefore make do, for say six months, with what I consider to be a second-best choice, but certainly a very loyal one.*

Templer set out three critical objectives:

* To restore public confidence in the police.
* To develop the information services so that the public would be made aware of government policies and the determination to win.
* To gear military operations to the flow of Intelligence.

In terms of his first objective Templer recognized that the police had, under Gray, become a para-military force rather than a police service. He was convinced that he had enough troops to win the jungle war and it was, therefore, in keeping with the context of 'hearts and minds', imperative to get the police back onto local duties policing the towns, villages and highways. With the staunch support of Arthur Young, the remodelling of the police

* Quote in *Templer, Tiger of Malaya*, p. 211.

was a rapid and great success. Trust was engendered with the civilian populace again and police training was thoroughly overhauled.

When it came to the business of revamping the Intelligence effort, Templer was well-equipped from his personal experience as a former Director of Intelligence. He could see immediately what was necessary. There was to be a Director of Intelligence personally responsible to Templer. He would also be a member of the Director of Operations Committee; his Directorate was to be co-located with the Deputy Director of Operations and the Police Headquarters. For this onerous task Templer chose Jack Morton, the officer responsible for regional security under Malcolm MacDonald.

Morton was an inspired choice and he set about the detailed restructuring with a will. He acknowledged that, though the police and military had much to contribute in the business of Intelligence gathering, the spearhead had to continue to be the Special Branch which in turn needed to penetrate the Min Yuen. Once the supremacy of Special Branch had been accepted as the ultimate arbiter which controlled the pace and direction of the war against the CTs, tremendous progress was made.

It has been said that Templer was a workaholic before the word was invented. He fired off minutes left, right and centre and then found that the recipients did not respond with the same sense of urgency. The Malayan Civil Service had its own pace and tempo for action and such habits of a lifetime were not about to be disturbed by some outsider, and a brass-hat at that, from London.

So battle was joined and the conflict proved to be short, sharp and, from Templer's point of view, decisive. He introduced a variation on the Churchillian system of wartime memos which were headed 'Action this day'. Templer's were called 'Red minutes'. Typed in red and numbered consecutively they were delivered to the addressee by hand, and despatch rider if necessary, and each carried a deadline for a response. The word soon got around that the answer was required on time – or else. Those on the staff and throughout the Civil Service who failed to measure up faced the threat of certain censure, if not possible dismissal – and some heads did roll.

Overall on the security front Templer introduced what he

called the 'Federal Priority Operations' which required the concentration of resources upon particular locations. The first to be
chosen was the Seremban District of Negri Sembilan. There were
three phases to the operations:

Phase One: Special Branch and Intelligence resources
were concentrated to build up a complete picture of the Min
Yuen; their contacts, the personalities – no detail was too
insignificant. This phase could last for up to two months.

Phase Two: Began on the say-so of Special Branch.
Additional troops and police were drafted in to provide what
Templer referred to as a robust police presence together with
food denial teams. The area was subjected to very tight
control with innumerable road blocks, spot checks, random
searches, etc. The objective was to flush out the weaker CTs
who were then to be 'turned'.

Phase Three: Templer graphically described this as the
'killing phase'. CTs forced to seek food because they were
denied contact with the Min Yuen were caught in ambushes
or the 'killing zones'.

The tactic was successful and in the words of one of his frequent
reports to Lyttelton the 'districts fell like dominoes'. But Templer
also recognized that while such harsh measures were effective
there must also be a more positive approach, one which married
rewards and benefits. So, in the autumn of 1953 he introduced the
policy of 'White Areas.' Once the Intelligence Services were
convinced that the hard core CTs in the District had been
eliminated, then it was recommended that the District should be
allowed to return to normality. All the restrictions and constraints
on movement and travel were lifted, the military and police
presence became far less intrusive; rationing was removed and
personal freedom restored. But always there remained, like a
sword of Damocles, the threat of punitive measures if there was
any backsliding or reversion to political violence.

Those punitive measures could be very harsh indeed and on
one occasion Templer, using the powers he held under the
'Emergency Regulation 17D', which allowed collective punish-

ment, ordered that in Tanjong Malim, for a period of fourteen days:

* There was to be a curfew for 22 hours a day.
* Shops would be open for only two hours a day.
* Nobody would be allowed to go to work (except the shopkeepers), and schools would be closed.
* Nobody was allowed to leave the town.
* The rice ration for adults was reduced by half.

It was an ambush, in March, 1952, in which a young Assistant District Officer (R.M.C. Codner) had been killed which incurred Templer's wrath. He pointed out that the CTs had only been able to operate in Tanjon Malim because they had been fed and protected by the local inhabitants. But he also appreciated that intimidation was probably rife. Every householder was visited and given a sheet of paper upon which they could record, anonymously, what they knew of CT activities.

Twenty-four hours later the papers were collected and taken to Kuala Lumpur where Templer broke the seals of the ballot boxes in which they had been transported. Nobody knows, of course, how many sheets were blank and how many contained scurrilous, or viciously false information, or a grudge hate against a neighbour. Suffice to say that, before the 14 days were up, some 40 Chinese in Tanjong Malim were arrested on suspicion of being members of the Min Yuen.

Did Templer overstep the mark? The barrage of criticism in Parliament at Westminster was matched by the press both at home and overseas. Politically the answer is that Templer was too harsh in his treatment of Tanjong Malim, for thereafter every step he took in Malaya was carefully watched by Parliament, and this must have reduced his freedom of action. The military would argue that it was an astute and necessary move; after all it never had to be repeated.

Templer was a man who was feared, respected and admired by his subordinates and perhaps these are not the best qualities in a leader, but he was precisely the man for the job at the time. A paternal and in many ways benevolent dictator, he led a very successful team and placed the Federation firmly on the road to victory and independence. The police was rid of its divisive elements and regained its professional esteem and self-respect. The military were working with a new sense of purpose and being properly directed in accordance with the best Intelligence available. Incoming battalions were being given the opportunity to undergo basic jungle training before being committed to 'Red Areas' and morale was on the upturn. It was Templer's drive, energy and commitment, his sense of urgency and mission, together with the ability to settle on straightforward and achievable objectives which won the day for him. In the 2½ years of his tenure 60% of the CTs were eliminated; the incident rate declined from 500 per month to 100 per month and the casualty rate, for both military and civilians which was 200, fell to 40 per month. Of course he was lucky and that is an important element of success, not one to be belittled. But he properly managed his share of luck by taking advantage of the opportunities to propel the country in the direction of recovery.

What did all this mean to the SAS? With a more professional approach adopted by higher command the quality of their support improved by leaps and bounds. With the refining of the Intelligence Service they were getting much better working information and a greater sense of purpose generally benefitted the unit. As the soldiers and officers of the line battalions improved their knowledge of the jungle environments so the SAS were to get more and better-trained recruits into the pool from which they selected their reinforcements. They were themselves growing in experience and professionalism and throwing themselves energetically into a business which they all enjoyed.

13

HEARTS, MINDS AND SOLDIERING

For the two years following Operation Helsby the SAS was committed to a number of the 'normal' operations much along the same lines as had been set by Calvert and followed up by Sloane. The Regiment was now on a sound administrative footing and quite a few soldiers had fallen by the wayside to the dreaded cry of 'RTU' (Returned to Unit). Even as the weaker ones were weeded out, so good, professional leaders were beginning to emerge in strength as jungle mastery slowly took place. But some of the events of early and middle 50s were to have far-reaching effects on the future of the SAS.

John Woodhouse had returned to the United Kingdom to take up the post of Adjutant to 4th Battalion, The Dorset Regiment, a Territorial Army post. He left Malaya with the distinct conviction that it was a theatre to which he wanted to return. Furthermore, despite the shambles which it had been, he considered that the SAS, given certain extra dimensions, was the unit in which he wanted to serve. He recognized that there were three fundamentals: that the men for the Regiment must be carefully selected volunteers; that the internal discipline and administration must be of a high standard (this was already improving beyond all measures under Sloane's command) and that Calvert's tactics, together with the risks inherent, must be accepted as the key to success in Malaya.

There was a somewhat fortuitous period before Woodhouse took over his Adjutant's post when he was asked to go to AFD, Aldershot and take over command of the volunteers who were being assembled for Malaya and to work out some form of selection for them. He had no support of any kind, not even transport, and the best he was able to achieve was to collect what rations he could from the cookhouse and take his band of men by rail to Wales where he set up a course of sorts in Snowdonia.

The principle was simple in that elementary training in the all-important facet of navigation took place along with basic tactics and as much physical stress as could be manufactured under such conditions. The hardest worked of all was Woodhouse himself who developed malaria! The session did, however, solidify his convictions regarding a selection course properly administered on a regular basis and on the strength of this and his Malayan experience he was able to write a convincing report along those lines to General Sir Miles Dempsey, then the Colonel Comman-dant, SAS. Dempsey was enthusiastic and also lent a hand in smoothing out relations with the Parachute Regiment at the AFD, even eliciting their eventual support.

A regular selection course did evolve from Woodhouse's efforts and he was instrumental in setting the high standards which still exist today. Obviously there was great emphasis on the physical side of life in order to ensure that the soldier who became exhausted still had the desire to join the SAS; more importantly it had been recognized that the Regiment needed men who were capable and willing to act sensibly on their own in the absence of orders. It became a rule that troops were not to be inspected before an exercise or operation. It was to be their responsibility to ensure that they had all the necessary equipment, rations, maps, etc. This was made clear to them right from the start. They were told that there were to be no 'nannies' and if they did not turn up for the truck at, say, six o'clock the next morning then that truck would leave without them and there was no point in their being in the camp when it returned at the end of the exercise! The principle worked well. The selection course was not the complete procedure for entrance into the SAS. There was still the training operation in the jungle to be survived and full acceptance into whatever troop the soldier joined. Today jungle training still remains an important part of a soldier's selection course.

Another event of 1952 which was to influence regimental development was a commitment of the SAS to operations which revolved around the siting and construction of jungle 'forts'. These forts were the alternative to relocating aborigines to areas many miles away from their natural or chosen habitats and putting them into hutted camps where often misery, disease and death followed. The principle was that a fortified camp would be constructed as a safe haven from the CTs; the aborigines would be moved in and a system of protection by Malay police would be put into effect. Such forts would be within the natural areas of the tribes and were designed to provide a barrier from CT persuasion. Eventually selected aborigines were armed with shot-guns by way of a 'Home Guard'. Although it has been argued with some merit that this type of operation was a misuse of the SAS, it did have a number of spin-offs which were to be of great use a little later. SAS members became more aware of the aborigine and his ways, medically trained patrol members began to practise their craft and improve beyond all measure from the rudimentary training they had been given (which was all the RAMC would allow). Fortuitously many men began to learn the language with some fluency.

From the early 50s onwards there was to be a greater emphasis placed on the whole business of 'hearts and minds' and this concentration of regimental effort was to stand the SAS in good stead in later years in Borneo and Oman. That the aborigines were an integral part of the war cannot be denied; though they had been drawn into the conflict as non-combatants, both sides used them. To the CTs they were an early-warning 'shield' and providers of food. To the Security Forces they were, initially at any rate, a cheap and handy source of porters and guides.

An operation typical of the SAS task in line with the concept of the jungle forts would be for a troop to be committed to a designated area and conduct the initial reconnaissance for the site along, perhaps, with a Malay Police Field Force unit. The troop would then split and patrol the area during the construction phase. In the early days most of the chosen areas required a long, arduous march-in from the nearest roadhead and one of the first tasks was to cut an appropriate DZ for the necessary materials to be air-dropped in. Aborigines formed the labour force (for which they were paid) and as much naturally available material as possible was utilized. The initial, quite primitive forts were later replaced, using more sophisticated building materials, and the introduction of the Whirlwind helicopter meant that the construction crews and police contingents could be flown onto the site. From 1953 onwards the short take off and landing Prestwick Pioneer became available and it then became routine wherever possible to incorporate an airstrip close to the forts.

This, on paper, sounds a relatively easy task, but indeed the siting of the forts was critical, as was the show of willingness of the Security Forces to remain in the area for many months. Even in 1953 there was scant knowledge of the areas in which the aborigine were living. The General Malay Census of 1947 had estimated the number of aborigines as being in the region of 35,000. This included all three recognised tribal groupings. The Negritos (in Malay – Semang and Pangan) lived to the north in Upper Perak and Kelantan with traces further south and to the east of the central mountain spine in west Pahang and even as far across as parts of Trengganu; the Senoi (in Malay – Sakai) tended to be a little further to the south also in Perak but spreading down as far as northern Pahang and the border of Perak and Selangor; The Aboriginal Malays (in Malay – Jakun) would be found in all areas to the south as far down as Johore Bahru. The popular tendency was to lump all aborigines together under the term commonly used by the Malay forces, 'Sakai'. Sakai translates more or less literally as 'dog' or 'slave' but can also be used in the sense of 'retainer' or 'follower' of a native chief. The word can properly be ascribed to the Senoi but other tribes find it insulting. The aborigines would often use Malay terms such as Orang Bukit (hillman), Orang Dalam (man of the interior) or Orang Laut (man of the sea) and even Jakun when describing themselves and other Aborigines. Interestingly the School of Languages in Malaya used the term Orang Darat – 'darat' literally meaning 'of the dry land – not the sea'. Small wonder the confusion to the Security Forces.

The Security Forces, including the Malays, were often insensitive and ignorant in their attitudes to the aborigines and this caused a resentment and hostility which the CTs were quick to seize upon in turning the nomads to their cause. The aborigines, in the early stages of conflict, were regarded by the Security Forces as something of a dangerous nuisance because of their apparent conversion to the cause of the CTs and as they formed only approximately 1% of the overall population their importance in the scale of things was not reckoned to be significant until Calvert's report.

Even though this 1% of the population was deemed almost insignificant in the early stages, it puts a slightly different context into the equation when it is considered that 70% of them lived in the interior from which the CTs were operating. There were very few, if any, deep jungle areas where the CTs lived without aborigines and where they had stayed for any length of time. Indeed many such associations had begun during the days of Force 136. The only exception was probably the Belum Valley and there the CTs had the support (albeit forced) from the Malays in Kampongs Belum and Sepor as we have seen. Only at the end of 1954 did the Department of Aborigines finally succeed in their task of identifying and mapping the hereditary areas of all groups of aborigines.

The very early members of the Malayan Scouts had some cause to distrust contact with the aborigines after the strange disappearance of Trooper O'Leary on 'Operation Prosaic' in early 1951. A variety of articles from Malayan newspapers of the times and Hansard allowed John Leary, himself an ex-Trooper of 'A' Squadron, to piece together an account of the business in his Historical Thesis written in 1987:

The loss of Gunner or Trooper J. O'Leary epitomized what the relationship between the British soldiers, the aborigines and the CT was like in 1951. O'Leary had a reputation for being tardy and often was late starting on patrol or dropped behind during patrols thus getting to an overnight halting place or base camp late. He apparently was fascinated by the few aborigines that 'A' Squadron met during its first operation and spoke of the free life they led. He was reported missing, believed killed, on 2 March, 1951, but the official announcement was later changed back to missing only. It was only by persistent lobbying of their local Member of Parliament by the O'Leary family that the matter was brought to light in the House of Commons in November, 1951. O'Leary had not caught up with his unit on the evening in question and a search for him had proved fruitless. Later that month the body of a British soldier was found by another SAS patrol, and it was tentatively identified as O'Leary because of a gold earring it wore. O'Leary was a very unconventional soldier for his time, and wore a gold earring on patrol.

Gradually the story of O'Leary's death came out in subsequent questioning of aboriginal suspects. O'Leary exemplified the British soldier, blundering through the unfamiliar jungle, trying to find his unit or a friendly aborigine encampment. He was found by an old aborigine, the Batin (Headman) Bujang, and two others. The aborigines did not know what to do with this armed stranger but they treated him hospitably. The Batin went back to his village, leaving O'Leary with the two other aborigines. There, according to Tanah, a witness to the incident, and later one of the accused, the Batin told four CTs about the armed white man. The CTs instructed the Batin and two other aborigines to go back and kill the white man, allegedly threatening to kill the aborigines if they did not do what they were told.

The aborigines faced a dilemma that many other aboriginal groups were to face in the coming years: whether to obey the directions of armed men who had lived amongst them and who had offered them protection in the war years and thereby face the possible retribution of the soldier's friends if they killed him. The Batin selected Tanah and another to go and kill O'Leary. They went back and found the soldier asleep, with his two aborigine guards. Waking the two guards, they hacked O'Leary to death with their parangs. They took his body to a tributary of the Endau River and left it there, where it was later found. Tanah, who was being held under the Emergency Regulations, confessed to the killing and he and four others were tried for O'Leary's death. Meantime the old Batin had died. After a trial lasting well into 1952, Tanah was sentenced to be hanged and the others to various gaol sentences. O'Leary's gun was recovered by Kampong guards in action against CTs in the Mersing area of Johore in January 1952.

If this was a downside to operations with the aborigines before a mutual respect and confidence evolved then there were quite a few early incidences when information derived directly from the tribesmen led the SAS to contact with the CTs and a number of kills resulted. The SAS was now operating deeper and deeper into the jungle and certainly often into areas which had never seen the presence of a white skin before. What is more, they stayed there for long periods and often their bases were taken over by rotating squadrons and it was this continuity of presence which made the breakthrough with the aborigines.

Of course, it was not just the presence; it was also the manner of treatment of these remarkable little men of the jungle. Many of the SAS soldiers were quick to realise what a marvellous, if simple, sense of humour the aborigines possessed and were soon able to create laughter and merriment in a very short space of time. This in itself was a considerable change to the serious CT attitude; there were no threats of death either, quite the contrary. These white men were a source of clothing, parachute nylon, sometimes cosmetics and a host of other items enjoyed by the aborigines. There was an occasion during Operation Galway (October, 1953 – June, 1954) in the north-west sector of Pahang when Lieutenant Fotheringham of 'B' Squadron took his troop on a typical task to make a reconnaissance of the area with a view to locating the site for a new fort (Fort Dixon).

The Squadron HQ was based on the Sungei Telom and in close proximity there was an aboriginal camp. The troop was fully aware that a large party of aborigines was due to arrive in the squadron base area and they were not long into the patrol when they heard the aboriginals 'chatting like a tree full of monkeys' heading towards them. They moved off the track to allow the party free passage making no serious attempt to conceal them-selves. They were spotted almost straightaway and immediately came under accurate small arms fire from a group of CTs who had concealed themselves amongst the aborigines. Fotheringham was killed in the first stages of the fire fight during which the SAS was inhibited by the presence of the aborigines. None of the aborigines were killed, neither were there any reprisals of any sort. They were treated in exactly the same way as the others when they eventually found the courage to arrive in dribs and drabs into the base camp area. It was this sort of stark contrast to the treatment the CTs would have meted out to the aborigines that was another factor in the slow cementation of good relations.

This was not a unique experience, though it was the only one which involved the death of an SAS man that we have come across. As often as possible the SAS patrols made their movements unpredictable, but eventually they had to return to the same areas in order to carry out the task of winning over the aborigines effectively. Medical treatment was, of course, a very powerful weapon in the armoury and the troop or patrol medic was viewed as a key person. It was not unusual for a trooper who had the knack of getting on particularly well with the aborigines to pose as the medic with the real incumbent alongside him giving advice from the corner of his mouth.

Apart from the usual cuts and fractures which were part of every day life to the aborigine, they tended to suffer tinea, yaws, tuberculosis and malaria to a considerable extent. The SAS represented the only form of effective treatment for any of these diseases and, though the CTs had formerly had the great asset of permanence and continuity, the SAS was also now offering this and, furthermore, if the aborigines supplied food or labour they were paid. The soldiers were quick to learn the politeness that the aborigine takes for granted; the compliments on his skill as a planter of bountiful crops; his abilities as a builder and a great prowess as a hunter. They learned not to take offence as the aborigines laughed at the quaint customs of the 'Orang puteh' (white man).

They learned about the aboriginal devotion to (and fear of) the 'hantu' – the spirit of the jungle. Their life was controlled by their 'dreams'. A bad dream could totally change a planned move at the last minute or cause a family to move an almost completed house. There was a 'hantu' for almost every circumstance. 'Hantus' made the crops succeed or fail, they guided the poisoned dart from the blowpipe, it was the 'hantu weweh' who decided if a man was to get lost in the jungle. The butterflies which abounded in the ladangs and along the rivers were the spirits of the aborigines' ancestors and it was not a good thing to kill these for collections. Mutual confidence was built up and though some aborigines may have complained about both terrorists and Malay soldiers mistreating their women, such a complaint was never levelled against the SAS. They were not particularly attractive to

European eyes anyway, but the job in hand, that of winning them over, was a serious business.

The long patrols also took their toll on the SAS men. It was arduous work and the business of first making contact with a headman was not without some stress. It was a venture into the unknown and possibly a CT ambush. The principle was that the patrol commander would, on arrival at a longhouse, enquire after the headman and would often be invited into the house on his own at first. He would generally introduce the medic to the villagers and then try to gauge the headman's feelings through questions about the CTs. The aborigines loved to talk and could do so for hours without really saying anything and it took endless patience to sit and listen with an expression of interest, and all this on the first meeting in a strange longhouse which could well be surrounded by CTs for all the patrol knew.

All the 'fort' type operations were conducted without forfeiting the need for aggressive fighting patrols. Obviously there was a lot of luck in whether or not a squadron or troop found itself in an area where contact with the CTs would be made. The regimental 'kill' rate was low at this stage and there is no doubt that some members thought this detracted from their standing in the overall scheme of things, but this is a false viewpoint. On many occasions it was the effort of the SAS patrols which forced the CTs to the jungle fringes and into the ambushes of the infantry battalions and the police. All of this engendered by their success in making the interior unsafe for the enemy through a long-term presence and the winning over of the aborigines. It is certain, from so many reports of near misses i.e., the finding of recently deserted CT camps and ladangs and the locating of recently used tracks by parties of outgoing terrorists, that in many cases they were forewarned by their aboriginal supporters of the presence of SAS. It took time to win the hearts and minds campaign and in many instances some of the aborigines would sit on the fence reporting to both sides while they made up their minds in which direction to go.

Not all the CTs lacked an understanding of the aborigines. One famous character was Ah Tuk, who, with his band of half a dozen other CTs and a few aborigines, operated in an area roughly 35 miles to the east of Taiping. His was a highly mobile group and he was very popular with the aborigines and rarely did they give away any information about him to the Security Forces. It was known that Ah Tuk was the man responsible for aboriginal support for 31st Indepedent Platoon (CTs) who, under command of a hard man named Pak Chuen, operated in the fringes of the jungle in this area. The platoon was well organized and there is no doubt that Ah Tuk's aborigine informants played a large part in their success in evading the Security Forces. He is mentioned because of a strange feud which built up between him and a member of the SAS.

Bob Turnbull joined the regiment in early 1952 from the Royal Artillery. A blunt-speaking Yorkshireman he was physically strong and with a real bent for jungle operating. On one of his early patrols he had missed shooting a terrorist with his carbine and vowed that such a thing would never happen again. On leave he would go off to the ranges and, with his new pump action shotgun, would pour round after round down the range until he reached an outstanding level of efficiency. He took his professionalism even further by teaching himself Malay and developing his talents as a tracker with the assistance of an Iban called Anak Kanyan. It is said by many that his ability eventually outmatched that of his tutor.

Turnbull's path had crossed that of Ah Tuk on a number of occasions as 'D' Squadron kept returning to the same area of operations and he was often to say that he would like 'to have him'. He got his opportunity in January, 1957. Moving off after a halt, Turnbull spotted a terrorist's head some twenty yards distant. A witness said that Turnbull fired with such speed that the three shots blurred into the sound of one. The echoes were still reverberating round the jungle when Turnbull was seen standing astride the corpse to check that he was dead. It was Ah Tuk, whose diaries were to prove of great use to Intelligence and explained many incidents, courier routes and aborigine sympathizers. But this was by no means Turnbull's finest hour.

Much interesting information was gleaned from the diaries and other papers recovered after Ah Tuk's death. It showed that the Regiment was working along the right lines in terms of its treatment of the aborigines. Ah Tuk had developed his own approach to the subject of propaganda and listed it in a pamphlet disseminated to all his subordinates. They would talk to the aborigines along the following lines:

> Are not all of you wanting a peaceful and secure life? Everybody knows the British Imperialists have penetrated into your homeland by setting up a number of fortified points. This is a move to subjugate you for ever. Why are they doing this? The Party and the aborigines have lived like brothers since the days of the Japanese. They succeeded together in bringing the Japanese to surrender after nearly four years. For this reason the British fear that we shall save you from starvation and sickness. Another reason is that the party have instilled knowledge, out of brotherly love, into your minds; in so much as you will no longer stand for exploitation and enslavement. The British invade your homeland on the pretext that they come to deal with the 'bad men' [our phrase for the Communists; in Malay 'Orang Jahat']. In reality they come to keep an eye on your movements. They aim further to part you from your wives and children, to use you as cannon fodder. Don't you believe from this that the British have sinister aims?

This was, of course, a poor case well presented, but it must be remembered that many aborigines had lost their lives in bombing raids and as a result of Security Forces actions and 'cannon fodder' would strike a basis of truth, as did the fact that the CTs had lived so long with the aborigines. The weakness comes in the fact that it is the British who are presented as the sinners and not the unscrupulous Malay and Chinese traders who had exploited the aborigines for years.

In 22 SAS Regt at that time (and for many years afterwards) was a Chinese named Ip Kwong Lau. Ip's route into the British Army had been tortuous. In 1942 he had been interned in Hong Kong by the Japanese at the age of twenty-one. Eventually he was to escape to China where he was picked up by Nationalist soldiers who thought he was a Japanese spy. It took a year for his story to be proved and he was sent, as a British subject, to India. He was incarcerated in a camp there with other British subjects until Calvert called for volunteers for his 77 Chindit Brigade. Ip volunteered and went as personal escort to Colonel Claud Rome on the second Chindit expedition into Burma where he saw many fierce actions against the Japanese. Ip's reasons for staying with the British Army are vague. He would certainly have made much more money in Hong Kong. In Malaya he spent much of his time with John Woodhouse who supposed that Ip's motives were pride in Hong Kong and the British connection. Woodhouse was to put Ip's appearance and talents to good use:

In the winter of 1957 'D' Squadron found itself again in the Gunong Chingkai area on the hunt for the remnants of 31st Independent Platoon. Ip Kwong Lau rejoined the Squadron from HQ and came complete with a communist uniform. He would be attached to different patrols and be sent into aboriginal settlements in his Chinese outfit at which point he would claim that he had become lost after a skirmish with the British and that he wanted to know how to rejoin the communists. This never led to any decisive success but on one occasion he was given two chickens and he insisted that these were carefully noted and put down to Ah Tuk's account!

Operation Gabes North took place between May, 1956, and December, 1957, along the Perak – Kelantan border. It was mounted on information from two sources; air reconnaissance had shown a large increase in cultivation along the Perak side of the border and this was assessed as being far in excess of the needs of the known aborigine settlements in the area. The second source was a surrendered CT (Wong Tung Shin). He claimed that there were up to thirty terrorists normally living in the area around the Sungei Klub which was, he stated, the centre of a communications route leading from the Central Committee in Thailand, through the Belum Valley and the Klub to the rest of Malaya. He also claimed that a year before that he had been ordered to bury a quantity of wireless equipment which he was later told had been recovered by Sze Yong and three radio specialists and it was assumed that they could well still be in that area.

On moving into the area, 'B' Squadron had an early contact with three enemy during which one CT was killed, one wounded and all three weapons were recovered. It looked promising, but the keys to control in the area were two aborigine leaders Bongsu Helwood and Along Serbin, a small number of whose groups had been armed by the CTs. Both Bongsu and Along were found within a few weeks and were easily convinced that the SAS was a better option than the Chinese and so, in less than two months, the majority of the enemy's labour force and warning screen were lost to him.

7 July brought confirmation of Wong Tung Shin's story; a 'B' Squadron patrol found a one-year-old camp high up on a mountain. It had last been used about two months earlier. Above the camp was a waterfall and a beautifully made wooden wheel which was used to drive a hydro turbine which had obviously been used to power a generator. Several batteries and radio parts were also discovered. This was enough for the then Commanding Officer, George Lea, to commit 'D' Squadron in a wide arc to the north, west, south and south-east of 'B' Squadron on the principle that the enemy had moved outside the area. Two troops of 'A' Squadron began to march northwards from the area of Fort Brooke. A half troop under Donald Hobbs was to parachute alongside the Sungei Perias to come in from the east and close the circle.

All these troops were to be in ambush positions by 18 July. On the afternoon of that day a 'scratch' force from the HQ Squadron was to parachute into the centre of the area under command of Captain John Slim, the son of Field-Marshal Sir William Slim, a big, exuberant officer and very much the front line soldier. He had just returned for his second tour with SAS after a staff liaison job in Australia. He must have had mixed feelings on such a command but he was certainly the right sort of leader for the job. (After this operation he was to take command of 'A' Squadron and, eventually, 22 SAS.) One of the great bugbears of jungle parachuting was to immobilize Slim's force soon after landing when a serious injury, a fractured spine, meant that they had to clear a LZ so that a helicopter could fly out the injured man. Not surprisingly, there were no CTs to be found afterwards.

A number of 'finds', kills and close misses followed over the next month and a half as the area was scoured for enemy. Throughout this period Sergeant Turnbull had been intermittently following enemy tracks. When they were lost he began a process of deduction and managed to pick them up again; on 4 September, having lost the trail again, a tip off from another troop gave him the lead he needed. He and Anak Kanyan, his Iban tracker, with three troopers picked up the tracks and stayed with them for some twelve thousand yards before losing them again. Then they came across a small, partly overgrown ladang where they saw fresh prints.

With caution they began the follow-up, conscious that they were very close. Suddenly, a slight movement about fifty yards ahead alerted them to the fact that they were very, very close! What they had seen was a leg; a human, khaki-clad leg. The rest of the body was invisible. It was obviously a sentry. The patrol melted back into the cover of the jungle. The situation was not good. The time was two fifteen and somewhere behind the sentry had to be a camp. There was no way of telling how large it was. Turnbull reckoned that the tracks he had been following were of four to five men, but there could well be others in the camp and who was to say whether tracks also went in from other directions? The camp was in a bamboo thicket and the dead stems lying around made silent movement almost impossible.

The only quiet approach was along the track. True, they could kill the sentry from where they now crouched, but Turnbull was an adherent to the SAS doctrine 'always take a chance and play for the higher stakes.' If they killed the sentry the rest would be off in a flash with no hope of catching them in the bamboo. Turnbull decided to wait for dark, but was hopeful that the usual heavy rain would not let him down. That at least would serve to dampen down the noise. In silence they waited, cramped and uncomfortable, for the next two hours. Then the rain came, a slow steady monotonous, chilling rain. The patrol began to shiver in the cold, but still Turnbull waited. Then it happened! The sentry disappeared. Had he gone to rejoin the rest in the shelter of the camp or had he just answered nature's call? There was no way of knowing.

Turnbull waited a few minutes more and then decided to take his chances and close in. He led the patrol himself. His four years of jungle experience showed as he moved, cat-like, straight into the sentry's recently vacated position. The patrol moved at five yard intervals behind him, ready to swing to either flank if contact was made. From the sentry position Turnbull could hear voices. In front of him was a low bank. It was not possible, because of the bamboo, for him to commit two men to an encircling movement and anyway the sentry might reappear at any second. He hand-signalled the patrol to come up line abreast of him and, still unaware of the enemy strength, he motioned the patrol to attack.

It took but two fast paces to breast the bank and in a split second they noted the four terrorists sheltering from the rain. Two CTs were cleaning their weapons; some yards to their left were three aborigines. Even as shock distorted the faces of the CTs, Turnbull opened fire with his automatic shotgun. As ordered, nobody else fired. Three of the four CTs died instantly, but the fourth, badly wounded, staggered away. Turnbull called on him to surrender, but he attempted to reach the cover of the bamboo. The patrol opened fire and brought him down. None of the aborigines was injured. Turnbull's men swept through the camp but found it empty.

The wounded CT was made as comfortable as possible, but he was in a bad way. He told them that his name was Wong Hoi and that five of the CTs had left the camp only two days before. Unfortunately Wong Hoi died before he could give any other information. After the bodies were searched and photographed the camp was pulled apart. Radio parts, documents and the presence of a pistol and sten gun, weapons normally carried only by communists leaders, served to tell the exuberant patrol that they had scored an important success.

There was great joy in the Squadron base that night with congratulatory signals being received even from the High Commissioner. If that seems to be a little extreme for four kills it must be remembered that in that year (1956) ten terrorists killed by a battalion in a year was a very good average. In August only sixteen had been killed in the whole of Malaya. Furthermore this had been achieved without any information other than that won by the patrol's own skills. Aborigines, in close proximity to the enemy, had remained unharmed – a story they were to relate to others later.

As to Turnbull's action; he was later to say that there was nothing special about it! In the opinion of many, however, he was to become the best troop sergeant (and commander) that 22 SAS had and he went on to take his place as a very perceptive member of the selection team at a crucial time of recruiting. Such names as Turnbull's pepper the pages of the SAS archives: Roger 'Olly' Levet; Frank Williams; Bob 'Crockett' Creighton (commissioned); Roy 'Striker' Ball (commissioned); 'Jesse' James; Bill Mundell (commissioned); Herbie Hawkins; 'Lofty' Ross; 'Gipsy' Smith; 'Lawrence' Smith; 'Whispering Leaf' Hague; Peter Walter (commissioned); 'Bosun' Sandilands and many others apart from those already mentioned.

Meantime actions were taking place in the rear echelons that would again affect the evolution of the SAS.

14

THE SECOND FRONT

In London, back in 1952, Major 'Leo' Hart had written a document regarding the organization and control of the SAS which had largely gone unnoticed in the Far East. Later this became more significant as the Regiment's reputation was enhanced; a regular selection course was set up and approved and regimental administration in Malaya became more professional. The question of control and representation in the United Kingdom became more pressing as it seemed probable that the SAS future may not end in the Far East.

Sloane was looking to the future in other areas and, indeed, some of the training during the Rest and Retraining periods became oriented to this possibility. Lieutenant-Colonel Oliver Brooke took over command from Sloane. He had a similar background in that it was his first experience of specialist troops and he was equally determined that the essential was to have discipline and administration firmly established and with this in mind he built on Sloane's work, albeit in a somewhat more explosive manner, in keeping with his temperament.

John Woodhouse, who during his period in the United Kingdom, had been given the chance to command a company of 21 SAS Regiment's 'Z' Reservists during their annual camp in Yorkshire, had his eyes opened by some of the wartime SAS members who told of their operations in Europe. He began to think of the possibilities for the new SAS in any future conflict against the Soviet Union. Hart's paper had outlined, at an early stage, a particular and immediate need for the SAS.

Extracts from his document will explain:

ORGANISATION AND CONTROL OF THE SAS REGT

INTRODUCTION

1. The SAS Regiment is now a separate Corps in the Army.
2. The Corps at present consists of:
   (a) 21st SAS Regt (Artists) TA
   (b) The Malayan Scouts
3. 21st SAS Regt has under command:
   (a) 21st SAS Regt Signal Sqn (R.Sigs) TA
   (b) RHQ The SAS Regt
   (c) Supplementary Reserve Depot, SAS Regt
4. The present intention is that other SAS units will be raised in various theatres as required, and disbanded when the need for them disappears.
5. At present there are no co-ordinating or supervisory arrangements for the SAS other than:
   (a) The RHQ just authorised
   (b) Directorate of Land/Air Warfare
6. The functions of the RHQ have not yet been laid down, but will clearly consist only of the traditional 'A' matters, such as dress, regimental costumes, etc., and, possibly selection of personnel.
7. Land/Air Warfare is a small Directorate (of which the Director is also DMT) and is primarily concerned with Army/Air Co-operation, Air Liaison and the Airborne Division. It has not, in fact, had an SAS officer in it.
8. The SAS is the only Corps in the Army which has no Director in the War Office.

REQUIREMENT

9. The proposed formation of 'M' Independent Squadron and of the Malayan Scouts has produced concrete evidence on which to base proposals.
10. Experience gained in these cases has shown:
    (a) that there is a need for co-ordination and supervision of all SAS units;
    (b) that no co-ordination now exists;

(c) that if there is no co-ordination and supervision it will be impossible to consider the various units as part of one Corps. The RHQ may be able to control dress and even selection of personnel, but the most important aspect for a new Corps are General Staff aspect of the role, employment, establishment, training methods, staff teaching, etc.

11. It is essential that, if the policy of grouping all long range, small party units under the 'umbrella' of the SAS is to be effective, there is some officer, or staff, charged with the responsibility for ensuring a measure of co-ordination and the acceptance of common principles. It is appreciated that the various theatres in which some units may be formed will to some extent produce different characteristics, and some difference in role, but if the inclusion of 'SAS' in the title is to have any meaning, there must be some means of integrating the various units.

12. This cannot be done by a RHQ Major. It is in fact the normal function of a War Office Director.

PRESENT POSITION

13. At present the co-ordination of other units would have to be effected by either:
    (a) the Colonel Commandant
or (b) the CO of 21st SAS Regt
or (c) the RHQ Major

14. It is submitted that:
    (a) the Colonel Commandant should not be burdened with such day to day matters of detail as are continually arising;
    (b) a civilian (who, if of the standing required to be a TA SAS Commanding Officer, would probably have important business interests requiring his prior attention) would not have the time, nor could he reasonably be asked to control in any way the activities of a regular Lt. Col.
    (c) the RHQ Major has not the proper standing, nor could he carry out the duties without continually

referring to the TA CO or the Colonel Commandant.

15. As a result many things have occurred which could have been avoided, and which are undesirable. To quote instances:

    (a) the carrying out of operations in KOREA by so called SAS parties, about which neither the War Office nor 21st SAS Regt had any knowledge until after the event, and which had no SAS approval. 'M' Independent Squadron, which had been intended for KOREA, was withdrawn as a matter of policy: yet an officer of only slight SAS experience, who had been turned down for the Sqn, subsequently was permitted to operate as SAS.

    (b) the doubts and misunderstandings which still exist, as to SAS mobilization plans, policy and employment, etc.

    (c) the delivering of lectures, and the training of Staff Officers at the Staff College and other schools, on the SAS and SAS policy without the knowledge or approval of the SAS or the knowledge, even of L/ AW.

16. These are instances of what has happened and could and should be avoided. In addition, and perhaps more important, it is considered that a great deal of positive action could and should be taken to:

    (a) formulate, crystallize and propagate SAS teaching and policy;

    (b) ensure that the SAS is accepted and understood as a permanent and valuable part of the Army;

    (c) ensure a proper common standard among the SAS units, and standardization of training, establishments, equipment and techiques so far as possible;

    (d) propose, and/or advise on, the use of SAS units as and when situations arise in various parts of the world, both in peace and war;

    (e) ensure a proper standard of recruits, including the training of reserves.

PROPOSAL

17. There appear to be two alternatives:
    (a) a Directorate in the War Office, or SAS representation in an existing Directorate;
    (b) a SAS HQ with the above mentioned powers.
18. It is not considered that the present size of the SAS justifies a Directorate, and it is felt that a Staff Officer within an existing Directorate would not have the necessary powers.
19. It is considered that a small SAS HQ is the ideal solution. The main requirement is, in fact, to have an officer supervising all SAS units and policy, with no other commitments and with sufficient seniority. He should also have War Office backing, as he will deal to a large extent with overseas Commands and Allied HQ. He would be, to all intents and purposes, an Inspector of SAS.
20. The proposal is to disband the present TA Permanent Staff and RHQ, and substitute 'HQ SAS Troops'. The functions of the latter would include:
    (a) The channel for all War Office dealings with SAS.
    (b) Inspection and co-ordination of all SAS units.
    (c) Control of recruitment for SAS.
    (d) The normal functions of a RHQ and Colonel Commandant's Office.
    (e) The training and supervising of 21st SAS Regt (with which it would remain), and other TA units which may be raised.
    (f) Training of reservists, including the Supplementary Reserve.
    (g) On mobilization the raising of additional SAS units and reinforcements.
21. Since the Commander SAS Troops would have, to a considerable extent, to control and supervise other Commanding Officers, it is considered that he should have the rank of Colonel. It is, however, of great importance that he himself should have experience of SAS, preferably as a unit commander.

SPECIAL NOTES

22. It must be emphasized that one of the aims to be achieved
    by this proposal is the avoidance of any confusion and
    misunderstanding about the SAS which may easily lead
    to prejudice and irritation, resulting finally in serious
    danger to its continuance in the Army.
23. Without this HQ, the SAS cannot be considered as a
    Corps in any sense of the word. Each unit that is raised
    will acquire its own characteristics, and the chaotic
    situation of the last war with regard to 'Special Units'
    will be perpetuated.

Major L.E.O.T. Hart
The SAS Regt

Not until March, 1954, did the SAS succeed in getting to grips
with at least part of Hart's proposals. The delay was due not least
to a degree of antipathy or ignorance on the part of the War
Office. In some quarters the Regiment was still viewed as a beast
which would shortly be disbanded as the Malayan situation
became more controlled; elsewhere there was the antagonism
which had been faced by Stirling in 1941 – the view that private
armies were to be actively discouraged – this despite the Corps
status of the SAS. It also has to be said that with postwar
redeployment and recognition of the threat from the Soviet
Union, along with the fact that the British Army was scattered to
all corners of the globe, the War Office was a particularly busy
place and the troubles of the SAS were rated somewhat lower in
the scheme of things than the Regiment would have wished.

The Directorate of Land/Air Warfare saw the SAS as being
properly grouped within the Airborne Division and so long as
AFD was hosting the recruits and providing limited training
facilities then all should have been well. A decision was made that
Hart's efforts would be bolstered by an officer who not only had
the SAS at heart but one who could speak with wide authority
about the Malayan theatre who also had his own strong ideas on
post-Malaya deployment and policies. Major C.L.D. 'Dare'
Newell, MBE (later OBE), was the chosen incumbent.

Newell's qualifications were impeccable. He was that strange combination of a deep thinker and an action soldier, but he nearly didn't get into the army at all. Paradoxically, his first instincts on reaching maturity had been to join the priesthood; this changed as he developed a love of the countryside and he diverted to the Forestry Commission where he worked happily until the Munich Crisis. He decided that war was inevitable and looked to the army for a short term commitment. On advice he rang the Adjutant of a famous Yeomanry TA Regiment only to be asked whether or not he owned his own horse. His negative reply caused the Adjutant to lose interest.

Shortly after that episode the Forestry Commission workers were informed that their work had been classified as a reserved occupation and that any attempt to leave would incur dire penalties. Newell became more and more frustrated and the Battle of Britain was the last straw as far as he was concerned. He simply walked out, telling nobody and enlisted into the Royal Armoured Corps. To his disappointment he was sent, as a newly commissioned subaltern, to command the motor-cycle section of a training regiment. Battles were being fought, won and lost while he vegetated in the north of England. Eventually he was rescued when a notice appeared asking for: 'Volunteers for operations of a hazardous nature; applicants must have a knowledge of wireless and be prepared to train as parachutists. Applications may not be withheld by units.'

A matter of weeks later Newell found himself in Cairo where he underwent his training with the Special Operations Executive to find himself, three months after that, parachuting into Albania. That is another story. After the Balkans, Newell moved to the Far East where he dropped into the Malaysian jungle with Force 136 in January, 1945, and during this period he met Chin Peng.

After the war Newell found himself discontented in a number of jobs and eventually he rejoined the army, gaining a commission in the Suffolk Regiment and thence a return to Malaya and to the SAS in 1952. As troop and then squadron commander he got his experience early and his past operations with guerrillas and with Force 136 made him an invaluable acquisition for Sloane and Brooke, both of whom were held in esteem by Newell. He relates an amusing, if well-known story:

Oliver Brooke came out in 1953 to replace John Sloane as Commanding Officer. John had been evacuated back to England with a very bad leg injury and I don't think Oliver had even had the chance to speak with him. Anyway we were hosting him in the Officers' Mess and after a very good dinner we were standing around drinking and with all of us trying to get our point across at the same time it was quite noisy. There was suddenly a bloody great bang and one wall of the Mess disappeared and the table was hurled over to roll into a corner. We were silent for a few seconds but the remarkable thing was that Oliver didn't seem to even notice. He just nodded and carried on talking as though someone had just farted.

The members of 'B' Squadron who had decided to welcome their new CO in this unconventional manner (using a small explosive charge) were soon to get the measure of him. The very next day, which happened to be a Sunday, seventeen RTU'd soldiers left the camp before lunch.

Newell's arrival in RHQ SAS at Dukes Road, London, strengthened the sense of purpose, but he was quick to realize that it was going to be a long, slow haul to achieve the recognition and establishment outlines in Hart's proposals and he doubted if it would ever really come to fruition. His first letter to the SAS Colonel Commandant, however, was purposeful:

General Sir Miles Dempsey, KCB, KBE, DSO, MC,
c/o DMO.,
The War Office,
Whitehall, SW1.   11 October 1954

Dear General Sir Miles,

As I have now been here for some six months I would like to report very briefly on what I have been doing, and to draw your attention to the problem of recruiting.

I have concentrated mainly on overcoming the decided antipathy to the SAS that I found to exist at the lower Staff levels, and have established better relations with those sections of the Staff that are concerned with the day-to-day matters that affect the Regiment in Malaya. I have made no attempt to further the expansion of our activities to other theatres as I feel that this is a matter that should be dealt with at a higher level than mine.

I have also taken steps to see that the Regiment has Standing Orders and Dress regulations and drafts are at present being studied by Colonels Brooke, Franks and Lapraik. I hope to get an agreed draft to you for your consideration by the end of this month.

The major outstanding problem at present in connection with the Regiment in Malaya is that of recruiting. This is far below what it should be, both in officers and men. There was a tendency in the past for the Regiment as a whole to lay too much stress on the excitement that sometimes attaches itself to this type of soldiering, and to forget that an officer or man must first be a good soldier before he can be a 'special' one. As a result of this, a number of most unsuitable men found their way into the Regiment. Their behaviour created a distrust in many quarters that we are only just beginning to overcome, and which has proved a stumbling block when recruiting from some of the better regiments.

A further difficulty has been the ignorance at battalion levels as to the role of an SAS Regiment and that of the 22nd in particular.

I therefore put up a letter to the Adjutant General's Branch for circulation to all Commands, outlining the type of operation at present being carried out by us in Malaya, and stressing the necessity of a high mental and moral standard amongst other ranks. I also added a note to the effect that this type of operation was ideal for developing both self-reliance and a sense of responsibility. This letter was in due course issued as a War Office Memorandum.

I next propose a somewhat similar course of action with regard to officers, and suggested that the War Office should circulate all Colonels of Regiments. I have now been asked by AG14 if we would agree to a postponement of this idea until we see the results of certain steps that are being taken within the AG Branch to increase the flow of recruits. I feel, however, that whatever is done within the Branch will have little effect in regimental circles until regiments understand that service with an SAS Regiment is not a glorious holiday. There are very many young officers, I feel sure, who are only too anxious to serve a tour with us but who are blocked by their Regiments.

This difficulty in obtaining good officers is, of course, having an adverse effect on the Regiment, and now that such a high standard is required of the men it is unfair to inflict inferior officers on them.

I do not like to bother you too much with regimental matters, but I feel that perhaps the stage is being reached where steps should be taken to settle this problem once and for all by a War Office statement for Officer recruitment.

I shall be in North Wales from 12 to 20 October with our Monthly Selection Course, but will be back in the office on 21 October.

Yours,
Dare Newell

The present authors asked Dare about his initial tactics and in particular why he had harped back to the business of early mistakes in recruiting the 'wrong type' of man; after all this was 1954 and surely discipline and administration were now in good order? His explanation was simple:

You see, we had all admitted to ourselves the mistakes and we were all aware of what great improvements there had been all round in the Regiment under COs like Sloane, Brooke and later George Lea. But, what you have to realize is that in the War Office and at regimental levels around Britain you had regiments which had returned from tours in Malaya and officers taking up War Office appointments who knew little, if anything, about our progress. All they remembered was what has now become known as the 'bad old days'. Leo Hart had been kept rather in the dark in the early stages and he was really fed on rumour and the rumours were not pretty. I felt that I had to start almost from the 'confessional' and say 'Look we've made our share of cock-ups but we've got it right now. How about some support?'

You must also remember that there were very many Staff Officers whose experience of the SAS during the war had been confined to rumour and sometimes harsh treatment by some of our more forthright officers of the time and many had failed in their attempts to join. They had no reason to love us. Dempsey was, in fact, a tower of strength and support in those early days. He was always ready to grasp the nettle once he was sure that he had all the facts at his fingertips.

Another factor was that on paper our recruiting figures looked quite healthy, but one of the squadrons was from New Zealand (the Rhodesians left in December, 1952) and one squadron really belonged to the Parachute Regiment. We desperately needed to reach regimental strength in our own right. It is true that the rapid turnover of individuals had decreased dramatically as a result of our having a regular Selection Course but we were far from being where we wanted to be.

We asked Dare his opinion of 'C' Squadron (Rhodesian):

Of course we owe them a debt of gratitude. Their numbers swelled our ranks at a time when we desperately needed them and they had some very fine soldiers. There are criticisms, of course, I don't think they were as at ease with the aborgines as the Brits but that is understandable given the background and they had a lot of trouble with jungle diseases. The quacks have said that British resistance to disease was in no small way due to a more deprived way of life in childhood. I can't say whether that is true but it seems a reasonable school of thought. They were disciplined and well-trained as infantrymen when they arrived, but, like the rest of us, they had to learn as they went. They produced some outstandingly good individuals and they certainly put the Malayan experience into practice during their own war in Africa later on. Peter Walls, of course, was a great leader and went on to command all of their armed forces. Later on, of course, we had the Kiwi Squadron who performed magnificently.

This is an opportune moment to give a little detail of the 'Kiwis'. The New Zealand Special Air Service Squadron, to give it the full, formal title of that time, was formed up in 1954 especially to link up with 22 SAS in Malaya. Within the original group there was a number of soldiers who had already seen 'special' service with the British Army through the Parachute Regiment, the Long Range Desert Group and 1st SAS Regiment. From the start Major Frank Rennie, MBE (later Colonel and CBE), the Officer Commanding the Squadron, imposed a rigid form of selection and by the time it was ready to be committed to Malaya the Squadron was a tightly-knit fighting force with immense pride.

The 'Kiwis' moved to Malaya at the end of 1955 and were operational soon after completing the parachute course by now established at RAF Changi. After an initial training operation in Pahang during which time it became quite obvious that they were able to get on with the aborigines remarkably well, the Squadron began to operate on a wider front in conjunction with the other SAS Squadrons. By the time they left at the end of 1957 they were held in the highest regard by all who had served along side them. They were disbanded, but, due in no small way to their Malayan reputation, they were included in the Order of Battle of the New Zealand Regular Brigade Group when it was created in late 1958. An article from *The Free Glance*, the Journal of the New Zealand SAS Association, February, 1993 Issue, describes a typical 'Kiwi' patrol in Malaya. Rather poignantly, it is this issue which also records the obituary of Colonel Frank Rennie:

Pahang, Malay, 1956. The men moved stealthily, every foot movement, every hand movement made slowly with great care. But their eyes moved ceaselessly. Now watching where a foot was to be placed, making sure no twig would crack; now looking up to search the undergrowth for any sign of the enemy, now down again for the next footfall.

They breathed silently through partly opened mouths as their lead scout tracked the faint sign on the ground that led them closer and closer to their quarry. Their ragged green shirts and jungle hats were now black with the moisture of their sweat. A few mosquitos hovered around the back of each man but they no longer felt the regular little stings as tiny tubes pierced their skin in search of blood.

It was now six weeks since they had commenced the operation. They had moved into this new area eight days ago, after their last resupply. Their packs were lighter now, and so were the men; angular, bony joints visible through their sweat-stained uniforms. The anticipation of an early result had waned as the weeks had passed. Reports from other Troops indicated no better luck. They had settled into a routine, always searching, never relaxing, never making a noise; every possibility checked out beyond any doubt. But nothing – until yesterday.

Yesterday they had found sign, fresh sign. They had been checking out an abandoned Temiar ladang. It was clear that the CT had collected food growing in the ladang and had prepared and eaten a meal while they were there. The men had followed the sign for the rest of the day, right up until it was too dark to go any further. First thing this morning they were on the trail again. Whenever they came to a stream the CT would move up or down the watercourse, sometimes for a considerable distance before moving out to continue their march.

But time and again their lead scout had picked up the sign and here they were now, still on the CT's tracks. They sensed, rather than knew, they were getting close. The men were tense, every sense alert. Had the CT also sensed they were being trailed? Were they even now lying in ambush? The hunted waiting for the hunters?

Unexpectedly, they heard the CT before they saw them. Chopping! Someone was chopping kindling for a fire. The patrol quietly removed their packs and left them with a sentry. As they advanced in the direction of the sounds, they came upon bamboo. The CT were making their camp in the bamboo for the protection it offered. The men took care not to make a noise. Any pressure on a bamboo and it would crack like a rifle shot.

They could now smell the smoke from the CT's fire. The Troop Commander silently signalled his support fire group to a position at right angles to his line of advance. The assault group slowly fanned out on either side of him. As they advanced, as quietly as they could, he saw a flicker of a fire, then uniformed CTs working unconcerned, unaware of the patrol's presence. They moved closer. Then something gave them away and the CT started shooting. The assault group charged.

To an observer it may have seemed chaotic, disorganized, but the attack drill they had practised so often, worked perfectly. Four CT lay dead. A fifth, wounded, got away through the bamboo and could not be located in the oncoming darkness. Best of all, none of the Troop had been hit.

In fact the New Zealand Squadron were to eliminate 26 of the enemy (15 killed) in exchange for only two of their own casualties before their return home. A Malaysian tour to be proud of in anyone's language.

So, the regimental strength when Newell took over as the RHQ Major, was in the order of 550 officers and men. 'A', 'B', 'D' and the NZ Squadrons had been further bolstered by the advent, in late 1955, of a Squadron of the Parachute Regiment under the command of Major Dudley Coventry (later to move to join 'C' Squadron back in Rhodesia). It is generally accepted by the Malayan veterans that the soldiers of the Parachute Regiment were not particularly successful in Malaya, but, equally, it is admitted, that one of the main reasons for this was not the individual but the fact that they were sent to the Jungle Training School which existed for the purpose of training the infantry. It is a fact that when the Parachute Regiment squadron was disbanded, the SAS benefited from many first class men who opted to join them rather than return to Aldershot.

Newell's struggles with bureaucracy and prejudice were legion. Suffice to say that the team working in the United Kingdom – Dempsey, Newell, Hart, Franks, Burt and Lapraik – through selfless devotion and not a little personal expense were to see the Regiment through some dark years when, to quote Newell: 'disbandment was only one cock-up away'. Perhaps the closest call was the threat of incorporation into the Parachute Brigade. This made sense only to those who were blind to the philosophies, character and potential of an SAS Force based on small patrol work. Newell's work in lifting the blinkers was sterling indeed and on occasions his language was harsh as an extract from a letter to Colonel Lapraik on 22 March, 1956, shows:

Dear Colonel,

I am enclosing a draft of a letter to L/AW . . . I had originally intended taking next week as leave, but as I think it is rather important that we should make our views known as soon as possible, I shall be in the office on Monday. If you could find time over the weekend to deal with the draft and let me have it in the Monday morning post, I will get the finished article in that day.

I think the time has come when we should get the General briefed on the situation in general as we see it and, although I can keep him informed of what is likely to happen, he will, quite naturally pay more attention to the views of yourself, Colonel Brian [Franks] and Colonel George [Lea]. I would like, therefore, to suggest that all three of you tackle him simultaneously. The major danger, as I see it, to the future of the SAS is that it may not be sufficiently recognized at CIGS level that small party operations require a very definite type of man and that great care must be taken in the selection and training. There is undoubtedly a tendency in many quarters to think that the role could be carried out by the Parachute Regiment by merely detailing them to the task. This has already failed in Malaya where the Parachute Regiment Squadron of 22nd, after a year with the Regiment, is still not able to send out 3-man patrols without an officer, or Senior NCO. A large proportion of the men are quite capable of doing so with proper training but normal infantry training is not designed to produce men to act as individuals.

Being a complete sub-unit, the Para Squadron has not learnt this lesson. We are about to hammer home this point on behalf of 22 SAS but it will have to be done by my working from the bottom upwards. If you can get the General to take an active part in the campaign as a whole we are much more likely to achieve success.

Should it be finally decided that there is no requirement for a Para. Division in a global war, it may well be decided to convert some of the Regiment to an SAS role. Well and good, if it is done in the light of our experience and on our lines but fatal to ultimate success if their selection, training methods and, above all, 'man management' remain those of the infantry.

Dare Newell

Assistance from Commanding Officers of the Regiment in Malaya was limited of necessity. They were required on the ground and it was to Newell that fell the lot of co-ordinating their support for a cause which was often distant to their immediate problems. Of course, the far-sighted individuals such as Lea and Woodhouse were prominent in the 'Whitehall Campaign', but much of the credit has to go to Newell who shouldered the burden of one thousand and one minute, often boring details which are the mortar to building any structure which is to last. Newell was, in fact, destined to become Regimental Adjutant to the SAS and serve loyally in that position until his retirement.

15

THE END OF THE BEGINNING

The improvements were enormous. The infantry training methods became more sophisticated and effective and Templer's insistence on the jungle fringe and plantation ambushes and working to good intelligence had proved itself. This was reflected in the growing number of kills. Within the line battalions, company-sized bases started to become a feature of life. The base was a mini-fort which often included a troop of armoured cars and a detachment of 25 pounder howitzers as part of the garrison. The company would have its area to guard and patrol, and there it was likely to stay, frequently for the duration of the tour. This meant that soldiers gained from local knowledge of the neighbours and the terrain and the kill rate improved even more.

Even in the best of circumstances continuity was impossible to achieve. The bulk of the private soldiers in a battalion were conscripts, and once their time was up they were sent home; this meant that there was a constant trickle of soldiers in and out of platoons and sections, and it did not make for a settled existence. In one particular battalion during one three-year tour 73 officers and 1646 soldiers circulated through the companies, the equivalent of two complete battalions.

Then, of course, there was the contribution made by the Royal Air Force which in the early stages seemed to wage its own war against the CT with little reference to the needs of the ground forces. The exception were the air supply sorties flown by the RAF Valetta and the smaller Pioneers. The Valettas parachuted supplies into the jungle often in very turbulent weather conditions. Indeed, in 1951–52 the RAF air crew suffered more casualties than the infantry. The Pioneers were invaluable as

STOL transports. During the period of the Emergency the Air Force deployed eighteen different types of aircraft in twenty subsidiary roles. The helicopter first made an appearance in the early fifties and proved an invaluable taxi, especially in later years of the campaign, lifting patrols deep into and out of the jungle. As we have seen, helicopters added a new dimension to the jungle war, but they were not all flown by the RAF. The Fleet Air Arm's Squadron No. 848 was equipped with 10 Sikorsky Whirlwinds and began to operate in Malaya in 1952. This squadron lifted 14,000 troops in the first year of operations.

The RAF also used Sunderland Flying Boats and the Royal Navy deployed numerous coastal patrols to sanitize the Malayan Peninsula and keep reinforcements and supplies from reaching the CTs. The newly independent Indonesians despatched some Sumatrans and some supplies in support of the CT effort; these were easily infiltrated across the crowded waters at night.

Templer had 26 battalions of infantry and two armoured car regiments at his disposal. He reformed the 17th Gurkha Division at Seremban in the south. In this, the heaviest concentration of troops, the Division deployed four full-strength brigades as follows:

* 26th and 99th Brigades in Johore
* 48th Brigade in Pahang
* 63rd Brigade in Negri Sembilan

The 18th British Infantry Brigade in the centre of the peninsula covered Selangor, Pahang and Perak. Ipoh was the divisional headquarters for the 6 Malay, 1 Gurkha and 4 East African battalions. The latter, 1st (Nyasa) and 3rd (Kenya) Battalions, King's African Rifles and 1st Rhodesian Rifles, were normally only as good as their heavy complement of white NCOs and junior officers. The Fijians, by contrast, were splendid jungle troops. Their logistic arrangements were a shambles and their weapons a disgrace, but these exuberant troops had an irrepressible fighting spirit. When they ambushed they would pursue the CT, run him to the ground and club him to death with a rifle which earlier had jammed.

General Sir Geoffrey Bourne followed Templer to become the

Director of Operations and introduced reforms of his own. His insistence that the line battalions should remain responsible for a particular stretch of country paid dividends as soldiers got to know their 'patch'. He also built upon the work of his predecessors in confirming the supremacy of Special Branch in the field of gathering and analysing intelligence and dictating where military operations should be concentrated. When such forces were working in harmony, the effect could be devastating.

An early success came with Evan Davies, nicknamed 'The Bishop' when in Winston Churchill's bodyguard because of his paunch, very much a case of the pot calling the kettle black. In 1956, Davies (his brother Rupert later made a name for himself as the actor playing the role in Maigret) was a senior officer in the Malayan Special Branch. Despite his girth (the Chinese called him 'Fai Chi' – The Fat One) Davies was an extremely effective operator. He was given the task of tracking down a CT leader called Goh Peng Tun, a particularly nasty individual who operated in Johore.

Davies infiltrated a local CT unit by subverting the platoon commander named the 'Raven'. The 'Raven' was persuaded to lead his unit into an ambush in which all his men were killed; they were replaced by members of the Special Branch, some of whom, of course, were turned terrorists themselves. Davies sent them back into the jungle to track down Goh Peng Tun. In an operation which became a classic of its type the SB undercover team worked closely with the local British infantry battalion, in this instance the South Wales Borderers, as they quartered the jungle.

Eventually the camp of Goh Peng Tun was located on an island surrounded by mangrove swamp and deep, near-impenetrable jungle. There was no way the position could be stormed by conventional infantry assault. The only option was to use air power. Even though air co-operation had improved considerably, the bombers still had to circle a likely target to ensure they were in the right place and to avoid civilian casualties. These were laudable tactics except that they invariably gave the game away and the CTs were able to scuttle off, leaving a deserted camp to the bombers.

On this occasion the infantry sited a radar beacon on a hill some

5,000 yards from the camp. The attack was launched at night with Australian Lincolns directed along the beam and straight onto the target area, a rectangle 700 yards by 400 yards onto which, and from a height of 5,000 feet, they dropped 90,000 lbs of bombs. The Lincolns were followed by RAF Canberras which strafed the target area with rockets and more bombs.

At first light Lieutenant-Colonel Meirs personally led a company from his battalion of the South Wales Borderers onto the position. The undergrowth was so dense that he had to use his bugler to relay instructions to the platoons. The camp was utterly devastated. There were fourteen bodies recovered including Goh Peng Tun.

The Air Force loudly proclaimed their success which they saw as a vindication of pinpoint bombing strategy as a vital part of the arsenal of counter-terrorism. The irony was that the CTs had spotted the beacon being established and had quickly moved camp. The Australians bombed off the beam but by some fluke hit the new camp fair and square. This was not discovered until some time later when one of the surviving CTs surrendered and revealed all, much to the embarrassment of the Air Staff.

The Briggs Plan, with Templer's modifications, had eventually proved itself, but as the country moved towards independence, (Malaya became independent, within the Commonwealth, on 31 August, 1957) it was becoming essential for the Security Forces to further reduce the terrorist threat. The British were aware of the precedent set by the French in Indo-China where a continuous stalemate was eventually to prove so politically counter-productive that the Government risked all on a military showdown at Dien Bien Phu, and with tragic consequences.

The Malayan Emergency could not be allowed to stagnate, so Bourne proposed a three-phase joint operation to reduce the CT menace.

The now highly respected and very professional SAS were deployed along the spinal mountain range to prise out the CTs from their jungle lairs and win over the aborigine tribes. In the meantime the army and the police in the field would be used to dominate known terrorist routes along the edges of the jungle and through the rubber plantations. The main purpose was to make the soldiers as familiar to the area and its people as the local terrorists. Finally the police and local civil authorities assumed greater responsibility for food control and distribution.

A good example of the food denial and jungle domination scheme was in the still troublesome state of Pahang. Called 'Operation Apollo', it was based upon the SAS moving deep into the jungle while Bourne deployed the Gurkhas and the King's African Rifles to interdict the main north-south lines of communication used by the Min Yuen to carry despatches and deliver food. He also beefed up the units patrolling the jungle fringe. At the same time rationing and movement restrictions were increased throughout the state and the amount of food and medicines which were allowed to be sold openly was further reduced. These two measures immediately hampered the effectiveness of the Min Yuen. Eventually the CTs, starved and abandoned by the aborigines and harried by the SAS, moved into the jungle fringes where they were caught by the ever-active and vigilant patrols. The Min Yuen lost heart, many turned informer and within a period of six months fifty dumps of food, clothing, etc., were also discovered.

It has to be recognized that, even though the skills improved, locating and destroying a jungle lair of hard-core CTs remained a difficult and dangerous task. Despite claims to the contrary by the air forces, these camps were very hard to pinpoint from the air and next to impossible to take by surprise from an approach march by men in strong numbers. In the case of the larger and more important camps, there were CT pickets set well out to warn of the approach of the Security Forces, and escape routes, often booby-trapped, were well-planned with all such contingencies rehearsed frequently.

For the line battalions this was especially pertinent, operating as they did in platoon or company strength. In deep undergrowth, even if the pickets could be silenced without giving the game away, the task of surrounding a camp and deploying a 'cut-off' or cordon sufficiently close to prevent the CTs making good their escape and yet disciplined enough not to fire on assault troops as they pursued the enemy, was fraught with risk. Field commanders constantly lived with the fear of 'blue-on-blue' casualties.

How then did the SAS cope with this scenario? For a start the individuals within the Regiment by this time were the equal of the CT in jungle craft. Operating in small numbers, they were able to move quickly and quietly through the jungle. Their navigation was precise, but, above all, they had developed the animal instincts which come from living close to nature and adopting the principles of both hunter and hunted. The use of such luxuries as soap and scented toothpaste were confined to the base camp area. Uniforms were worn until they dropped off. There was no alien smell to give away their presence. Their patience in ambush was unrivalled as was their ability to ignore the hundred and one minor irritations such as bees, ants, leeches, mosquitos and the like which swarmed over the body of a soldier lying in wait in the undergrowth. In short, they were at home in the environment.

Some notable members of the Regiment developed their tracking skills far in excess of what would normally be considered possible for a 'civilized' man. They knew that the CT, when making his camp, had certain requirements. He needed camouflage, a good defensive site or one which was difficult to approach, and access to food and water. Though it would appear to be a contradiction in terms, there are large areas of the jungle where water can be a problem, particularly at higher levels. The CTs were past masters at disguising their watering points. One technique was to use the trickle of water from a very small tributary and, by carefully laying apparently naturally pieces of dead bamboo, bark, or even sturdy leaves, pipe the water across a distance of many yards to a point close to a camp. To the untutored eye these bits and pieces of wood and bark were accidents of nature, but not to the experienced jungle soldier.

Maps were constantly improving as the quality and quantity of air photography got better. One spin-off of this was that it became possible to apply the CT's requirements to the map and, by careful study, predict those areas which were likely to conceal the enemy and avoid those which were probably non-starters. The standard of navigation across the board of all ranks in the SAS had become very high indeed. If people like Woodhouse or Ross (see later comments) were to ask a member of the patrol where they thought they were, it would be no use the hapless trooper putting his finger on the map and saying, 'There'. He would immediately have a small twig or pointed leaf thrust into his hand and be told to be precise, the point being that the end of a man's finger covers five or six hundred yards on a map.

The four factors dominant in a troop's success ratio were jungle craft, patience, the ability to get into the CT's mind, and luck. We have discussed jungle craft already. An enormous amount of patience was required to move into an area and search it, often grid square by grid square; to sit for endless hours with aborigines, trying to cut through their interminable chatter in the hope of picking up information which may be casually dropped into the conversation; the slow, difficult business of following a track laid by terrorists skilled in anti-tracking measures; losing the spoor and then the agonizing procedure of circling ever outwards to pick up the sign again.

The ability to get into the mind of the CT was not given to everyone. Perhaps one of the greatest exponents of this art in the SAS of the Malayan days was Bill 'Lofty' Ross who was later to become Regimental Sergeant Major of 22 SAS. This six-feet-six-inch-tall, athletic product of the Green Howards became something of a legend in his time. He was often to be seen in the base camp or overnight basha site, sitting completely motionless in the attitude of Rodin's 'Thinker', focusing all of his attention on the map on his knees. He was, during those moments, to all intents and purposes a CT commander thinking through all the possibilities of movement through Ross's own area; choosing his camp sites and deciding which of the aborigine villages or ladangs he was going to visit next.

These mental exercises worked for Ross. He had remarkable successes in tracking down CT camps and generally making those within his area feel very vulnerable through forcing them to be constantly on the move. Ross was awarded the Military Medal in 1957 and, reading between the lines of the citation, it is possible to get a measure of his effectiveness:

For gallant leadership and devotion to duty as a Troop Commander during two years of jungle warfare. Due to his skill and determination the terrorist system of communication in the Hutan Melingtang area was destroyed.

Everyone needs luck. The secret is, however, to recognize this fickle factor and manage it to advantage. It is often hard to distinguish between luck and skill in jungle operations. Turnbull, in the incident described earlier, was undoubtedly lucky to be in the right place at the right time; it was certainly not luck, however, which made him spot the target, make an instant decision and go for the kill. That was Turnbull's professionalism. He was also awarded the Military Medal for his outstanding performance over a period of four year's jungle patrolling.

Though the SAS would have shrugged it off, there was another factor – courage. In the jungle environment where visibility was so restricted, it was usually not possible to get a clear view of the enemy. When Turnbull attacked the CT camp there was no way of knowing how many terrorists were in occupation or nearby. To follow up after a head-on contact was not the most comfortable business in the world; the jungle lends itself very well to the pursued using the tactics of the African buffalo and setting a hasty ambush to turn the tables on the pursuer. Undoubtedly the selection course process, good training and the confidence of the SAS soldier in his own abilities and those of his comrades were significant factors, but it would be wrong to ignore courage as a key element to success on many occasions.

As the number of active CTs dwindled it became harder and harder to seek them out, though balanced against this was the fact that the SAS continued to get better and better in all respects. The esprit de corps so necessary to permanence was growing; inter-squadron rivalry was intense, but above all a sense of belonging began to pervade the Regiment. Individuals were enthusiastically resisting the rule of returning to their own units after two tours; fortunately many of them were successful. Back in the rear echelons Newell's team was working wonders in refining the selection course procedures, smoothing out the administration and putting the case forward for the retention of the SAS in the British Army orbat.

16

TOWARDS A CONCLUSION

When Lieutenant-Colonel George Lea took over 22 SAS Regiment in 1955 he inherited a far better prospect than any Commanding Officer before him. The soldiers were much more disciplined and relatively well behaved when out of the jungle; they had a sense of identity and a fierce pride was taking hold. Lea's concern, after analysis and discussion with his Squadron Commanders and Senior NCOs, was that perhaps there was still room for improvement in battle discipline and operating procedures and it was in this area that he focused his main attention.

Obviously he was dependent on his Squadron Commanders to weed out those who were still reckoned to be unsuitable, but this was becoming very much the exception rather than the rule as the effects of the selection courses being run in the UK were showing up. Over the next two years experienced officers and Senior NCOs were to rotate through courses as instructors. They knew exactly what they were looking for and RTUs were becoming fewer and fewer. There were still the cases of officers and soldiers who appeared to be first class on the course only to find that the business of jungle operations showed up some deficiency unde-tected until then. If anything the process was harder on the officers than the rank and file because, if they were not right, then nothing else would be. The system tended to err on the side of severity and it is probable that some individuals were obliged to leave who would have made the grade given a little time.

During the same period squadrons were encouraged to complete the laborious process of writing down their Standard Operating Procedures. This had a threefold benefit; it was possible for newcomers to the scene to read up on what was expected of them; it encouraged a cross-fertilization of ideas between squadrons and it allowed up-to-date tactics to be taught on the Selection Course. There was also the fact that if men were complying with a standard set of instructions under a given set of circumstances then the commander always knew what a troop, patrol or individual would be doing which was a great help if there was an emergency and communications were lost. As Calvert would have said, 'They are in my mind'.

If this sort of procedure is conducted in tandem with paper exercises and if that process is also subjected to the self-criticism and free-thought sessions which were encouraged then everyone had a voice and in this way ideas were stimulated in to how to improve and develop the Regiment's efficiency. 'Shop' talk is normally discouraged in many military canteens and messes but in the SAS it was and is an important facet of soldiering.

The SAS tactics in Malaya, with the exception of the 'hearts and minds' part of the campaign, were always offensive and this undoubtedly paid dividends. The enemy was badly equipped and not very well trained in the military sense, certainly not as well trained as the Security Forces, but he was a master of fieldcraft in the jungle and therefore something not to be taken too lightly. It was the regimental dictum that, if faced by the enemy, the force, no matter how small, would attack. This was a totally justified approach as the enemy almost always broke off the fight and by attacking there was always the chance of killing or wounding one of them. It was also very unsettling for the CT to know without doubt that, should he run into an SAS patrol, he would be met with aggression.

Time and again during the later years of the 1950s, the SAS was sent back to areas they knew well to flush out the last remnants of CTs. One such operation which combined all the skills the Regiment had learned was the hunt for Ah Hoi in the swamps of Telok Anson.

The Telok Anson operational area was typical of those permanent mangrove swamps to be found along the west coast of the peninsula. At the point in question the area of tactical interest lay some thirty miles or so to the north-west of Kuala Lumpur dominated by the delta of the Sungeis Selangor and Tengi. The ground, if it could be called that, was a morass of mud under brown water to a depth in places of five feet. Snakes were abundant as were leeches (not the normal leeches but the large, painful 'half-pinters') and mosquitos. Navigation was difficult as the smaller streams marked on the maps tended to just disappear and the larger rivers were not well defined, becoming almost lagoon-like in some places; compass bearings were the order of the day. Obviously soldiers suffer from being in water for the best part of each day and the only way to stay dry at night was to use a hammock or, if staying in an area for more than one night, to construct either a floating platform or a solid bed wedged into the large roots of the mangroves.

Intelligence sources had determined that two groups of CTs were still in hiding in the area embraced by Kuala Selangor and Kuala Tengi under command of Ah Hoi. This infamous terrorist was nicknamed the 'Baby Killer' after he had murdered the Malay wife of a suspected informer. The fact that she was pregnant did not deter Ah Hoi from hacking her to death in front of a selected group of villagers from her home. It is not germane to the operation but, not surprisingly, the CTs in that area lost all the support they had once enjoyed. 'D' Squadron was chosen for the task of rooting out Ah Hoi.

Major Harry Thompson, MC, who commanded 'D' Squadron, decided on a parachute entry for reasons of secrecy. It was an unlucky choice, as one of his soldiers, Trooper Mulcahy, had the misfortune to crash straight through the trees when his canopy collapsed. He fell across one of the mangrove roots and his back was broken and, of course, an immediate 'casevac' was required. This was effected by cutting an LZ for the helicopter to hover close enough to the swamp for Mulcahy to be eased aboard. It was a remarkable piece of flying and to the credit of the SAS medics and the pilot, Mulcahy made a full recovery but surprise in that immediate area was lost.

Operation Thrust began in February, 1958, and Captain Peter de la Billière's troop was tasked with making a search along the main line of the Sungei Tengi and, though they found many signs of hastily abandoned camps; there was no contact with the CTs, who appeared to be following the course of the river inland. This bore out the suspicion that the helicopter activity had been heard.

In conjunction with de la Billière's movement, Sergeant 'Bosun' Sandilands was moving on a bearing to intercept the CTs, though he did not know it at the time.

Sandilands had decided on a change of tactics and was moving mainly during the hours of darkness, hoping to pick up the smells or noise from a relaxed CT camp. He had also decided that the increased jungle noises at night gave him better cover for his own movement, and the lower canopy of the mangrove trees let him take advantage of a good moon.

Setting out earlier one day in order to cross a wide expanse of water prior to darkness, Sandilands saw movement sixty or seventy yards away across the open area. Settling into the roots of the trees, the patrol observed and calculated that there were two CTs also sitting on mangrove roots. The 'Bosun' had a problem; given that the CTs were under partial cover, the range was too great for a certain kill and how could they close the distance without being seen? He resolved his dilemma by easing a log from the tangled roots and, with one of his troops, slipped into the water and began to cross, using the log to shield them. They closed the range as much as they dared and opened fire from about fifty yards. One CT fell dead and the other disappeared into the gloom. They stayed in position that night and the next day they were able to follow a fresh track for a number of miles to a further newly abandoned camp.

There was now sufficient evidence to conclude that Ah Hoi was probably still in the area and Thompson's troops began to manoeuvre to close the inland river line. The whole of the coastal area was cordoned off by other Security Forces and, since security was no longer a problem, helicopter activity was deliberately increased in an effort to force the terrorists to move precipitately. The SAS took full advantage of the helicopter movement to take regular resupplies of fresh clothing and rations to ease the rucksack loads in that difficult terrain.

A few days later Ah Niet, Ah Hoi's courier, gave herself up to the Security Forces and delivered a message that Ah Hoi would be prepared to surrender on payment of a large sum of money and amnesty for his men. This was, of course, refused and she was sent back to her master with the news that Ah Hoi was surrounded and would be hunted to death. Less than twenty-four hours later Ah Hoi did indeed give himself up and he was followed a few days after by the remnants of the second gang.

The SAS group had remained in the swamp for twenty-two days and conditions had taken their toll in the myriad of ulcers and other infected sores which marked the bodies of every soldier. These soon healed up with a few days exposure to the sun and certainly did not detract from the feeling of euphoria which comes from the knowledge that a difficult job has been done well. The outcome showed that the SAS was still not stereotyped in its tactics; Sandilands had taken a deliberate decision to move by night which had paid off and it is also a tribute to the trackers that they could follow a track in swamp for five miles or so to locate the last of the camps.

'Bosun' Sandiland's part in the operation was just the prompt needed for him to be recommended for the Military Medal. Again the wording of the citation leaves much to the imagination:

> For his example, courage and tactical skill when leading jungle patrols over a period of twelve months spent on anti-terrorist operations. He was personally responsible for the elimination of several of the enemy.

By the end of 1958 and now under the command of Lieutenant-Colonel Tony Deane-Drummond, DSO, MC, the writing was on the wall for the SAS's future in Malaya. The figures stated at the time were that 6,400 terrorists had been killed with a further 3,000 captured or surrendered and their back was well and truly broken. It may seem that the total number of kills by the SAS (108) was small when compared to some of the outstanding British infantry battalions who rotated through the theatre but there are a number of things to take into consideration here. Calvert once put it succinctly on a briefing to 'A' and 'B' Squadrons:

> Be under no illusions about this business. We in this unit are not going to win the war. All that we can do is to play a particular part in it for which other Army units are neither trained nor suited.

Without a shadow of a doubt the SAS did play a major part in that war; in their sterling work with the aborigines; in their collection of intelligence; in their harassment of CT lines of communication; in their total disruption of CT 'safe' areas and the fact that many of their 'kills' in those safe areas were of high grade CTs; it was the loss of leaders which caused the final crumbling of communist resistance.

Above all they had proved their worth. In the War Office the SAS was being regularly mentioned, as different tasks for the British Army were projected. 'What about the SAS?' was now not an uncommon question and nobody was responding with the other question which would have been asked a few years earlier, 'What is the SAS?'

Perhaps the real finale of this first period of consolidation of the SAS was the remarkable transition from jungle to mountain and desert that occurred in November, 1958. At the end of October 'D' Squadron was again operating in the area of the Belum Valley close to the Thai border when they received the instruction to wrap up the operation. Within forty-eight hours they were back in Kuala Lumpur expecting to be briefed to go off to round up a few CTs in some other area. Far from it: they were to move to Oman in the Middle East. Many soldiers had never even heard of the country.

In less than a month 'D' Squadron were in pitched battle on the peaks and ridges of the 8,000-foot Jebel Akhdar fighting an aggressive, well-armed and numerically superior enemy. From sleeping in underpants and shrouded in flimsy parachute nylon they were now swathed in heavy sleeping bags and found themselves on occasions with frozen water in the mornings, whilst during the day there was little respite from a searing sun. Two months later they were joined by 'A' Squadron who repeated the speed of transition from jungle to mountain/desert. Working in conjunction with the armoured cars of the Life Guards and local Arab units, an enemy force of several hundreds of men was routed, with some sixty or so killed. The SAS losses numbered three killed. This spectacular victory was marked by the award of a DSO, four MCs, a DCM and an MM. How was this possible?

In the first place there was the idea from Calvert which seized the imagination of the many and in the second place there was the inspired leadership and farsightedness of officers like Sloane, Brooke, Lea and Woodhouse. In the 'battle at the rear' there was the drive of Dempsey, Hart, Franks, Lapraik and Newell. All these were instrumental in forcing the concept through against heavy odds and ensuring the survival, this time, of what Stirling had started so long ago.

But, on the base line, were the hundreds of soldiers who had answered the call for action. The men became totally dedicated to the SAS form of soldiering and approached it with amazing enthusiasm which refused to accept defeat. They became the foundation stones of the later regimental successes in the Middle East and Borneo. Many were to stay with the SAS for twenty years or more, many were commissioned and many well decorated. Of the officers some were to go on to command the Regiment with distinction and at least three reached the rank of General. ·

John Woodhouse certainly was to end his career on a high note in that it was he who was in command of 22 SAS when it was committed to operations during the Borneo Confrontation. That he himself enjoyed it is beyond dispute, but more to the point is that the Regiment could not have had a more experienced CO at that time. Most of the Troop Sergeants were Malaya veterans and the majority of the rank and file had benefited from at least one, two or three month post-Emergency training operations in Malaya. In short, very few were completely new to the jungle. At the time of the first deployment to Borneo in January, 1963, the Regiment was down to two-squadron strength.

The topography of Borneo is very similar to that of Malaya, but for the SAS most of the work was to be conducted along the central mountainous spine and main river lines. The major difference was the enemy. In Malaya the Security Forces were pitted only against the CT as an irregular guerrilla and, while there was an enormous (24,000) Communist element in the CCO (Chinese Communist Organization) in the urban areas they never entered battle with the exception of a few minor skirmishes in the early days. The real threat came from the Indonesian regular troops. Well trained, well equipped and well desciplined many of the officers and SNCOs had been trained at the Jungle Warfare School in Malaya by the British and they had certainly had

American advisors in the past. Forward troops had artillery and medium mortars at their disposal as well as rocket launchers and a variety of anti-personnel mines.

The SAS was committed sensibly in an intelligence role at the beginning of the war and the Malayan experience of 'hearts and minds' operations stood them in good stead. The patrols got on enormously well with the diverse tribes along the border, helped by a much greater degree of language knowledge. Much the same tactics were used as in Malaya in that a troop would be given its area and be expected to remain within it for a lengthy period getting to know all the natives; preparing LZs against contingencies, but above all setting up its own local intelligence network using the tribesmen. One essential difference was the aggression factor. During most of the conflict it was the order of the day for SAS patrols to 'shoot and scoot' if they made contact with the enemy. The task was to avoid them, observe them and report. The SAS became the 'eyes and ears' along a 900 mile front.

From such beginnings their task grew and the Regiment was given the authority to expand its manpower base. 'B' Squadron was reborn and latterly there was a further increase in the form of 'G' Squadron, drawn from the Brigade of Guards and Household Cavalry. If there were no sweeping changes in initial tactics then there certainly was in equipment. Gone were the days when it took a couple of aboriginal porters to carry the troop's wireless and batteries. The advent of the transistor led to highly portable, long range radios and communications of which full advantage was taken. Although regular resupplies of fresh rations were still part of jungle life, the day to day dehydrated rations were a great improvement in terms both of weight and calorie content to the rudimentary food carried in Malaya. Strangely, the British Army adopted Napoleon's dictum that, 'An army marches on its stomach', and did nothing about the dreaded canvas and rubber jungle boot. The answer, to the SAS, was simple, throw it away and wear ordinary boots.

Gradually, and much to the relief of the Regiment, there was a committal to more daring and more offensive operations as cross-border forays were authorised. At the start these were confined to close reconnaissance on enemy lines of communications and camps but later they were expanded into a role where the SAS patrols would guide companies of Gurkhas into a variety of targets. Towards the end the Regiment was allowed to conduct a number of aggressive operations in squadron strength all of which were successfully executed thus proving a further aspect of SAS flexibility, and ability to operate as tactical fighting troops if necessary.

All of this had become possible because of those few farsighted soldiers in the early fifties whose ideas were furthered and improved upon by the dedicated soldiers who followed them into the SAS. They set the right players on the stage for the wars in Oman and Borneo and thus firmly cemented the SAS into its place in the British Army orbat for all time.

More than this, perhaps the SAS 'message' is now truly international. Most armies of today have a Special Force of some sort or another apart from the well-known and well-proven SAS Regiments of Australia and New Zealand, the highly effective force in Rhodesia (now disbanded) and the Delta Force of the USA. The need for such forces is internationally recognized but 22 SAS Regiment remains still in 'pole' position because it steadfastly refuses to accept that it has reached the highest standards possible.

Appendix 1

OPERATIONS CONDUCTED BY
MALAYAN SCOUTS & SAS REGT

Initial Operation	Oct 50
Prosaic	Apr 51
Sunset	Apr–Jul 51
Warbler	Jun–Oct 51
Helsby	Feb–Mar 52
Hive	Sep–Oct 52
Demon	Sep–Nov 52
Lambley	Aug–Nov 52
Grease	Mar 52
League	Apr–May 52
Churchman	Oct 52–Jan 53
Copley	Oct 52
Hammer	Dec 52–Jan 53
Eagle	Jan 53
Hardcastle	Feb–Apr 53
Pageant	Apr–Jun 53
Commodore	May 53
Matador	Jun 53
Flame	Jun–Oct 53
Mustang	Jul–Aug 53
Biter	Jul–Oct 53
Boxer	Sep 53
Galway	Oct 53–Jun 54
Valiant	Oct–Nov 53
Sword	Jan 54
Termite	Jul–Nov 54
Axe	Oct–Nov 54

Hilt	Oct 54–Jan 55
Asp	Dec 54–Mar 55
Beehive	Apr 55
Unity	May 55
Shark	Jun–Aug 55
Subsidiary Op (South Jahore)	Oct–Nov 55
Gabes, South	Nov–Jun 57
Latimer, North	Jan–Feb 56
Corner Key	May 56
Gabes, North	May 56–Dec 57
Claud	Jul–Aug 56
Latimer, South	Sep 56–Nov 57
Cobble Shoe/Lagoon	Nov 56
Chieftain	May 57–Aug 58
Parchment	Jul–Aug 57
Goblet	Dec 57–Aug 58
Hippo	Dec 57–Jan 58
Dazzle	Dec 57–Jan 58
Ladder	Jan–Feb 58
Thrust	Jan–Feb 58
Ginger	Mar–Aug 58
Juno	May–Jun 58
Brooklyn	Aug–Oct 58
Boulder	Aug 58–Feb 59
Jumlah	Sep–Oct 58
George	Undated
Churchill	Undated
Medal	Ongoing (Forts)

Appendix 2

1953

2/Lt	C. Cherrington	MID★
L/Cpl	D. R. P. Coates	MID
Sgt	H. S. Davidson	MID
WO II	R. G. Hannaway	MID
Tpr	H. Kerry	MID
S/Sgt	D. F. Langston	MID
L/Cpl	J. McDonald	C-in-C's Cert.★★
Maj	C. L. D. Newell (MBE)	MID
Sgt	S. Pownall	C-in-C's Cert.
WO II	L. R. Pullen	MBE
Tpr	A. Rowe	MID
Capt	G. P. Smith	MID
Capt	P. A. Winter	MID
Capt	J. P. Williams (MC)	MID

1954

Capt	D. R. Boyne	MBE
Sgt	D. Cross	MID
L/Cpl	H. Johnson	MID
Cpl	O. R. Levet	MID
Cpl	P. McWilliams	MID
Sgt	W. H. Ross	MID
Maj	J. R. Salmon (MC, TD)	MID
Gnr	J. H. Stones	MID

1955

Sgt	R. G. Ball	MID
Sgt	H. W. Baxter	MID
L/Cpl	S. E. Dickson	C-in-C's Cert.
Sgt	J. Ferguson	C-in-C's Cert.
L/Cpl	F. Hague	MID
S/Sgt	T. W. James	MID
Sgt	O. R. Levet	BEM
Sgt	G. Merritt	MID
Cpl	D. McFarland	MID
Sgt	J. Morrison	MID
Cpl	J. H. Morgan	MID
L/Cpl	W. Mundell	MID
Capt	P. S. Rich	MID
Sgt	J. Saul	BEM
Sgt	L. Smith	MID
Tpr	D. Watkins	MID

1956

Sgt	H. W. Baxter	BEM
Lt	I. H. Burrows	MC
Sgt	G. Butler	C-in-C's Cert.
Maj.	E. W. Coventry	MID
Tpr	D. Duggan	C-in-C's Cert
Capt	D. F. D. Hobbs	MID
Pte	Tuan Anak Kanyan	MID
Lt. Col	G. H. Lea (MBE)	MID
Cpl	J. M. Morgan	C-in-C's Cert.
WO I	N. Reed	MID
Sgt	R. Turnbull	MM
Maj	J. M. Woodhouse	MBE

1957

Capt	G. N. M. Boswell	MID
Lt	I. H. Burrows	NSCGM★★★
Sgt	J. Dearden	MID

WO II	S.E.L. Doyle	MID
L/Cpl	R. S. Hurle	NSDCM★★★★
Lt. Col	G. H. Lea (MBE)	DSO
Lt	J. H. Mace	MID
Maj	C. H. Mercer	MBE
Capt	C. J. Moore	MID
Tpr	G. G. Otene	NSDCM
Maj	F. Rennie	MID
Maj	F. Rennie	MC
WO II	W. H. Ross	MM
Maj	H. A. I. Thompson	MID
Tpr	Watene	BEM
L/Cpl	R. P. Withers	NSDCM
Lt	E. W. Yandall	NSCGM

1958

Capt	P. E. de la Billière	MID
Capt	I. R. Cartwright	MID
Cpl	R. Copeman	MM
Dvr	C. Coutts	C-in-C's Cert.
Cpl	W. T. Hales	MID
Capt	T. P. Hardy	MID
WO II	T. W. James	BEM
Maj	A. A. Julius	MID
L/Cpl	J. Ladner	MM
Maj	P. L. Rawl	MID
Cpl	J. G. Ritchie	MID
Sgt	H. Sandilands	MM
Cpl	D. Swindells	MM
Maj	H. A. I. Thompson	MC
Capt	R. M. B. Walker	MID
Maj	J. P. B. C. Watts	MID

★ Mentioned in Despatches
★★ Commander-in-Chief's Certificate
★★★ Negri Sembilan Conspicuous Gallantry Medal
★★★★ Negri Sembilan Distinguished Conduct Medal

Annex A

LT. GENERAL SIR HAROLD BRIGGS K.C.I.E., C.B.,
C.B.E., D.S.O.

DIRECTOR OF OPERATIONS, made the
following statement to the Press
on November 27th 1951

I feel it necessary, before leaving the direction of operations in the capable hands of General Lockhart, to try to put the situation in Malaya in its right perspective.

The situation as I see it to-day does not justify any lowering of morale which some statements I have read in the Press must, I think, have tended to produce.

For instance, the impression has been given that our losses exceed those of the bandits. The figures of the last six months up to the end of October show 277 of our own men killed but during that period exactly 700 bandits have been eliminated and very many more active Communist agents arrested. In no month have the bandits succeeded in inflicting more than 50% of the losses they themselves have incurred. Contacts with bandits increased by about 80% over 1950 and bandits eliminated by 45%.

It has been said that an increasing number of civilians is getting killed. Two figures for 1951 up to mid November are 478 as against 646 in 1950.

I have given to the press to-day graphs which show clearly that the number of major incidents, causing casualties or damage, rose steeply up to August 1950, but that then this rise was checked and the numbers have remained generally steady thereafter. The types of incidents are however, more serious than previously due, no doubt, to experience.

This is not, as so many seem to believe, a purely military problem. It is a very complex one and one which embraces every aspect of the Administration, our economy and the psychology of the various races and communities which make up Malaya. It is a problem of maintaining the morale of the people while at the same time destroying Communist morale.

The Armed Forces are of course necessary to give security to the people whilst we build up our resources to combat our main enemy, that is the Communist cells in our midst and those who are their supporters. It is these organizations who use the cover of armed banditry, to terrorise the people and commit indiscriminate murders and atrocities among them, so that their identity should not be disclosed. Without these cells the bandits could not exist.

Our main object of these last two years had been to give added security where possible by intensifying our effort against the bandits, bringing in the isolated portions of the population for their own protection, and building up an improved intelligence organization, a psychological warfare department and a police striking force of jungle companies. I might add that without resettlement and regrouping of the population that task of the Security Forces would have been very much more difficult and that of the Intelligence and Information Services almost impossible.

One hears a lot about Communist penetration of Resettlement areas. I admit that in some cases the security given is still inadequate; but don't forget that among these squatters there were already many Communists and these could not have been discovered until they had been collected in. Since then our Intelligence Branch has had many big, if local, successes leading to the arrest often of complete cells. We have now resettled four-fifths of these exposed people and particularly the most exposed. This has been a magnificent effort on the part of the administration, police and army personnel engaged in this work often at the risk of their lives. To them the country owes a deep debt of gratitude.

These foundations could not have been laid in a day. They have imposed an additional strain on the planters and miners and others who are exposed to the rigours of the campaign but despite this their morale and determination remains unshaken.

The Communists have now been fully committed to the battle, deploying all their resources in order to exist. I will remind you of a period in 1949 when the lull in incidents gave a feeling of false security; but it is our intensified measures which have brought on the battle – as in any other war. We must not complain if we too have higher casualties, as long as they are justified by corresponding damage inflicted by (sic) the enemy.

We have much evidence to show that the Communists are putting their all into this battle. Life in the jungle is no longer the easy life it was: food is scarcer and they have to split into smaller groups and work harder to get it. Our improved information and intelligence made the bandit lairs and Communist cells daily less secure, in spite of their increased efforts to intimidate and murder the innocent. The Communists have their difficulties too, which are not so visible as our own. We have some way to go yet before the day comes when the Communist morale is broken, but broken it will be.

Our task is now to review and strengthen our machinery and in particular to commit all communities to play their full part in the defence of this country in which they live, without thought of personal gain, and to take a more active part in the defence and security of their homes, so that they may be emboldened to resist and inform against the enemy in their midst. It is only thus that speed in ending these atrocities can be possible.

It is only by service to a country that the spirit, pride and goodwill of a Nation can be built up. Politics alone will never achieve them.

KUALA LUMPUR, November 27, 1951 (issued at 1130 hours)

Annex B

Sabotage of Malayan Railway Track

Between June 1948/November 1951 the Malayan Railway track was interfered with by bandits on 389 occasions. This resulted in 129 derailments.

2. A railway track is very vulnerable to deliberate sabotage. The principal methods which can be used are:

(a) Destruction of track (or bridge) by explosives detonated by a passing train. This method has been used successfully on 41 occasions, the last being in 25th October, 1951.

(b) As in (a) but with electrical detonation from a distance. This method has been used successfully on 4 occasions.

(c) Placing an obstruction on the track, particularly a small obstruction fixed to the higher rail on a curve. This is a simple method which can be applied quickly, but so far has been used infrequently.

(d) Removal of the fish plates (which hold the rails together at the expansion joints) and slewing the track about 3" out of alignment. This operation requires from 10 to 20 minutes to complete and has been used frequently. A variation is to loosen fittings before passage of a patrol train but to defer slewing of the track, which can then be effected in a very short time, until the patrol train has passed thus causing derailment to the important following train.

(e) Removal of one or more rails. This can be done quickly by a large gang. This method, though unnecessary as (d) is fully effective, is, in fact, the method which, so far, has been most used.

(f) Removal of fish plates and some of the spikes holding the rail to the sleepers. This may be done as a deliberate plan or may result from the bandits being disturbed whilst removing the rail. The effect is to leave the track in a strong enough condition for a light patrol train but a heavier train causes a loose rail to overturn and a derailment results.

(g) Sawing through rail fastenings. This method has been tried and hacksaw blades have been picked up on the railway track.

(h) The track could also be made unsafe by removing spikes and widening the gauge or by the removal of ballast from under one rail but these methods have not so far been attempted.

3. Counter measures which Railway does, or could take are:

(a) Foot patrols by railways staff. Inspection of the railway track at day break by men from each Permanent Way gang is a standard railway practice. The men from neighbouring gangs meet and exchange a patrol token and this ensures that the whole of the track is walked over early each morning. This is standard practice.

(b) Strengthening of track fastenings.

    (i) The introduction of elastic spikes in places of the normal dog spikes baffled the bandits for a short time, but they have now learnt how to deal with these spikes.

    (ii) Fish plate bolts have been riveted over so as to make it more difficult to remove the fish plates. This, however, has not been effective as, by tightening the nut, the bolt can be broken; also the nut can be split with a hammer and chisel.

    (iii) Fish plates have to be removed about once per year for oiling to allow for the normal expansion and contraction of the rail. Two fish bolt nuts could be welded to each fish plate. This will not prevent the removal of the fish plates but it would make it more difficult and the initial cost and the increase in maintenance cost may be considered to be justified by the small measure of additional security given.

(iv) In each rail length a number of special dog spikes could be provided. The heads of these spikes would be altered from the standards pattern so that the spikes would be more difficult to remove.

(c) Patrol Trains.

These trains are made up as follows:

(i) a locomotive with armouring to protect the crew;

(ii) crash wagons which precede the locomotive.

These are low-sided vehicles weighted so as to detonate explosives under the track.

A device is fitted to the leading crash wagon designed to apply the vacuum brake on derailment, so that the Driver is warned and the severity of the derailment is reduced.

A number of crash wagons have been fitted with powerful searchlights and armoured sections to accommodate three men. These men examine the rail joints by the aid of the searchlight and give signals to the footplate staff by means of hand torches, the Pilot train running at reduced speed. Fish plates are whitewashed to aid in quick detection of sabotage. This counter measure involves slow running but has been effective in particularly bad areas.

(iii) An armoured cupola or a Fox Car mounted on a flat wagon. This vehicle follows the locomotive. The armed Police travel in the cupola. Searchlights are mounted on the cupola and they can be rotated from within the cupola.

Patrol trains run five minutes ahead of the following train and in the same block section. Speeds are reduced to give an adequate braking distance. The patrol train driver carries a Verey pistol which he fires when derailed to give warning to the following train. He also carries a walkie talkie set with which he can speak to the driver and guard of the following train. These sets are not effective when the train is running.

Wickham trollies are used on occasions to pilot trains running through the hours of darkness.

4. The Night Mail trains and the Night Military Mixed trains carry armed parties which are accommodated in specially designed armoured portions of each train. The trains also carry wireless sets and the operators are in constant touch with static wireless stations along the route. Armed parties also travel in armoured cupolas or on Fox Cars attached to the four principal Night Goods trains.

Armed parties have now been provided for the four Day Mail trains and four Passenger vans are being provided with armoured sections for protection.

5. The defensive counter measures taken by the Military and Police are:
(a) Foot patrols along the railway.
(b) Patrols with 12 Armoured Wickham trollies. These work in pairs and each carries four men.
(c) Patrols by armoured trains. Four armoured trains with space for 80/100 men are in constant use in Pahang.

More intense patrolling in South Johore has reduced the number of incidents. It is considered that similar measures should be taken in South Perak and North Selangor, where there is now frequent sabotage of the track, and be extended in future to any areas in which attacks on the railway are intensified.

6. The question of sabotage of permanent way was considered by the Railway Security Committee at its Eighth Meeting on the 29th of November 1950. The minutes record that it was the opinion of the Committee that 'neither spot welding nor other measures so far proposed would make interference with the permanent way appreciably more difficult'. Investigation of the possibility of using electrical devices to detect or prevent interference with the permanent way established that this method was impracticable.

22nd December, 1951.
G.M.R. Conf. 161(a).

INDEX

collective punishment, Tanjong Malim, 158–9.
Manchurian Railway, 37.
Manson, Douglas, officer Malay Scouts SAS, 52.
Mao Tse Tung, 17, 21–2, 26; Manchuria, offensive against Nationalists, 79, 155.
Masterson, police officer, Malaya, 155.
Mayne, Blaire 'Paddy', early SAS officer recruit, 6.
McComb, Trooper, 35.
McGonigal, Lieutenant, disappears with plane on first SAS venture, 8.
McLeod, Brigadier 'Roddy', commanded SAS Brigade until late 1944, 38.
Meirs, Lieutenant-Colonel, South Wales Borderers, 196.
Middle East, headquarters (MEHQ), 1; 3, 5, 7, 9, 206.
Min Yuen, 'The People's Movement', guerrillas supporting Malayan fighters, its 'Old Comrades Association', gathering of intelligence etc., 14, 19–21, 25, 31, 85, 90–1, 93; further activities of, 145–6, 159, 197.
Montgomery, Viscount Field Marshal Bernard, 39, 54; advice to Lyttelton on Malaya, 151, 153–4.
Morton, Jack, appointed Deputy Director of Operations, Malaya, 157.
Moscow, 11.
Moseley, L/Cpl, doggedness in face of acute pain, 122, 127.
Mountbatten, Lord Louis, Viceroy of India, 79.
Mulcahy, Trooper SAS, injured, 203.
Mundell, Bill, officer SAS, 176.

NAAFI, 108.
Nagasaki, bombing of, 37.
National Servicemen, 'Running Dogs', 51, 56, 103.
Negrito aborigines, 120.
Nepal, 136.
Newell, Major C.L.D. 'Dare', OBE, MBE, of SAS, 102; his background, and strong letter to Dempsey on quality of SAS recruitment, 182–6; explanations and opinions, 186–7; of his work, and letter to Lapraik, 190–2, 200.
New Zealand, SAS raid on compound, 6; SAS Squadron, formation and description of patrol in The Free Glance, 187–90.

North Atlantic Alliance, 147.
Norway, 9.

O'Leary, Trooper John, Malayan Scout SAS, the killing of by aborigines, 165–6.
Oman, 163; SAS at war there, 206, 209.
Operation Apollo, Pahang, food denial scheme against CTs, 197.
Operation Gabes North, Perak-Kelantan border, 172–5.
Operation Galway, 167.
Operation Helsby, 115; 117; detailed description of, Chapter 10; 161.
Operation Mustang, 128.
Operation Prosaic, 165.
Operation Roll-Up, 141.
Operation Thrust, the flushing out of CT leader Ah Hoi, 203–5.

Pacific Tin Corporation, 22.
Paddy's Ladang, SAS jungle base, 130.
Pahang, 14, 148; New Zealand SAS patrol, 188–90; 194.
Pakistan, 79.
Palestine, 23; Palestinian Arabs, 40, 137; 79–80.
Palestine Police, 81–2, 84.
Parachute Regiment, 50, 63, 105; support to SAS, 162, 187–8; record in Malaya, 190–1.
Parachute Training School, Ringway, 6.
Park, Colin, officer Malayan Scouts, SAS, 52–3, 114.
Pathan, fighters, 40, 137.
Peacock, Captain Ted, explosive expert, 48; 73.
Pearman, Mike, officer Malayan Scouts SAS (Aden Protectorate Levies), 52; swims across Sungei Belum, 123–4.
Perak, 14, 26; Civil Power, 87; military sweep, 87; Kuomintang bandits, 94; 112, 112, 194.
Percival, General, Commander-in-Chief, Singapore, 13.
Philippines, 12.
Pola, 50, 52.
Port Said, 6.
Prestwick Pioneer aircraft, 164, 193.
Prince of Wales, loss of, 13.
Private Armies, 40.

RAAF-RAF 124–5, 193.
Raffles, Long Bar, 26.